# CHRONICLES
## FROM THE
## DIARY OF A WAR PRISONER
### IN ANDERSONVILLE AND OTHER
### MILITARY PRISONS OF THE SOUTH
### IN 1864

Experiences, Observations, Interviews and Poems
Written in Prison, with Historical Introduction

An Appendix Containing Statement of a Confederate Physician
and Officer Relative to Prison Condition and Management

BY
# John Worrell Northrop
### Formerly Seventy Sixth New York Infantry

*Shut in a prison vast*
*A soldier languished, but not alone;*
*Thousands were assembled there,*
*Captives from armies of the North,*
*Who craved release to join the ranks*
*Of comrades in war's activities,*
*Prefering far the dangers there*
*Than rust and rot and pine and die,*
*In enervating squalor and privations,*
*Which was the fate of many, day by day.*
— From The Vision of North.

HERITAGE BOOKS
2024

# HERITAGE BOOKS

*AN IMPRINT OF HERITAGE BOOKS, INC.*

## Books, CDs, and more—Worldwide

For our listing of thousands of titles see our website
at
www.HeritageBooks.com

A Facsimile Reprint
Published 2024 by
HERITAGE BOOKS, INC.
Publishing Division
5810 Ruatan Street
Berwyn Heights, MD 20740

Copyright © 1904 John Worrell Northrop

Originally published by the author
Wichita, Kansas
1904

— Publisher's Notice —
In reprints such as this, it is often not possible to remove blemishes from the original. We feel the contents of this book warrant its reissue despite these blemishes and hope you will agree and read it with pleasure.

International Standard Book Number
Paperbound: 978-0-7884-2798-5

## DEDICATION

In the hope that the facts herein chronicled will instruct, interest and inspire patriotism and love for mankind, this book is dedicated to the **Sons and Daughters of Union Veterans** of 1861 to 1865.

BY THE AUTHOR.

WINING PRINTERY, 205 N. MAIN ST., WICHITA, ANSAS,

## PRELUDE.

Tears! Men had no time for tears
   When battle waves rolled fierce and high,
Could only fight; they had no time for fears!
   When comrades fell, could do no more than sigh,
Press to victory, or, if driven to defeat,
   Bow in grief when waned the battle's heat.

Comrades slain were scattered on the way,
   On fields, in woods where was met the foe
That came to kill where we had come to slay,
   Met as wave meets tide in ocean storms that blow;
But men who war must not seek time to weep,
   Must go where duty calls, though death shall reap.

Sad visions from distant and the yore
   Rise in the heart and in sad memories,
And oft some sweeter thought they stand before,
   Like shadows grim bedim the Veteran's eyes.
And yet this sadness bears sweetness all unfeigned,
   For hearts are blest where truth and valor reigned.

Far o'er the distant list to battle's roar!
   Time, like a valley mead, lies 'twixt us and the scenes
Where our fading lines shall march and fight no more,
   Nor countermarch the way that intervenes.
The shining river lies just on before;
   We shall cross, anon, where the van passed o'er.

O, may the deeds which higher justice sought,
   Which sought to strengthen Freedom's loftiest fane,
Be by no recreant head, or hand, unwrought,
   To grieve the souls who for the right were slain;
But let the work they nobly did bestow
   Be builded on, far better than we know!
                         —J. W. NORTHROP.

## PREFACE.

From boyhood to mature years I was accustomed to write occurences of personal and general interest, often daily, sometimes summarizing several days, noting what I read, heard and saw. After going into the army I practiced this custom as circumstances allowed, not for use publicly, but for self-entertainment and improvement. Becoming a war prisoner in 1864, I was naturally impressed to practice my diary habit. I had a burning desire to note everything, which led to finding a way, more or less crude and inconvenient, to write what I did. Prison life furnished an unwelcome but unique field for daily journalizing. To avoid the idleness and ennui incident to my misfortune, I made it an occupation to observe, to hear, to meditate, to write. A partly blank diary and every piece of paper I could get hold of, became precious. I wrote fine and skeletonized. In my "teens" I had "fits" of poetic composition. I indulged and invited the bent. For all of the imperfections of these effusions, they brought to my brain a new and pleasing vitality; a light to my mind that darkest shadows could not dim; a hope and a purpose terrible realities could not obscure. I grasped the idea that an active, cheerful mind imparted added life to the body and strength to the soul. Though bound in conditions conducive to indolence, sloth and imbecility, I sought and found occupation that kept Giant Despair at a distance. Keenly realizing pending evils meant squalor and death to the imprisoned multitude, I lived in my thoughts, feasted on the glory of a higher plain. At times I lived in a world distinct from all but a few comrades, though sharing the fate of all. Some ridiculed my devotion to my work. They could not, would not write of the dreadful daily happenings—they wanted to forget. Productions "inspired by prison grub" were anomalous. So I wrote without thought of publicity, feeling that my efforts, my ideals and silent aspirations brought a steadying element to my life and raised my mentality beyond the miasms of the "Slough of Despond." It was three years after the war before I copied my prison manuscript and partly published in a newspaper There are occasions when it is good to speak of disagreeable things and to think of ideals beyond the scope of inexorably painful conditions. It lifts the better-self beyond the harm of their

PREFACE. 5

physical effects.

The book that follows is a diary of prison life and events at Andersonville, Ga., Florence, S. C., and other places, journeyings from Virginia battlefields to those places, and the final restoration to the Union lines; a succession of interesting, sad, and unusual incidents and of patriotic sacrifices made by thousands of brave men for this country, and an exhibition of many phases of human nature under unprecedented circumstances of cruelty, adversity and deprivation. A number of the poems are contained in the order of the date of writing as part of the diary, and others follow the concluding sketches entitled, Prison Psalms.

Time is passing. Those who fought, suffered and survived to save coming generations from consequences worse than war, all of which must have entailed war, eventually will follow comrades gone before. Hence, I deem it a highly patriotic duty to place these annals, which it was the lot of but few to record, though many saw and felt, before the public. Here is chronicled what ordinary history has not recorded, and that which all lovers of their country and of mankind should read. Young men and young women without definite facts of prison life, written daily, cannot comprehend the weight of all the perils and privations borne by men who fought for their country in the war for "Union and Liberty * * * one and inseparable." Life in Rebel prisons tried men's souls as well as their bodies, showing grand loyalty and sacred devotion to justice and liberty bordering on martyrdom. If the Chronicles teach lessons of patriotism, the principal motive of the writer in publishing them will have been gratified. If they teach other lessons, so much the better. If they contain literary qualities they may exceed my claims.

Two historical introductions concisely detailing important events leading to the war, and immediately following the election of Abraham Lincoln, precede the Chronicles, the value of which for easy epoch reading, exceeds the price of the book.

That which is dead of the past, cannot be written into life. But there is that in all the past without which the present would be blind, the future blank. The past speaks to the future. Though behind, it is before. Even of its wrongs we learn lessons of truth, of right, of progress. The past links the future to that still beyond, that must evolve out of the past elements for better building and the glory to be. The wrongs of the past forgive; their lessons never forget. They are lights on the shore of billowy seas of moral advancement. The soldiers dead live; those living have more to live for, to hope for, to work for. While living, wait not to die. Let there be no straggling in the ranks of the army of freedom. We dwell in the present, our work is not done.

Forty years have passed since the beginning of the Chronicles, covering less than a year, but they are history written contemporaneously. Shall they remain inert? The value and vitality of history never depreciate; its virtues are ever new. Men die, but what they do for the true greatness of their country will live forever.

Men who fought on the other side, lacked not valor and endurance. We do not, in any sense, hold them culpable for the horrors we suffered in prison. They are our neighbors; they are citizens of the Union. The benefits of its preservation are theirs as they are ours. In fighting for it we fought for them. In loving our country we loved them.

The work concludes with a report of Dr. Joseph Jones relative to prison conditions as he found them in a visit to Andersonville, by direction of Surgeon-General Moore, of the Confederate government, in the interest of medical science; also the report of Colonel Chandler, representing the Confederate War Department, and his testimony relative to it, who was there about August 1, 1864. These reports confirm passages in my diary as to the wretched condition of prisoners and the wickedness of our prison keepers.

Wichita, Kansas,                      J. W. NORTHROP,
June 4, 1904.

# HISTORICAL INTRODUCTION

### CAUSE AND EVENTS LEADING TO CIVIL WAR.

The cause of the Civil War was slavery. African slavery in this country was an entailment coming through many years and peoples in other lands. It was an offspring of barbarism, despotism and Dark Ages. Before the beginning of any movement looking to independence from the rule of European powers, its existence in the Colonies, transplanted from those countries, was condemned by the best and ablest men of that time. It was one of the evils for which England was blamed, as the era of independence approached. Beneficiaries conceded its incompatibility with republican government when the time approached for its establishment. Among this class were the Tories of the Revolutionary period. After the Revolution, in the formation of the National Constitution, as in the Articles of Confederation, they demanded that slavery be left untouched, that some provision for its protection be incorporated in that instrument. Contrary to the conviction of the authors of the document the desire was gratified as the unity of all interests and all classes was highly essential, but with a mutual understanding that its abolition would naturally follow at "a more convenient season." Slavery was regarded as purely domestic, having no political or social significance, an abomity to be eliminated; but how and when, was an event of the future. The very fact that it was a class interest, left by concession, under a free government in which equality of human rights was a declared principle, made it seem plausible that some guaranty of non-intervention in its control be inserted in the Constitution. This compromise authorized Congress to pass a law for the recovery of persons held to service in one state who might escape to other states, and restricted Congress from abolishing the importation of Africans to be sold as slaves until 1808. It was a mistaken policy and opened a way for other demands, among which was a three-fifths representation in Congress based on slave population, which was granted as a compromise for a demand for full representation.

## HISTORICAL INTRODUCTION—PART I.

In 1784 it was proposed to cede to the general government, lands that belonged to Virginia, North Carolina, and Georgia, which lands now compose the states of Kentucky, Tennessee, Alabama and Mississippi. The ordinance designed to make the transfer was drawn by Jefferson. One stipulation was that after the year 1800 neither slavery nor involuntary servitude shall exist, otherwise than as punishment for crime of which the party shall have been convicted and upon this article six of the eleven states present voted in its favor, New Jersey losing its vote by the temporary absence of its representatives. The motion to strike out received seven votes cast by Maryland, Virginia, North Carolina and South Carolina, Jefferson of Virginia and Williams of North Carolina, voting for it to stand. The vote was recorded six states for the stipulation to stand, and three against it, North Carolina being a tie and not counted, the vote for slavery restriction being lost through the absence of a New Jersey representative, as the Articles of Confederation required an affirmative vote of a majority of all the states. By this accident all that rich and extensive territory became slave states, and but for which slavery would have been confined to the Southern Atlantic States. As it was slavery was rendered permanent and profitable, and the traffic in slaves was stimulated. In a few years Louisiana was acquired and added to the slave states. Thus in the early years of the Republic the country became sectionalized by the existence of slave labor, and the accursed traffic in men widened.

In 1787 the Northwest Territory was ceded to the government from which slavery was restricted.

Roger B. Taney—later Chief Justice of the United States Supreme Court—in defending as a lawyer, before a Maryland court in 1818, Rev. Jacob Bruber, charged with anti-slavery inculcations, truthfully set forth the revolutionary idea of slavery and the plea for leaving it undisturbed. He said: "A hard necessity, indeed, compels us to endure the evils of slavery for a time. It was imposed upon us by another nation, while we were in a state of colonial vassalage. It cannot be suddenly removed. Yet, while it continues, it is a blot on our national character, and every real lover of freedom confidently hopes that it will be effectually, though it must be gradually, wiped away, and earnestly looks for the means by which the necessary object may be attained. Until it shall be accomplished, until the time comes when we can point without a blush to the Declaration of Independence, every friend of humanity will seek to lighten the galling chain of slavery, and better, to the utmost of his power, the wretched condition of the salve."

This was said by a man born, reared and living in a slave State, but who, in later life, became a slave to the slave power,

## HISTORICAL INTRODUCTION—PART I.

and thirty-nine years after, as Chief Justice, declared to the astonished world that slavery had every right in the Territories of the United States that freedom had, and that no one had a right to protest, in the infamous Dred Scott case. His idea that "it must be gradually wiped away," was long before wiped out by the wrathful suppression of discussion of policies looking to its gradual abolition or against its further extension, thus bringing to a direct conflict the long "irrepressible conflict."

Slavery had triumphed beyond the anticipation of its friends or foes, so that when President Polk was inaugurated in 1845, of the twenty-eight States comprising the Union, half were free, half slave. In 1820 the line between free and slave territory had been made definite by the Missouri Compromise, giving all territory south of the southern line of Missouri to slavery; all territory north of that line to freedom. Nevertheless, Missouri had already become a slave Territory. Its admission to the Union with a slave Constitution at this time, caused great excitement over the country, which the Compromise Act designed to allay. Though it did prevent slavery north of the Compromise Line, except in Missouri, at the same time it sanctioned slavery in territory south of the Missouri southern line to the Pacific Coast. These conditions proved the insincerity of the South when the North was led to trust that slavery, if let alone, would disappear. From the adoption of the Constitution, it had been aggressive. From the hour of the first concession, the conflict became irrepressible.

Trade centers grew favorable to slavery for sordid reasons. They were the bulwark of pro-slavery in the North. Mobs were encouraged by their attitude, sometimes led by men of influence, to prevent abolition meetings and destroy anti-slavery literature. The press was used to pervert truth and condemn justice. Northern Legislatures were petitioned and threatened by Southern committees to pass stringent laws against tongue and pen that spoke against slavery. For thirty years free speech and a free press had been banished from the South, prior to 1860. On mere suspicion strangers were mobbed, deported and hung in the South. Efforts to bring about similar conditions North did not succeed, though they received serious attention by reigning powers. These but confirmed the convictions of anti-slavery people and made the contest more determined until the movement against slavery extension assumed shape.

Illustrative of the feeling of the controlling class in the South against anti-slavery people, I quote a few paragraphs:

"The cry of the whole South should be death—instant death—to Abolitionists wherever caught."—Augusta (Ga.) Chronicle.

"We assure Bostonians who have embarked in the nefarious

scheme of abolishing slavery, that lashes will be spared their emissaries. Let them come to Louisiana; they will never return to tell their sufferings, but they will expiate their crime by being burned at the stake."—New Orleans True American.

"Abolition editors in slave States will not dare avow their opinions. It would be instant death to them."—Missouri Argus.

"Resolved, That it is our opinion that any person who dares circulate any incendiary tracts or newspapers in this country, is justly worthy, in sight of God and man, of immediate death, and we doubt not that such would be the punishment of any such offender in any part of Mississippi where he may be found."— (Resolution passed at a public meeting in a church at Clinton, Miss., Sept. 5, 1835.)

"Let no Abolitionist come within the borders of South Caroline; if we catch him * * * we will hang him."—Senator Preston in United States Senate, June 4, 1838.

"The people of the North must go to hanging the fanatics if they would not lose Southern trade, and they will do it. * * * Depend upon it Northern people will never sacrifice their present lucrative trade with the South, so long as hanging a few thousand Abolitionists will prevent it."—Richmond (Va.), Whig.

Henry A. Wise, later the Governor of Virginia, who hung John Brown in 1859 for his appearance at Harper's Ferry, early prescribed "Dupont's best gunpowder, and cold steel" as the medicines for "Abolition fanatics."

Rev. T. S. Witherspoon, Alabama, wrote W. L. Garrison, editor of the Emancipator: "Let your emissaries cross the Potomac and I promise you that your fate will be no less than Haman's."

Rev. William Plummer, D. D., Richmond, Va., to a body of other clergymen, in 1835: "Let the Abolitionists understand that they will be caught if they come among us, and they will take care to stay away."

Pages of similar utterances exist; but my purpose is answered with these, as they show the feeling of slavery supporters South for forty years prior to 1860, and the spirit of hate Union soldiers faced, and the kind of treatment they suggested would be and was meted to Northerners who became prisoners.

Fugitive slave laws were a source of conflict, a firebrand instead of an olive branch. Before the year 1808 slavery had become an influential factor politically, commercially and socially, in elections, in trade centers, so that not until 1820 was the slave trade abolished against bitter opposition. As anticipated slavery was abolished where it existed in Northern States, some owners selling their slaves to Southerners where slave industry was more fostered, where slaves numerically increased and the area of slavery was extending. It soon became a paramount interest,

## HISTORICAL INTRODUCTION—PART II.

against which, it was believed, there could be no competition in Southern agriculture. The market for the chief products of the South was so general abroad, and the home demand for slaves so strong, that for several years after 1820 slave dealers carried on a business of smuggling imported negroes at Southern ports, and free negroes, wherever they could be kidnaped, were sold in slave markets until, at ,last, public sentiment against the illicit traffic rendered it obsolete, slave traders being driven from the sea rather than excluded from our ports. But as an instrument of political intrigue slavery continued a growing force, dominating both great parties, largely the press and pulpit, but making the Democratic party, after its subversion, its chief organ. Large commercial and financial interests in the great cities North became subservient, and socially it wielded a power North as well as South.

Slaveholders opposed a tariff on imported goods used by them. Some sections were strenuous for free exchange of their exports for imports. Not being successful in securing free trade, their purchases were made from large importers in New York, Boston, Philadelphia and Baltimore. As a sequence those centers were strongly pro-slavery. In November, 1832, South Carolina legislators assumed to nullify the National Tariff Law and to absolve the State from the Union. The movement was abandoned in consequence of the firm stand taken by President Jackson. Stimulated by tariff laws and higher considerations, New England States engaged in cotton manufacturing, furnished a home market for cotton and a demand for labor. Manufacturing interests grew everywhere North, agriculture improved and extended, population grew rapidly in the North while slavery restricted growth in the South, repelled population and capital. Slave interest must be preeminent, must be promomted though progress be barred! The situation embittered Southern rulers; new jealousies were fostered, hatred fired, fearing political results. It had been the aim to balance the two sections politically in Congress on compromise plans, but conditions of progress and growth rendered such tactics futile. The danger of slavery being civilized out of the country ultimately, seemed imminent to slaveholders and their Moseses—a thing intolerable to them. In 1850 the whole question was again opened to remove apprehensions. In order to admit California a free State, the Territories of Utah and New Mexico were organized open to slavery, in effect removing the compromise line between free and slave sections established by the Henry Clay Compromise Act of 1820. The energy of the South was more desperately bent to control the Executive, Judicial and Legislative branches of government than ever, to secure new territory for slavery. In 1854 the Kansas-

Nebraska Act, formally repealed the Missouri Compromise, and opened that Territory to slavery. In 1857 the Dred Scott decision held that neither a negro nor any of his descendants could be a citizen of the United States, that any territorial or congressional restriction of slavery from public domain was unconstitutional. A few days before Lincoln was inaugurated President the Territories of Colorado, Nevada and Dakota were organized open to slavery. Thus when Abraham Lincoln, pledged to oppose the extension of slavery into new territory, took the oath of office on the 4th of March, 1861, slavery existed in the Southern States by provision of State laws, and was admitted to all the public domain by congressional enactment and judicial construction. How significant these words of Lincoln, uttered at the Illinois State Convention in June, 1858:

"A house divided against itself cannot stand. I believe this government cannot endure permanently half slave and half free. I do not expect the Union to be dissolved, I do not expect the house to fall, but I do expect it will cease to be divided. It will become all one thing, or all the other. Either the opponents of slavery will arrest the further spread of it and place it where the public mind shall rest in the belief that it is in the course of ultimate extinction, or its advocates will push it forward till it shall become alike lawful in all the States, old as well as new, North as well as South."

Four months later Seward at Rochester, N. Y., declared that slavery had produced "an irrepressible conflict" between the North and South. Thus far the advantage had been with the South; all territory organized and unorganized was open to slavery; the issue was clearly drawn. Slavery or freedom must become National. Which should it be?

The cause of the Civil War was slavery; the occasion, secession of slave States and their aggressive defiance to rightful authority. The purpose was political power embalmed in the dreams of the most aggressive which pictured a vast territory, including Cuba, its government to be built upon the unrequited toil of slaves, to be administered relatively by a few. Gigantic schemes were drafted for the establishment of this powerful slave oligarchy among the nations of the world. Failing to do it within the Union they essayed to do it by disunion, and the highest aims of the hated Abolitionists was attained precipitately by the rash and fanatical action of the South.

## EVENTS IMMEDIATELY FOLLOWING ELECTION OF 1860.

The political and military situation at the South just prior to and at the beginning of the Civil War, is a marked and dramatic feature, historically, of that impressive crisis. Believing it valuable to readers in connection with this book, it is here concisely presented.

Abraham Lincoln was elected President, November 6, 1860. That election was made a pretext by leading statesmen South for precipitating secession. South Carolina took the initiative and passed its ordinance of secession by unanimous vote, on December 20, 1860. Georgia followed January 19, 1861; Louisiana January 26, 1861; Mississippi, January 9, 1861; Florida, January 10, 1861; Alabama, January 11, 1861; Virginia, April 17, 1861; Texas, February 1, 1861; Arkansas, May 6, 1861; North Carolina, May 20, 1861. May 24, 1861. Tennessee, by proclamation of Governor Isham G. Harris, was declared out of the Union, public sentiment being too strongly against secession for the adoption of a secession ordinance; but June 8, 1861, a formal act of secession was carried by a faction

Christmas day, 1860, President Buchanan sent this note to his Secretary of War:

My Dear Sir: I send you a telegram which I have this moment received from Pittsburg.. (The telegram read as follows):

"An order has issued from the War Department to transfer all effective munitions of war from the arsenals in this city to Southern forts. Great excitement has been created * * * by this order. We advise that it be immediately countermanded. We speak at the instance of the people, and if not done, we cannot be answerable for consequences." (Signed by five prominent citizens.)

At this time J. B. Floyd was Secretary of War; Samuel Cooper was Adjutant General; Joseph E. Johnston, Quartermaster General; Jefferson Davis was chairman of the Senate Committee of Military Affairs. Four days after receipt of this note, Floyd resigned and went South to become a brigadier in the rebel army;

14        HISTORICAL INTRODUCTION—PART II.

Davis followed and in a few weeks was President of the Southern Confederacy, Cooper was its Adjutant General, and Johnston a brigadier, each acting in violation of his oath, leaving high places in the Federal Government for the treasonable purpose of destroying it.

Four months later, Robert E. Lee, after the secession of one-half of Virginia, resigned as Colonel of cavalry in the U. S. regular army, and was made a General of the Secession Confederacy, commanding all military forces in Virginia, including forces sent there from other States. Two days before surrendering his commission to the Federal authority Lee wrote this letter to his son:

"I can anticipate no greater calamity for the country than the dissolution of the Union. It would be an accumulation of all the evils we complain of. I am willing to sacrifice everything but honor for its preservation. Secession is revolution. The framers of the Constitution never exhausted so much labor, wisdom and forbearance, and surrounded it with so many guards and securities, if it was intended to be broken by every member of the Confederacy at will. It was intended for perpetual union, so expressed in the preamble, and for the establishment of a government, not a compact, which can only be dissolved by revolution, or the consent of the people in convention. It is idle to talk of secession! Anarchy would have been established, and not government, by Washington, Hamilton, Jefferson, Madison and the other patriots of the Revolution."

And yet he violated his oath to sustain that government and that Union, to seek its overthrow by exerting a power no other man in the South could exert, his sole excuse being that his State, or a major part of it, had taken a decisive step to bring about the greatest "calamity" that could be anticipated, to the country. Secession was anarchy in his honest judgment; but he took up the sword of anarchy and oppression because his State had attempted to break a Union not intended to be broken by its founders, saying at last that he owed allegiance to dissolution rather than to loyalty to the government that had fostered and educated him to be one of its defenders.

Shortly after the inauguration of Lincoln, John C. Brekenridge, who, as Vice-President and President of the Senate, declared that the election of Lincoln was legal, and had been elected and sworn as Senator from Kentucky, resigned his Senatorial seat, after making a treasonable speech, and joined a Rebel army that had invaded Kentucky, and soon after was commissioned a Brigadier General, and continued in service until the close of the war. He was also a presidential candidate in 1860. This is another fact showing that the Executive branch of our government, for years, had been in charge of the enemies of the people.

## HISTORICAL INTRODUCTION—PART II.

On November 18, 1861, by a factional convention at Russellville, Kentcky was, by ordinance, declared out the Union, against a strong Union sentiment. The State Administration assumed to be neutral, so far as neutrality could be practical, although there were many brave Kentuckians in both the Union and Secession armies. The preponderance of popular sentiment was for the Union more than 3 to 1 and its representation in Congress was maintained. At the beginning of the war, Governor Magoffin, was a Secessionist and clandestinely aided Secessionists.

Missouri was greatly convulsed. Its Governor, Claiborne F. Jackson, favored secession and declared for the Southern Confederacy, but by timely action due to the wisdom and courage of Gen. Nathaniel Lyon and others a formal act of secession was averted, the government property saved and virtually the loyalty of the State preserved.

Maryland was divided by fearful agitation, but Governor Thomas H. Hicks was strongly for the Union, though a slaveholder, and regardless of much secession inclination on account of slavery, the State stood for the Union.

In June, 1861, Western Virginia, (now West Virginia), loyally repudiated secession, formed a new State government and remained loyal and was recognized by the government and contributed to the national cause. Such was the action of the slave States.

Each State Convention in States where secession unqualifiedly prevailed, assumed to sever the relation between the State and other States, and the national government; chose members to the first Confederate Congress that met at Montgomery, Ala., on February 4, 1861, with Howell Cobb of Georgia, as President. Cobb had resigned from the Federal Cabinet as Secretary of the Treasury after bankrupting it, to become prominent in the secession movement. In accepting the position he declared the secession of the South "a fixed and irrevocable fact, and that the separation is complete and perpetual."

Just one month before the inauguration of Lincoln, the Confederate government, as the instrument of rebellion, had been organized and was in full operation at Montgomery, assuming to perform all functions of national authority. On February 8th, the Congress adopted the Constitution of the provisional government; on the 9th it elected Jefferson Davis President, and Alexander H. Stephens Vice-President, of the Confederacy; on the 10th Davis was inaugurated with imposing ceremonies, and a full Cabinet appointed.

[Note.—In strict truth, legally no State had withdrawn from the Union for the people who compose a State in our Republic, had never been asked to sanction such change. Certain persons in certain States conspired against national authority and were in rebellion against it, had usurped the power and suspended the Constitutions of such States, and the confederation formed at Montgomery was a league of conspirators to disrupt the Nation, and not a Confederation of States. Had it been the action of the people of such States, they would still have been in rebellion because the consent of the people of other States had not been scured, besides the purpose of such confederation was in violation of principles on which our government is founded.]

Seven States had been declared out of the Union; South Carolina had taken possession of Forts Moultrie and Castle Pinkney on December 27 and 31, 1860, the arsenal with 70,000 stand of arms, the post office and custom house at Charleston and throughout the State. January 2, 1861, Forts Pulaski and Jackson, with the United States arsenal at Savannah, Ga., were taken January 4, 1861; Fort Morgan at Mobile, Ala., and Mt. Vernon arsenal containing a large amount of arms and ammunition; January 7, Fort Martien and arsenal at St. Augustine, also the Chattahoochee arsenal containing supplies; January 9, the Star of the West with supplies for Major Anderson at Fort Sumter, was fired upon off Charleston and compelled to retire; January 10, the guns and stores of the steamship Texas were seized; January 11, Forts Jackson and St. Phillips, New Orleans, and Fort Pike, and arsenal at Baton Rouge, La., were taken; January 12, the Navy Yard and Forts Barrancas and McRea, Florida, and the revenue cutter, Lewis Cass, were seized;; January 20, Forts Chadbone and Belknap with the fort and arsenal at Ship Island; January 24, the arsenal at Augusta, Ga., containing a large armament of guns and ammunition; January 25, General Twiggs, Department Commander, surrendered his command and stores valued at $1,300,000, besides a large number of mounted and dismounted artillery and 35,000 muskets to the State of Texas. Months before North Carolina seceded, Gov. John W. Ellis seized the United States arsenal at Fayetville and Fort Macon and fortifications commanding approaches to Beauford and Wilmington and Forts Caswell and Johnson, by State Militia, February 8, the arsenal at Little Rock, Ark., with many cannon and small arms and ammunition.

All this and more had been permitted to fall into the hands of the enemies of the Nation to be used against it. Edward A. Pollard, author of a history of the war from the Southern side, states that the number of improved muskets secured by these seizures without bloodshed, including those transferred by War Secretary John B. Floyd, from Northern to Southern forts after secession began, reached 150,000. Pollard's statement amounts

## HISTORICAL INTRODUCTION—PART II.

to a confession of treachery as he had a position in the Department.

It is seen that war had commenced months before Lincoln's inauguration, by acts of secession, the seizure of United States forts and property by armed, rebellious forces and by the marshalling of armies to resist national authority. This fact should have been promptly recognized by his predecessor and effective measures taken to maintain national authority, to protect government property, and suppress rebellion. Opinions varied regarding a definite policy. There was but one logical one; Buchanan did not favor that, so he drifted and let the nation drift on the rising tide of treason, which was equivalent to sanctioning secession and everything essential to its success. Events proved that a prompt, courageous repetition of a Jacksonian policy in a somewhat similar but less grave crisis, would have been logical. If not immediately as effective, it would have restricted the rebellion as to time to prepare, as to power, influence, territory and duration. I differ from the opinion that a vast proportion of Northerners would have been disloyal had Buchanan been equal to his charge. Seventy-five thousand, or four times that number of men would have responded to a call to arms from Buchanan to suppress rebellion in January, as quickly as they rallied under Lincoln, had it been made, and their equipment and maintenance would have followed.

But it was not so ordered. There were traitors in the Cabinet, traitors in Congress, in military service, sympathizers in plenty and abettors in every department of public service. Yet the great majority of the people, while deeply realizing the terrible gravity of the crisis, were loyal to principles the government was instituted to promote and were ready to meet the extraordinary demands required. The President, no matter when or by what party elected, was expected to fulfill the trust assigned. A call to arms from Buchanan would have met with as patriotic response as the subsequent calls of Lincoln. The prestige of such a call would have strengthened the North and more than proportionately weakened the South. Seward's idea of ending the war in three months might have been realized.

Superficial theorizers assume that, but for the firing on Sumter in April, the Confederacy would have been peacefully established; the North and South permanently divided. The conclusion is fallacious, discreditable to American intelligence, and contrary to the spirit of progress. The firing on Sumter was but a continuance of many seditious acts, many other as treasonable and warlike assaults. Hence a call for troops immediately after the first act of secession instituted for the purpose of seizing forts and resisting national authority by military force with or without the firing of a gun, would have been legitimate, patriotic and wise. Those who would have denied this at the time, denounced the acts of Lincoln just as unwisely after Sumter fell

It was thoroughly known in December what secession meant. It meant war or national ruin. It meant a perpetual slave empire, the overthrow of a free republic, and the North still subject to increasing, insolent demands of a triumphant Slaveocracy, to resist which would invite war, when the only policy of peace would have been cowardly submission to injustice, the final issue to be bloody conquest by one party or the other after generations of drifting, conflict, impoverishing conditions and fretful and destructive anarchy.

Many intelligent people in both sections were conscious of the probability of these consequences in the event of Southern success. To say that secession would have been acceded to under any circumstances is to belie the wise patriotism of Northern people and loyalists south who met the stupendous requirements of that unparalleled occasion.

As it was the work of conquest by the slave power or the confiscation of national property proceeded without official protest to the close of Buchanan's time, so at the beginning of Lincoln's term the Slave Confederacy was nominally established and harder to subdue than at the outset. The closing months of Buchanan's fiasco was consistent with the policy that had persistently fostered pro-slavery and causes leading to the final crisis. The character of his administration was shaped before he was President. He was surrounded by traitors in authority. Like clay he was molded to fit; a figure, a cipher to be looked to by loyal people while disloyalty carried into execution a plot to subvert or destroy the republic. His maudlin appeal to the North for conciliation served to kill time while rebels made read to kill. Rebels had made it clear after the election of Lincoln, that no terms of compromise acceptable to the North would be accepted by the South. Had compromise been possible it could only have been so by a firm, aggressive executive policy, not by an attempt at neutrality toward either a loyal or a disloyal constituency. It was an unnatural attitude for an Executive. It only served to establish a belief among all classes South and certain classes North, that disunion was acquiesced in, a conclusion that had to be overcome by powder, bullet and blood.

True there was a somewhat prevalent sentiment North that extenuated Southern acts and inferentially encouraged them. It is true that this sentiment was fostered by his course, and would have been less known had he been vigorously loyal, and less resigned to his own weakness. He made a pretense of reorganizing

## HISTORICAL INTRODUCTION—PART II.

Yet the total force assembled was but 630 men. This condition did not represent the needs of the people; nor did Buchanan's act represent their wishes. It had been the policy of the South, long supreme in Washington, to keep the regular army as small as possible, to scatter it to remote points, to leave insufficiently garrisoned Southern forts, using mostly Southern men; to enlarge and keep its State militia full, and recently had been drilling and re-arming. And notwithstanding the insufficiently garrisoned United States forts in the South, Floyd, of the War Department, had been transferring from Northern military posts arms and war munitions of all sorts to Southern arsenals for use in a prospective war against the national government, one order alone transferring 115,000 improved muskets.

May 1, 1861, the U. S. Mint at New Orleans was seized by a military force with $600,000 specie; also the U. S. Custom House with considerable funds. Cobb had bankrupted the treasury, Floyd had caused a defalcation in the nterior Department by complicity with a clerk, of over $1,000,000, and both had joined the host of treason. Buchanan, on leaving the presidency, after showing formal courtesy to his successor, Lincoln, repaired to the house of his friend, Robert Ould, a United States district attorney, who was preparing to go South to become active in the service of rebellion, though his home was in Maryland, expecting, probably, that it would e'er long be incorporated in the Slave Confederacy.

Such was the political, military, financial and moral status of the outgoing of the last administration of the irate slave power. "Time honored" we had been told was their rule, yet nothing could be more rotten in an ethical sense, more dishonorable politically, more savage, more disgraceful to the country. Study the horrors of history, the bloody treachery of ages, the plots of tragedies, nothing more wickedly planned and savagely executed is apparent.

# CHRONICLES
## FROM THE
## DIARY OF A WAR PRISONER

### OPENING CAMPAIGN IN 1864, IN VIRGINIA.

In camp near Culpepper, Va., May 3d, 1864.—Weather delightful. Rumors of marching tomorrow morning. Marching orders we have been expecting several days, but this is the first rumor for some time. It has been mysteriously quiet. If, instead of May and fine weather, we had had dead of winter, storm and mud, we would have been provoked with five or six rumors daily. So that's nothing;; but we shall march soon. Usual drill forenoon and afternoon; march an hour under knapsack. Go to Culpepper with several for examination for commissions in negro regiments. At 5:30 o'clock drew one day's rations. This task is assigned me this week, for my company. At dark, orders for three days' more rations. Had a tedious task lasting until 9 p. m. Quartermaster is getting everything ready to leave and hinted we should move at 12 midnight. Got orders at 8 o'clock to strike tents, pack nothing unnecessary; build no fires. Everything soon ready; we are waiting, the boys are jolly, full of spirit. At 11 o'clock we marched—winter quarters again broken.

May 4th, Morning at Stevensburg, Va.—Taking a southwest direction we passed northeast of Stony Mountain and came in conjunction with other marching columns and moving trains. Our ears were filled with confusion, noisy jests, rough questionings and "blowing" of different regiments. Marched fast. Inspired by excitement, our boys were not to be beaten; it was a grand show that nobody saw but the performers. Our course was principally southeast until we reached this deserted village, Stevensburgh, at daylight. Here are fields of artillery and cavalry awaiting us. We rest awhile; I lay on the mossy plank steps of what was a tavern. Grass is in the streets. Buildings old style; paint has seceded. It is a pleasant site, overlooking grand country; had been a desirable place in better days. This movement is to throw our forces together to the right of Lee's position south of the Rapidan, cutting the latters' connection with Fredericksburg and to go on to Richmond, if he does not come out to fight us. This will bring our base of supplies south to points accessible to the coast.

On Field, South of Rapidan, Noon—We took a southerly course to the river, halting but little. Beautiful morning, splendid view of the glorious landscape; rich country. Occasionally stately dwellings of the comfortable Virginia style are left on terra firma and inhabited.

Sun came out hot. Those who had scruples about throwing clothing away on the start, felt the necessity. For an hour and a half the road was strewn with coats, blouses, shirts, blankets and other things, so thickly that we could not march in files without treading upon it, which made marching tiresome. Miles of ground was literally covered.

Men were sun-struck and fell as if shot dead; one who fell as we moved along a narrow dugway, rolled down the hill and lodged against a tree. It is a frightful moan they give as they fall, slamming their guns on the ground. The aid they get from comrades in the ranks is slight; we can only cast a pitying look and pass on. I came near falling. Friends applied water from canteens to the back of my head, neck and breast, which proved a relief. Capt. Swan told me to fall out but I felt determined not to leave the ranks; threw away my woolen blanket and got better.

About 11 a. m. our (Fifth) corps reached the Rapidan River at Germania ford and crossed on pontoons. Several cannon were in position commanding the heights beyond. It was a proud sight to see the columns winding up the rocky slope on the south side, as we descended from the north. They crossed a drove of cattle by driving them through; some were drowned. There was once a bridge here; the stone abutments remain.

The Second (Hancock's) corps crossed at Ely's ford several miles east. His advance surprised and captured a Confederate force this morning that had been watching our army. The Sixth (Sedgwick's) corp crossed five miles west of Germania. The positions of these grand divisions of the Army of the Potomac, in these movements, indicate their respective positions in coming battles, namely: Hancock's corp on the left, Warren's in the center, Sedgwick's on the right. The Ninth (Burnside's) corp is a few miles behind, moving in three columns to be used in emergencies. Cavalry divisions are generally in advance and on our flanks contending with the enemy's detached forces, or harassing his rear, miles away.

Hard fighting is expected by officers and men. We feel the final movement on Richmond is on. It is the beginning of the end—a big butt-end! We are to meet the enemy in regions where fighting has been mostly favorable to the Southern army, in its chosen, often fortified positions. Officers assume that our corps will make the first attack, or will be first attacked. The enemy is familiar with the country where battles are likely to occur. During winter suspension of hostilities, he has moved forces about this country to acquaint them with it. Leading officers know points of natural strategy, hence have many advantages. Naturally he will make a desperate attempt to crush us at a time most opportune to him. His position we shall find when revealed by the attack, or by our skirmishers and scouts. Our men understand this; are nerved for the crisis. Our fate rests with officers.

They were strongly fortified here and a half mile back, but forces in charge retired after a few shots. We lay down behind these fortifications two hours, taking refreshments, rest and sleep. A heavy body of troops are assembled in this vicinity.

Near Wilderness, Sunset.—Bugles sounded again; columns of infantry and trains of artillery move out by brigades, the corps having divided into several columns for convenience in forming for battle and to make closer connections with the left and right wings. It appears, by the way we move, the enemy are not disposed to check us today; all is quiet as if there were no such thing as battle. We move cautiouly, through heavy wildernesses on old roads—about 4 o'clock p. m. struck the plank road and were soon near portions of the old battle grounds about Chancellorsville.

The column soon broke off by regiments on either side. To our delight, we were told that we would probably stay the night. There is a broad field covered with troops of all arms; heavy supply trains and artillery, no doubt 40,000 armed men. Generals Grant, Meade, Warren and staffs arrived soon after we camped, also several other generals and staffs. General Wadsworth has been riding among the troops of his division and passing a word with us. The old gentleman is as good natured as ever. He wears the regulation cap, rides a light gray horse, his gray hair cut short and side whiskers closely trimmed. The boys all like the old "Abolish." A have been to a creek and bathed, feel pretty well. Headquarters bands are playing beautifully. The scene is sublime; the red sun hangs just over the woods, the trees are brilliantly green and filled with happy birds. Men by thousands are boiling coffee and frying pork and hard tack.

There is an old mill near, long silent for Secessia's sake, now receiving attention from the boys; they are not likely to slight it until they run it—into the ground. Some are running through it seeing what can be picked up; others are knocking and pulling pine boards from its sides. It is not a stranger to soldiers, they have been here before, both Union and Rebs; Stonewall himself, perhaps; like enough "Fighting Joe." It was about here the former made his last dash. Two of us lug off a wide door for a bed. Of course the boys talk about where we are going; some think they know exactly; it is to Mine Run again, or it is straight to Richmond. We have marched thirty miles. Fog appears as the sun sinks. We lie down early; had no sleep last night; pitch no tents. Probabilities are for an early stir in the morning. We have plumb six days' rations, expect to need them.

### OPENING THE GREAT WILDERNESS BATTLES.

Thursday, May 5th, 1864.—Before day bugles blowed, drums beat; men get ready to march. At dawn troops were moving; at sunrise our division marched. A mile out we discovered indications of the enemy. More skirmishers are thrown out (56th Pennsylvania of our brigade) and a battery accompanying it. Heavy picket lines move on the right and left of the advancing column. In an hour we move southwest, into thick woods. The road became so crowded by troops and artillery that moving was difficult. At last we moved rapidly, the artillery halting to give us a chance. We struck the plank road leading to Orange Court House from Fredericksburg, and reached a clearing about two miles on, our brigade leading, formed for battle, and halted, having come up with our skirmish line that had met a check. Several generals were riding on the line. In a few minutes General J. C. Rice, of our brigade, ordered three companies of the 76th N. Y. to deploy as skirmishers. Companies F, K and B advanced along the edge of the woods to the left and deployed. Advancing into the woods we were ordered to lie down, General Rice superintending at the time. Sharp skirmishing was taking place to the left between cavalry which grew heavier and nearer. Our line was being driven in by a stronger force, Rebels yelling as they came on. Firing nearly ceased, then came a sharp volley that shook the woods. The Rebels yelled and fell back, we following. This was the first fire received by our part of the line since deploying. The fight grew sharp; our line trembled but we heard artillery hurrying through the woods having to cut roads. The enemy again attacked us. Presently we heard cannon booming heavily, we rallied and Rebs fell back. The lines on our right and left seemed to have changed; then firing nearly ceased. We pressed forward and came up to a heavier detachment of the enemy and had a lively brush, taking three or four prisoners and driving the enemy. Our orders were to advance two miles, if possible, and we pushed on firing and maneuvering every way, part of the time lying flat, loading and firing. We took seven more Johnnies

Meantime firing began on our right earnestly, an incessant roll of musketry for two hours. It was between our Fifth corp and Ewell's. It began about noon and lasted half the afternoon, but little artillery being used on our side on account of the woods. It appeared they had turned our left flank, which cut us off from any support.

We found the enemy's skirmishers on our left, right and front in heavy force and connections with our forces broken. We sent men to find the brigade that we might get relief or orders, and they never returned. We were dealing with an enemy more than ten to our one who were trying to decoy us. It proved we were behind Lee's fighting line and in the track of his reinforcements, as then constituted. It was impossible to maintain a position against their assaults. That we might more safely retire. and to deceive them as to our force the line was assembled, and we gathered nearly 500 men, some of the 56th Pennsylvania, and fragments of eastern and western regiments that had been scattered. To extend our line we advanced boldly single rank, fixing bayonets, loudly cheering, firing rapidly as we located the Rebs who disappeared over the ridge, behind a high, thick hedge, when we suddenly moved by the right flank and file right, double quick. We thought ourselves lucky when we got out of this predicament.

We had lost seventeen men out of our three (76th regiment) companies. During our direct movement, before retiring, we passed over several dead Southerners. The movement became confused, some of the men breaking off from the column and came in contact with another body of the enemy. In getting out I barely escaped running into this body. As I approached they cried "Come in, you Yank!"; their pieces were at a ready, but I plunged to the right into a narrow gulf down an embankment through the brush to the bottom, despite whistling bullets, and soon came up to the officers and most of the men. One of the boys who was taken at this time escaped without hat or equipments.

Several bullets came near hitting me during the forenoon. At one time I stood by a hickory tree charging my gun, when a bullet struck it within two inches of my face. I cast my eye to the spot when another ball struck the tree an inch below and glanced away, throwing the bark in my face. Others struck a log, behind which I lay, and glanced over me.

The woods were very thick and we ran as fast as possible and reached a small clearing. Some thought it the place where our brigade formed for battle in the morning and where we were detached as skirmishers; I did not recognize it. It was now 3 o'clock and quiet all around. We were perplexed, tired, hungry and hot, besmeared with powder and dust, clothing torn and faces and arms scratched with brush. We lay down and ate a hardtack, hoping for the better. In our retreat we paid no attention to prisoners and only one, belonging to a North Carolina regiment, was with us. Contact with the new force of Rebels from which I escaped, convinced me that we had been drawn purposely on and that this party, which seemed numerous, was swinging to our rear and that our movement was timely. I informed the officers of what I had seen and believed and, while they were consulting, a young "darkey" whom Captain Swan recognized as his father's servant, who was Captain in Co. D of our regiment. He was much excited and came running from the woods and said there was Rebel cavalry "right out dar," pointing in the direction we hoped to find our army. An officer immediately rode to the edge of the woods but came back hastily, falling us in and we moved to the west as fast as possible. We had not reached the woods before the cavalry came out on the other side thundering and rattling and quickly formed. We were not thirty rods distant when they formed. We immediately formed and moved into the woods and prepared for a fight feeling confident that if we could not whip the cavalry we could not out run it. A few men were so excited they could hardly be kept in line.

A Rebel officer came out the road; (a mere by-road). Discovering us ready, he returned. They immediately changed their course and we went on. We moved as fast and as cautiously as possible, for the woods seemed full of the enemies scouts with whom some shots were exchanged. Turning north we passed through a dark swamp and came out near a clearing. A portion of the ground had been fought over. Dead and wounded were scattered along. Mostly Union, but I saw two dead Southerners. For a ways guns, knapsacks, hats and blankets were strewn. From the position of these we judged our skirmishers had been overwhelmed, slaughtered, driven in or captured. Coming near the edge of the woods we halted and, after consultation, Lieutenant Cheesman of Rice's staff rode out to an old house at the edge of the clearing. He found an old man and a fair looking young woman who asserted their ignorance of the presence of any of Lee's army and consented to go with us to show the way to Chancellorsville. In about half a mile we came to where the road forked. They told us to take the right and at a cetain point to turn to the right again, and we would reach Chancellorsville in about four and a half miles. They were dismissed by the officer in charge and were observing us pass when I noticed the dis=

graceful and humiliating conduct of a lieutenant of the 95th N. Y. volunteers, an insignificant looking fellow who thrust his face close to hers and used insulting language, calling her abusive epithets. She shrank from him. Those who saw him hissed and cried "pimp, louse, fool" and other epithets. He threatened to put us under arrest for using disrespectful language to an officer. They called him a scoundrel, saying "if we get to our lines we'll report you." He sneaked off to keep from being clubbed by their muskets. Officers hearing the row ascertained the cause, reprimanded him and told the men they did right. Capt. Swan apologized to the woman.

## SURPRISED AND MADE PRISONERS OF WAR.

We had gone scarcely half a mile before we were in the midst of the enemy again. The first intimation we had of it was the clicking of their muskets as they cocked them and I saw two officers on horseback to the right of the road ahead and their lines rose up in front and on both sides of us. Our officers were too confident of escape and neglected to put out an advance guard after talking with those people, although we had a rear guard. It was an overwhelming surprise. Officers and men stood speechless, huddled together. But one order was given, that by Orderly Sergeant G. W. Mattison of Co. F 76th N. Y., to "wheel into line and fire," which we did quickly and commenced to reload as we fell back. The Rebel fire was directed to the huddle of men, twenty-two of whom were killed and wounded and among them the lieutenant of the 95th N. Y. was shot through the bowels and killed; Lieut. Cahill, Co. B 76th N. Y., through the right arm, breaking it, but none of our company were injured; three others were killed as near as I could learn. I saw several fall in the Rebel ranks. There was confusion and fright, most of the men scattering, flinging away everything hoping to escape. Lieuts. Cheesman and Call flew on Cheesman's horse. Our company broke, the men hoping to escape. Tbout twenty of us re-formed back in the thicket and rallied to fight them, when someone from the front cried "hold on, boys, hold on, they are our men; don't fire for God's sake!"

At this point I saw Captains Swan and Clyde in the midst of the Rebels waving their hats not to fire. Exultant at the thought that we had met friends instead of foes, for the thicket we could not see that they were, we eagerly rushed forward shouting "Good!" Then I saw the two captains throwing off their belts and swords, holding their swords up by the points. The Rebels rushed at us screaming "surrender you Yanks," "throw down them guns." Some were for running, some for renewing the fight.

I heard Captain Swan say "Its no use, better surrender;" Some attempted to break their guns against trees, but Rebel bayonets were so near and so many, that we desisted. The wounded in our midst begged us not to fire. Plunging the bayonet which I had fixed to my Springfield, into the ground I said, "Boys you've got us." "Come heah," they said, and I did, cutting my straps at the same time. I tore the bugle from my hat, not caring to indulge the Rebel craze for Yankee trinkets. Just after an officer rode up to the next man and said, "Gimme that bugle on your hat sah" (a brass ornament for hat or cap.) Jonnies mixed freely with us to trade canteens, knives, caps, rubber blankets, tobacco boxes, etc. Excitement chiefly over we marched about 30 rods to a strip of clearing where we found a division of Hill's corps in line of battle to receive us. One said to me that they had been watching for us all the afternoon. "We'ns reckoned there was a heap more of you'ns; you'ns played right smart or we would had you'ns befo'."

He said the woods were full of cavalry looking for us. They got nearly 300 men

It was between 5 and 6 o'clock p. m. when we stood before that long line of men saying all sorts of things to us, asking all sorts of questions, what we thought about other battles that had been fought where they had been successful, how Grant was getting along, what we thought of Bobby Lee, and if McClellan would be our next President and other things, while the officers prepared to move the column to the rear. I was very thirsty and was glad to trade my canteen for the sake of water. Cannonading was lively, shells screaming through the air almost over head. We found ourselves between our right and Lee's left flank but nearer to Lee's.

Looking easterly I saw the Union line advancing, muskets gleaming, smoke rolling in front as far as could be seen, probably over two miles. Batteries were in action on both sides. The Confederate works were indicated far and near by the smoke of musketry and cannon. The ground shook from the force of rapid firing. As I looked about it seemed like the beginning of sorrow, a day of trouble and danger passed and worse to come. I forgot to say that Capts. Swan and Clyde threw themselves flat on the ground at the Rebels first fire and that each was grazed by bullets on the cheek. They had got but about two-thirds of our party. In a few minutes the Rebel command "Attention," was given and the column left faced and moved off, prisoners marching by their side. As we double quickened up the hill the rattle of musketry mingled with the roar of cannon and the bursting of shells was terrific. As we approached their lines it seemed to be in confusion, shifting batteries, digging rifle-pits, throwing up breast works, cavalry golloping and reserve infantry rushing to the front. Excitement was intense as we passed through their lines and were hurried back, our own shells cutting the woods around us. We had been taken charge of by a detail of guards, the troops that escorted us in, being assigned to a position in the line of battle. We were halted about sixty rods to the rear from the line of battle behind the woods where we found other prisoners crowded together as thickly as possible, surrounded by Rebel troops. Faint and thirsty we sat down to take it as easily as possible. There came a lull in the battle but in a few minutes the quiet was broken by an outburst of firing close at hand. Great confusion prevailed; shouts of distress and sharp commands mingled; teams with and without riders came flying back; down the road, through field and wood, fled fragments of infantry, officers shouting halt, flourishing swords and revolvers. Guards yelled, "The Yanks are coming, the line is broken, fall in right smart, get out of har Yanks."

It was a scarry time for us, though we rejoiced to see it. Bayonets in hands of excited Rebels, some so enraged as to be anxious to use them. We expected the whole line might be thrown dismayed upon us, and our bullets might whittle us. The stampede was soon checked, fresh regiments hastening forward and it became quiet. Though we had not gone a rod an officer came along and in a kindly manner said, "Sit down, boys, and take it cool." Yanks began to inquire of Rebs about particulars of the excitement, when an officer told both parties to "shut your heads, its nothing but a d——d nigger let a span of horses loose." About sunset the battle was resumed. The roll of musketry was terrible and incesant, cannonading almost continuous until after 8 o'clock. Before dark we were marched about two miles to near Barker's store where we found other prisoners. We got over the trenches, rifle pits and breast works and lay down for the night. It was very dark, and we were closely guarded and not allowed to speak to the guards.

### BEHIND THE ENEMY'S GUNS; LEE AND LONGSTREET.

Friday, May 6th, 1864—Up at earliest dawn. Feeling quite well. The sound of battle was in our ears. The ground is very foul here; a winter camp and a fresh battle ground. Dead cavalrymen, killed yesterday are in our midst, our men bury them. At daylight Longstreet's corps came up on a forced march, moving close to us; it was two hours passing. General Longstreet and staff call at General Lee's headquarters, a hundred yards distant.

The fore part of last night several batteries were hurried past, sent, I think, to Lee's right. I think this early fighting is to facilitate a movement by our left wing around Lee's right. Hard to get water. They let a few men out with canteens under guard.

When Longstreet returned to his column he was accompanied by General Lee. A short time they stood together dismounted, with bared heads, opposite us on the other side of Longstreet's cheering columns hastening to battle. Grave concern was on their faces. Magnificent men; but I felt oppressed with the fact of their attitude toward their country, fighting to disrupt it, to maintain a claim of right to perpetuate slavery by unlimited extension; to curse the whole country as it curses the South. Educated to serve the Nation, sworn to do it, they break their oaths by acts most treasonable, justifying their course by the flimsy pretext of the acts of their states in seceding because a president, not their choice is elected. It is apalling how men of large ability and boasted dignity, stultify themselves! the greater the men the greater their responsibility for wrongful acts. The roar of deadly battle this good morning witnesseth their and their associates sin. What wretched perversion of the sentiment of patriotism! Their cause fails, God rules! General Lee and staff passed close to me at 7 o'clock, galloping to the front. He has a pleasant face, peculiarly impressive but stern; an imperative temperament that inspires confidence, admiration and fear, the austere features lighted by geniality and persistent characteristics signifying strength of nature, but liable to act from illogical and dangerous influence that appeals to prejudice, narrow pride, warped by false traditions; a bent of character when once it espouses illegitimate conclusions, devotes his best ability to accomplish ends his better judgment had condemned.

The battle had opened at 5 o'clock, our sixth corp attacking. Firing terrific, nearer this point than last night but farther west, came nearer steadily, our forces driving till Longstreet's corp reached the field, overlapping our line and regained the position from which our forces had driven them. Had our attack occurred an hour earlier, decisive defeat of the Rebel forces engaged must have resulted before Longstreet could have arrived. Our lines are reported in confusion and falling back.

The rest of our party who avoided capture last night, are brought in after trying all night to escape. Officers are as humble as privates, look full as serious over prospects. Talk of exchange as soon as the campaign is over, July at the farthest. But the duration of this campaign is uncertain. A great disaster on either side would need it. If there are no decisive results, and a prospect of transferring the struggle to the vicinity of Richmond—Butler is already near there—it will be longer than any other Virginia campaign. Lee will get no peace as long as Grant maintains a position between Fredericksburg and Richmond, until he is in his stronghold; then Lee's fate will be settled. Fortunate we shall be if we see our lines by September. By 8 a. m. fighting ceased; wounded coming in fast. Confederates taken to field hospitals, our wounded put with us. Some have lain all night, are chilled badly. It is hard to see so many bleeding men shot through faces, arms, legs, bodies, broken limbs, distorted mouths, one with eye-ball dangling on his cheek, blood clotted on his face, neck and breast. They let us help them from ambulances. They cry for water, some stupid, some shaking with chills and crying for blankets. Rebels claim they whipped us yesterday; but they have no advantage except in position; in that they are losing. They admit two generals killed and Longstreet wounded. Fog clears away; gets pleasant.

### LEAVE BATTLE LINE FOR PRISON—INTERVIEW REBEL OFFICER.

At 10 a. m. about 700 prisoners started for Orange Court House. Day hot, road dusty. We meet supply trains, ambulances, troops and a few conveyances with civilians pushing to the front, and for twenty miles groups of stragglers limping on, some lying down, the hardest looking lot of men ever seen trying to get to their commands. As we met the troops they cried, "What brigade's that?" "Are you on to Richmond?" "Where's Grant?" We were told that already a large portion of his army was north of the Rappahannock. Sneers, jeers and words of contempt we did not notice; but when they told us we were whipped we replied bitterly, "You fool yourselves." Till noon we march fast, the guard keeping ranks closed up, threatening if one lagged. We suffered with thirst, wallowed in a constant cloud of dust, panted with heat and chafed over our terrible luck.

Our guard claims to be General Lee's bodyguard; better men than the general run of Rebel soldiers. They grew sociable and easy with us. We halted at noon near a creek in woods by the roadside, until lately an army camp, and rested an hour. Bathing my head and neck freely in the stream, I felt better. A man about forty years old, a Captain, was eager to talk politics. I saw him talking to one of our soldiers who was irritated by his secesh notions, which he put forward in a good natured but overbearing way. The boy could not stand it and "blew on him" and took another seat. Anxious for a little Copperhead philosophy from a Southerner, I took a position nearly in front of him, my friend Thompson on my right, and called him out. The group that listened were convinced that Northern sympathizers are of the Virginia stripe, the same bird that can see only in the night of slavery and Southern rights and the art of secession; and while he believed in secession he was not of the "fire-eater" temperament but would have preferred the further way round to the same point. That is, he preferred that the slavery question be settled in favor of slaveholders in the Union.. But "Black Republicans" and "Nigger Stealers" had seized the bridge, and the South had gone all one way by the Secession route." "We conservatives fell in at last feeling elated and sure," said he, "that when we get secession, friends at the North will help us to pin to the wall the radicals, hang abolishionists, suppress every newspaper like old Greeley's and stop the incendiary preaching against slavery, and reestablish the Union on Southern ideas proclaimed by Alexander H. Stephens in his inauguration speech, making slavery the chief cornerstone of a new government."

We accepted his declaration as very frank and representative of so-called Virginia conservatives. Consequently they rejoiced to see a party crying down the administration, praying that that party shall rise to power, in Northern States, hurl every man from positions of trust that does not believe in the policy of the extreme Southern leaders on the slavery doctrine, with the fiercenes of vigilance committees. I had read much of this many times in stanch newspapers, ratification speeches and in platforms. While in his mind lurked a love for Union, he said: "First and always the independence of the South must be the end of this war." If Northern "doe-faces" would still whine for a Union on "time-honored principles" namely, on any terms dictated by Calhoun disciples, their manhood and patriotism is a nullity. A thousand times have I wept and raved that Northerners should palaver over this deliberate treason of the South, failing to see the issue so plain that he who runs may read. There never was a more direct conflict of principles than this in which America is engaged.

To detail all was said is impossible. I give some points to show his logic. I open by saying it was foolish to "flare up," that we ought to be able to talk even if we were prisoners, but if we could not express our views we had nothing to say; that if free discussion had been allowed by the South for the last thirty years instead of hanging Northerners for expressing opinions we would thought better of each other, the problem would have been solved without war.

Tis home is at Leesburg, Va., in Union lines. His wife resides there. He had known General Lee many years and from the first was ready to follow him either way in this contest; so was all northern Virginia. He confirmed my assertion that if Lee had stood for the Union and offered his services, that the majority of Virginians would have been on the side of the Union, and there would have been no State of West Virginia; also that Lee deprecated secession, regarded it revolutionary and contrary to the intention of the founders of the government, and if successfully it would multiply the very evils slaveholders complain of. But he justified his ultimate course by the fact that his State had seceded, that it had a right to secede, and that his duty to Virginia was paramount to his allegiance to the national government.

"A majority of Southern men are States rights," said he, "and when it appeared that the South would secede, State after State, it was plain to Southerners that the Union had gone to pieces,—nothing left to hang to, even if every Northern State should legalize n'gger slavery and embellish all Northern political platforms with Southern notions about that 'peculiar institution.' Southern rights, secession, and slavery is the prevailing trend, out and out slave confederacy the aim. No man of character can live in the South and attain success without slaves, or an heirdom, pecuniarily or socially. A slave holder has standing; it is a certificate of character, a credential that takes him everywhere, to be master and owner of labor. He holds the church in his hand, and in his grip the politicians and the state. The press must be his tool. He is master of society as well as his slaves; commands respect from centers of fashion and trade, even in England and France regardless of professed aversion to slavery. You had not a merchant in New York, of wealth and influence, who did not cater to the hated slave-power; always will out of the Union the same as in."

He owned slaves when the war began; he had thirty-three. He said: "You nigger stealers get all but one, and he is a cook in Lee's army." Then to my surprise he said:

"I never did believe slavery right; it began by stealing and piracy, and you fellows mean it shall end the same way. It is practically the curse, of the South, degrading to the master morally; degrading to the mass who never did and never can hold slaves; yet the mass are the bone and sinew of its strength. Slavery is to be the cornerstone of the Confederacy; but that stone rests upon the bare backs of the non-slave holding rank and file. They must be our military strength. They are not and cannot be our industrial strength; that belongs to the slaves under the whip. The wealth, social and political power, lie with slave owners; they are the land owners; they rule the white mass as effectually and at less cost than they control the blacks. The future of the South is a military empire and necessarily a wealthy power."

I endorsed his prophesy, if the South should succeed, and asked: "If slavery is not right, why are you fighting to maintain it? Why will it not be abolished?" He said:

"The South has made it a permanent system not only of domestic importance, but a state policy, a source of social, economical and political strength. The abolishionists are not strong enough to abolish it; secession has placed it beyond their reach. It is an accomplished fact. If the Confederacy is not recognized this summer it will be be after the fall election. The wealth power of the North, then, through commercial and financial interests, will be weighed against you."

"You are deluded, Sir, in assuming that secession, if successful, will put slavery beyond the growing power of abolishionism. Freedom is progressive; your boast arrays civilization and progress against you. Again you are wrong in assuming that the Confederacy will be recognized this year or next. The rabid spirit of the slave power has called into greater force the love of liberty, the principle written in the Declaration of Independence, than has been known for ages. The very fact that your great men of Virginia today repudiate Washington, Jefferson, Henry and Madison, convicts you of treason to the spirit of '76. Your apparent chance of success as it seemed to exist has gone. You stole States, forts, arms, men trained at government cost, until we had nothing left in the South and but little in the North. We then proposed to coax you to old fashioned loyalty patched with a new slavery grant. But you thought you had it all. We now propose to restore the Union and purge it of slavery. Instead of recognition you will see that secession will go to pieces and your Confederacy will collapse. We were unprepared for this fight, you boasted you were ready. We are now ready and your power must wane. It will cost less to save the Union without slavery than with it. Should you now offer to accept our first purpose, to save the Union, with slavery, the North would scorn it. The trend is against your scheme of a black Utopia, a slave owning, slave breeding, slave selling, slave working empire.

"Had the Democrats of the North done as they might have done you would not have been here, boys. Abe Lincoln could not have carried on the war. The abolishionists will have a sweet time up North this fall if they run McClellan for president."

"What did you expect they would do?"

"Do what they said they would, oppose the draft and war by force, not let the abolishionists rule."

"Is it possible you expected what you call the Democrats would assist you?"

"We cal'lated their opposition to Lincoln would prevent war, but they kept still and let him control the people and gave him power in Congress and had not nerve to oppose him."

"But it was your party that gave him power in Congress by seceding; they boasted North that Lincoln could not choose his Cabinet except by sanction of a Democratic Senate."

"Yes, but we had seceded, and there would have been less bloodshed had they shed some."

"You deceived yourselves."

"Should not have been deceived had Seymour led the New York riot. When he was elected Governor the South rejoiced; New York would send no more men and when that riot came up we expected great things; but instead of running it he let it run itself; he might have helped us there."

"What, you don't suppose Horatio Seymour is in sympathy with secession! He will stand for the Union till the last." My aim was to make them believe that the North is a unit. So I added: "The people of the South have, and will rely in vain upon this element; the mere difference of opinion never will injure our strength. The North is as one man on the question of Union and never will give it up; they can whip you and will do it."

"See what they will do if they elect McClellan, he is your best man; you never ought to have removed him."

"Will you come back into the Union if he should be elected?"

"Never; we'd be d——d fools to come into the Union then. Never; until all States shall have adopted policies favorable to slavery!"

He said the administration would have interfered with slavery if they had not gone to war. I quoted from the Chicago resolutions, speeches and the resolutions of Congress after they had seceded and left the power in the hands of the Republicans, showing they were anxious to give them every guarantee not to interfere with the local establishment of slavery by legislation; that they persisted in revolt and measures were adopted accordingly. "You invited war," I said, "and that invites the use of the war power against slavery. After it is over you may resume rightful relations in other matters but slavery will be ended."

"Well, niggers run into Pennsylvania and they would not let them come back."

"Recognize your Confederacy; will not the nigger go over? Will it not be an inducement to run away? Will your fugitive slave law apply?"

"Yes, they may run away."

"Will we as a nation give them up?"

"I don't know; reckon not."

"What will you do if we don't?"

"We'll fight for them."

"What have you gained there?"

"It's a state right to secede; you deny it, we establish it."

"Could you maintain a Confederacy three years?"

"I presume not; South Carolina'd kick up a muss in six months and raise h——l."

"Then the other States would have to assume the obligations of the Confederacy; this would produce discontent; what would you do?"

"Well, I s'pose we'd whip her back."

Taking him by the buttonhole, I said: "Where are your state rights, man?"

Amid the shouts of the boys he laughed, frowned, colored, and was much agitated, and said:

"Damn her; she and Massachusetts ought to've been shoved into the ocean years ago."

"That can't be done; you'd whip her back and that is precisely what we are doing only on a larger scale. Can you blame us for whipping you back?"

"Never can do it. We will have our independence; without that there will not be a slave in the South; a man is a fool that thinks we are fighting for compromise, or will give up till we are whipped, or force you to concede our rights."

"So we might as well have it out and end the matter, slavery question and all."

"Yes, sir; we agree on that."

"We are going to do it," shouted the boys.

Giving him a Union hardtack and receiving one of his, feeling heartily thankful that we had over an hour's talk with an officer of Lee's bodyguard, we pursued our dreary journey, considerably rested.

## TALKS AND INCIDENTS AT GORDONSVILLE.

Passing Mine Run we got a view of that formidable position which we invested in December last and realized the wisdom of General Meade's caution in retiring. The most important place on the route is Old Verdersville where we raided her public wells. Many of our men were overcome with thirst, heat and cramps. Griffith and I had some dried currants and Jamaica ginger which we distributed much to their relief. It was eight in the evening, and very dark when we arrived at Orange Court House. They put us in the court house yard which is paved with cobble stones and surrounded by an iron fence, so crowded that there was not room for all to lie down. We had come 25 miles, was faint, tired, dejected; had eaten but little all day, piecing out the remnant of rations drawn May 3 and 4, not knowing when the Rebels would issue any.

Saturday, May 7th—At 1 o'clock last night we were aroused by guards shouting "Get out o'har, you'uns, in five minutes to take ca's for Richmond," punching us through the fence with bayonets, others coming through and kicking those who had not arisen, driving us out like a pack of hogs. It was evident, by the dialect, we had changed guards. Though much confusion and hurry followed, it was an hour before we moved to the train, and when aboard we stayed till daylight. They were box cars, so crammed we had to stand. At daylight officers ordered tents and blankets thrown out. The guard in our car repeated the order aloud, then whispered "Hide them." Some were thrown off and the train moved.

The landscape was beautiful, clothing herself in robes of spring. Morning delightful, a sweet air, the sun shed its rays on the land and spake peace to every heart. Nature was heavenly, her voice is ever, "Man be true to thyself;" the same in war and in peace, to the rich, the poor, the high, the low. Oh, could we be like her! "Only man is vile."

As we approached Gordonsville we saw the heights, fortifications and the southwest mountains. In seven miles we are there. They marched us into a lot, searched us and registered our names. Before being searched I sold my rubber blanket for $5.00, Confederate money, to a guard. While going to the house to be searched I cut my tent into strips, feeling sure it would not aid and abet a Reb and bought bread of a woman, having nothing to eat. They took blankets, tents, knives, paper, envelopes, gold pens, razors and other things. Money was generally taken care of, but some was taken. My money I had tucked into the quilted lining of my dress coat. Many of us had nothing left to put over or under us; this was my case. All I had was my clothing, portfolio containing blank paper, envelopes, a few photos and a partly written diary, pencils and pens, which they took from me, but I prevailed upon the officer searching me to return them, for which I thanked him.

Searching over, we took another part of the field near some houses. There were some citizens, one from North Carolina who inquired particularly about Northern affairs. The coming presidential election is the rage among soldiers and citizens. They believe it will effect the interests of the South. Prejudice and pride are the levers by which the Southern mass have been moved. Through these the Southern heart has been fired by the ruling class. Their eager enthusiasm over prospects of realizing the hope of the permanent adoption of their absurd theory about

Southern civilization and scheme of empire with slavery as the cornerstone, is evidently waning. Our side of the story was new. They seemed to doubt the soundness of the old doctrine of Southern extremists, hence desired the triumph of the "conservative" party north more because leaders favored it than for a real understanding of the matter. They had had no idea of taking up with the seceded States, had they been able to maintain their armies along border States, or quarter them in the heart of the North.

Their motto was "All the South must be given up along the Southern to the Western coasts, and all slave States. Picturing the inconsistency of their demands, the improbability of their being yielded, made them look sober. They had supposed the North cared nothing for the Union worth fighting for, and as the Democratic party never opposed slavery, should it rise to power the war would cease and all disputes would be settled by treaty. A soldier of prominence said the mere existence of slavery led on our armies; that if we had the power to abolish slavery we would acknowledge the South.

Then came the usual tirade about disregarded Southern rights contented negroes, their unfitness for liberty. This summary of sentiment, be it true or false, sways the mass, fills the ranks and yields supplies. Yet it is noticable that the mass admit a belief that slavery is wrong, a weak system of labor; but that there was no other system for the South and what would the North do without it? They assumed that Northern commerce and industry depended upon slavery; that the climate is against white industry, white men being unable to endure labor; to which we replied by reminding them of the ability of both Southern and Northern white men to endure the hardships of war in the South.

These people had little knowledge of the character of the North, the value of the Union and the nature of the general government. It was noticable how frankly they admitted the cohabitation of some masters with slaves, or white with black, as more prevalent than is generally supposed, a fact that is evident by looking over the yellow complexioned slave population of Virginia. This intimation was offset by repeating the Jeff Davis calumnies uttered in one of his noted senatorial speeches of the degraded and wicked state of Northern society, and elicited this sentence: "Right or wrong it is the South's business," which came so hotly as to suggest danger.

One of the older citizens said: "Young man, you exercise more liberty of speech than is allowed in this country," which I conceded to be true and begged his pardon.

They do not see that when they forced slavery into a national territory and demanded its protection in Northern communities, it was the North's business. Much of present belief is new. There is a portion of the older class contiguous to the days of Washington and Jefferson, who entertain different sentiments politically and socially. Beliefs, as well as physical wants in the mass, conform to circumstances nearest the mind. We held that originally the negro question was incidental, but modernly became the cause of all difference; the grand issue being free government and the maintenance of the Union the best means to that end. Without slavery this issue would not have occurred.

An old man said he had always loved the Union, but had given it up; if the country could be restored to peace in the Union he would be glad, but he should not live to see it, "neither will you, young man," said he. It is a fact that the privileged youth of the South, wealthier and more favored, I mean, are stronger secessionists and more luminous in their ideas of empire than those whose days reach to the earlier period of the republic, because State rights, which always means slavery, have been the cause of the prevailing mania for a generation. Older citizens have been deposed, practically. Young men who have political views are invariably of the Southern Rights school, disciples of Calhoun and Yancey, who taught the new civilization with slavery as the cornerstone.

These young nabobs look us over as if surprised at our near resemblance to themselves and innocently inquire, "Do you think the nigger as good as the white man? Do you expect to reduce us to the level of the nigger?"

As to those who claim no right to know anything about politics they are like the old lady and daughters whose house I visited near Culpepper, Va.: They wanted the war to end and "don't care a plaguey bit how."

We lay at Gordonsville all day and night between the embankments of the railroad. Here I got my first sesech paper; it gave meager accounts of battles, stated that a force was within two miles of Petersburg and Richmond.

Wrote a letter to be sent home which a citizen said he would put in the office. About a hundred rations of hard bread and beef was issued to 700. I got none. A train of wounded Confederates came down from the Wilderness battlefield bound for Charlotteville; Gen. Longstreet on board. I climbed into the car and got a look at Longstreet as he lay bolstered up on his stretcher.

## VIRGINIA GIRLS OF SWEET SIXTEEN DID NOT LOVE US.

Saturday, May 8th.—Weather hot; two more trains of Rebel wounded pass. Report that General Wadsworth and others of our valuable generals are killed. At 2 p. m. our train moves for Lynchburg. It is composed of horse and cattle cars all crowded. Charlotteville is beautifully located in a fertile valley. About one mile west is the University of Virginia, founded by Thomas Jefferson. In the vicinity of this edifice were about twenty-five girls. Observing us, they waved their hands in greeting; we waved. We were going slowly; they ran across the green toward us. Discovering their mistake they bounded up and down and cried "You damned Yankees!" Screaming contemptuously they went back as fast as they came. Procuring a Rebel flag they flirted it at us.

      Sweet Virginia maids,
        You love the soil where born;
      But you bear a flag that fades;
        Yet I forgive your scorn.

      You know not what you do,
        Nor do I court debate;
      I'll fling a kiss to you,
        As you bestow your hate.

      I wish I had a flower;
        I'd toss it on the lea.
      It might perfume this hour
        You sour so on me!

      Indeed, I love you, quite
        You so much remind
      Of Northern girls as bright,
        Sweet girls I left behind.

      Your scorn is hot and keen
        As Yankee girls, I trow;
      Though you are sweet sixteen,
        Still sweeter girls I know!

      But when this war is o'er
        And purged your blood, that's bad,
      The Union we'll restore
        And you'll not be so mad.

Yes, when this war is over
 And the Union is restored,
You may want a Yankee lover,
 And not try to feel so bored.

Coquette with old Secech!
 Indeed,, it seems quite sad
That such could make a mash
 On girls and be their fad!

Some brutal nigger-driver,
 Who glories in his lash,
Some slavery conniver
 Might favor such a mash.

But your dear Alma Mater
 Is Jefferson's own school;
He was a slavery hater;
 T. J.—he was no fool!

Haughty maids, good-day—
 When shall we meet again?
You don't seem to like my way,
 Mad maids of Old Virgin.

Observing a large crowd to see us in town, the boys sang national songs, as the train drew in, which the officers stopped. The normal population of Charlotteville is 5,500. The greater portion of the crowd were women who looked at us with apparent interest. There are several hospitals here which are being filled with wounded. Four miles further the engine lost power and half our train is left, I being on the rear car. Before dark guards were stationed and we were ordered out of the cars and camped by the side of the railroad to remain all night. To the left of the road was a high steep bank; on the right a steep declivity, on the west the South Mountains. We had a pleasant talk with some guards who expressed Union sentiments, one, a North Carolinian. When home in April, he said, corn was worth $14 per bushel Confederate scrip; only 50c in silver.

A woman passing, said: "It is hard times; the people had not reckoned on the possibility of failure; for myself I did not deem it possible that all their lofty expectations would be realized."

Monday, May 9th.—About 10 a. m., the train having come back, we got on for Lynchburg. I had a flat car next to the engine, exposed to the sun, smoke and cinders. The passage was very disagreeable. The only place of account on the way is Amherst Court House. Arriving at Lynchburg, 3 p. m., we marched through the town exposed to the wondering gaze of all classes. A motley crowd gathered at every corner, blacks and whites indiscriminately mixed, some the dirtiest objects generally found in the filthiest portions of cities. Had I seen so many black and white heads together in New York or New England my conservative inclinations would have upbraided my abolishion sentiments about amalgamation, about reducing white folks to the level of the niggers. The town is dirty, dilapidated; streets cluttered with business, it being a depot for military supplies and a rendezvous for troops, situated on the right bank of the James River and on the Kanawah Canal and the Virginia and Tennessee Railroad; population about 13,000. They marched us a mile out of the city, and stopped in a deep hollow by a fine stream. On one side is a high, rocky hill. Here are all prisoners recently captured, except officers, who are locked up in the city. Our guards are mostly citizens, boys and old men, equipped by themselves or with such guns as the provost could pick up. Most of them are impressed and drilled by invalid soldiers. I observed one man about fifty, very corpulent, good naturedly inclined, dressed in common citizen's coat and pants, white vest, white stove pipe hat, with a weed, armed with a shotgun, pacing his beat. He said he would like to converse but dare not. From the brow of the hill several cannon command the camp. I saw several citizens imprisoned in the city on parole who sympathized with the North. One guard inquired as we came out from the city, what we did with deserters from their army. He said they were told they were hanged by our authorities. He is a sergeant, had contemplated deserting; had a brother who deserted last winter. I gave him all information I could and intimated that a few of us would like to strike for the Blue Ridge that night. He said it would be death to attempt escape. We soon became convinced that it was quite impossible. I here learn of some I knew, being killed and wounded; that our division was badly cut up, and the loss of Generals Wadsworth, Rice and Robinson. Nothing to eat. No rations seen today. I spread my coat on the ground at night and lay down to sleep.

        The Nation's in a sorry fix,
        Tremendous family jar!
        'Cause freedom and slavery couldn't mix,
        The Johnnies went to war,
        And when we meet them in their tricks,
        Whine, "What you'ns fight we'uns for?"
        We fight you for your cause is bad;

Your leaders honest blood have shed;
In South have human rights forbade
And wrongly have your hearts misled.
You challenge us to fight this war;
Our rights in Southland are effaced.
That's what "we'uns fight you'ns for,"
Or stand before the world disgraced.
The average Johnnie does not know
The baleful nature of his cause.
He's heard Davis, Toombs and Yancey blow,
And joined in brainless, wild hurrahs
To 'lect Buchanan, and so and so,.
Pledged to enforce all slavery laws,
Slaveholders asking "Mo', give mo',"
Demands that never brooked a pause.
We've often warned them to go slow,
To curb their cursed maws.
Then they rebellious teeth would show
And gnash their wrathful jaws,
And swear they'd from the Union go
Or dictate all its laws;
For government, from long ago,
They've grasped with greedy paws;
Persistently have lobbied so
For some new pro-slavery clause.
They fell down in their Kansas muss—
They forced a savage fight—
Then started up this bigger fuss,
And we're in it up to sight.
I know not when the fuss 'll end;
It has been hard and hot;
But to the finish we'll contend,
And they'll lose every slave they've got,
The power they so long did wield,
We'll break forevermore,
And bleach its bones upon the field
And Freedom's cause restore.

## LYNHBURG TO DANVILLE—DREW ENEMY'S FIRE.

Tuesday, May 10th.—My throat and lungs sore this morning, caused by heat and smoke of yesterday and drenching dew and chill of last night. Get rations today for the first time since taken; I was very hungry and could have eaten all at one time. We understand the bread was baked by citizens; it was very good. A number of citizens come to see us, appear courteous and friendly. There was one group of ladies and one man enthusiastic for the Union and said more than was safe to say, even spoke when the guard remonstrated. One said:

"We would be glad to see you out of here; we are sorry that men have to be so treated for this worthless government." The man said the Rebellion had ruined him. He took some Confederate money and tore it up saying it is "worth just that." He looked upon us in tears. The guard threatened to shoot him when he tossed a roll of money among us, and was about to leave when he was arrested, roughly treated and taken to the city. After this no one was allowed to speak to us or we to anyone, not even the sentry. More prisoners arrive from the battlefield and crowd our quarters.

Wednesday, May 11th.—A chilly day. Shortly after noon it began to rain and continued all night to which all prisoners are exposed. Drew a little more bread and bacon, not one-half as much as we needed. Prisoners continue to come; report our army south of Fredericksburg having had quite a race with Lee; fighting has been almost continuous. They report we have taken about 4,200 prisoners in the movement. About 2,000 of our men were sent away at 9 a. m., it is supposed, to Danville.

Thursday, May 12th.—Still rainy. When I awoke this morning I lay in water; no shelter, no wood; consequently I am wet all day. All the wood we have is green brush and roots they let us pick from the bank. This is very little; we use it for cooking.

Friday, May 13th.—Cold and wet. Throat and lungs sore, head and bones ache; I am nearly sick; got no rest. It grew warmer about 10 a. m. I lay down to get a little ease when orders came to get ready to leave. After a long parade, a great deal of threatening and ordering by officers to "slap the bayonet into them," we started out. In passing the guard we marched by twos. Going up the hill I slipped and fell behind. The officer that counted us was enraged; seized me by the collar, pushed me down the hill, then jerking the other way struck me across the shoulders with his sword a blow that staggered me. Had it not been death I should have struck him in the face, it was my first impulse. Our eyes met, I wanted to know him if we should meet again. He flourished his sword and with an oath ordered me on. It rained hard so there was not many to look at us on the street. Nearly noon I got aboard the car. It was after dark before we reached Burkville, a junction of the South Side Richmond & Danville Railroads. The most important place was F rmville, 70 miles west of Richmond on the right bank of the Appomattox River, a place of nearly 2,000.

Near this place we passed a high, long bridge. The car I was in was an old-fashioned coach with seats, although not cushioned we thought they were doing well by us. Shortly after dark I got as much out of the way as possible, for the boys were inclined to be "gay and happy still," and lay down on the floor. I felt much worn; my throat pained me constantly. Fortunately I had some camphor gum, sent from home during the winter, a pill of which I frequently took, which gave relief.

Saturday, May 14th.—Owing to wet clothing and a chill I could not sleep. Before day I was watching the country. At sunrise we were alongside the Little Roanoke River near its confluence with the Staunton. On the bridge over the Staunton several guns were planted, one so near the track that the engine swept it off. This was in expectation of a cavalry raid. We were 46 mlies from Danville. Here they retain their slaves and agriculture is in its usual state. As we approach the Dan River the country is admirable, rolling land, rich valleys. The road runs near the river several miles north of Danville, then sight is lost of it. At this point I judge it is larger than the James at Lynchburg. It was after 3 p. m. when we got off the train at Danville and marched through the place, and an hour later when we get into quarters in a large brick building formerly a tobacco warehouse. In passing through we tried to buy bread of women who offered, but guards would not allow. Several buildings were filled with prisoners. As we got near the building we were to enter I saw a man taken at the battle of Chickamauga eight months before, who attempted to talk but was driven away. He was on parole building a high fence back of our prison. We were crowded so thickly into the building that there is scarce room to lie down. While waiting for rations a man passed through with tobacco at $1 in greenbacks and $3 in "Confed" a plug. At length rations came, corn bread and bacon warm. This was new, men had a great relish for it. It was the third day's ration drawn during the nine days we had been prisoners. Danville is four miles from the North Carolina line on the Dan, a branch of the Roanoke River. It has water power for manufacturing, but not developed; lies in a fertile country; the river is boatable to the falls in the Roanoke 40 miles east to Clarkville. Population, 1,900. Close confinement, not being allowed to get faces to windows, although they are heavily barred with strips of oak plank, the nature of our rations and conditions in general, began to work perceptibly on men. Water is insufficient and bad, taken from the Dan, muddy in consequence of rain. Diarrhoea is becoming universal. Bread is coarse, no seasoning.

Sunday, May 15th.—Those who complained bitterly of soldiering in our ranks, are very gloomy and wish they were back to their regiments, saying they never would complain again of the service. We can only hope and wait for events to bring things right. Patience at home in the midst of friends is indispensable. Here deprived of liberty, in the hands of enemies, we cannot dismiss her. If needed then it is needed much more now. Guards frequently fire into windows, on getting a glimpse of someone, scattering glass and splinters in our faces. In going down stairs to the recess three men were bayoneted in the legs and two taken out under threat of being shot for words they had said. Twelve hundred men are in the building on three floors, so crowded that at night it is impossible to move without treading on someone, in the total darkness.

Monday, May 16th.—Appearances and talk on the streets last night indicated that they had news that worried them. This morning I learned from a sergeant, that General Stuart is killed. Our cavalry are troubling the railroads, the long bridge mentioned near Burkville, they destroyed. Several hundred start from other prisons to Georgia. There are some wounded here, thus far no medical attendance. Considerable excitement in the street occasioned by several bodies of troops leaving for the front to join Lee's army.

Tuesday, May 17th.—Wounded men are taken out from among us to be sent back. All windows are ordered closed. Owing to this order two of our fellows rigged up a skeleton dummy and dressed in blue and a cap which they stood at the window. Soon after it was fired upon, and an hour later it was poked up at another window and two guns banged at it. Soon after they swung it up at another window. Two more Rebel guns burned powder. Every time the glass was scattered over the room to the annoyance of men, but when they growled the fellows yelled out we have got to have air. This time a sergeant and several guards with bayonetted guns came up to look after the dead and wounded, but found none. The boys dissected their artificial Yankee and the event was a mystery to Rebels until in the afternoon at a later performance, the trick was discovered by a man posted on the stairway and an officer of the prison came up and vented his wrath very savagely, but did not find the fellows who had fooled them.

Wednesday, May 18th.—"Grant defeated, sho'," exclaimed a lieutenant who appeared on our floor this morning. We draw no rations today. Tomorrow we expect to start for Georgia. Savannah, Americus and Macon are points named.

Buchanan sat in Federal chair
While Rebs purloined our cash and guns.
They stole our forts,—'twas all unfair,—
From office every Rebel runs,
With none to him succeed,

And took these guns and turned about,
While several States secede,
And boasted they were brave and stout
And sneered the North they'd bleed,
And "Yankee armies put to rout
For we've stole the stuff they need;"
And in the Northern face did flout
Insults their crimes did breed.

Buchanan turned with mien devout—
A Nation's brittle reed!—
Said: "North, I said, 'twould thus come out,
If their threats you failed to heed;
I begged these States not to go out,
But can't help it if they do secede.
Now, friends, if you would win 'em back,
Drop down upon your knees,
Like slaves who fear the lash's crack,
And try again to please;
For, if you fail this act to do
Secession stands—alack!—
For if these States shall choose to go,
You can't coerce them back!"

So up they hoist a Rebel flag;
They shake it in the Nation's face—
An insolent old slavery rag—
To all the land disgrace!
Then Lincoln to the loyal said:
"What will my brothers do?
You as the people, I the head,
To Justice must be true!
Come forth to meet this traitorous horde;
Defeat them where they stand;
They'd wreck the Nation with the sword,
Come and redeem the land!
They challenge us; shall we be brave,
Or cowards shall we be?
From basest treason shall we save
What God proclaimed was free?"

"We're coming, honest Abraham,"
Replied the loyal North,
"The plea of tyranny we'll damn;
By thousands we come forth;
For slavery we much abhor,

We've borne its insults many years,
And though we mourn the woes of war,
Our honor knows no fear!"
Thus awoke the loyal host,
E'en where Treason claimed to reign;
And though they strive, and threat, and boast,
Their striving shall be vain.

### DANVILLE TO COLUMBIA—WAYSIDE NOTES IN SLAVEDOM

Thursday, May 19th.—Awakened by the guard at 4 a. m.; at daylight go on the street receiving a small day's ration, the fourth issue since our capture. Rain is over; we are delighted to get out-door. I shall not soon forget the morning. We are starting on a long, tedious journey southward dependent on the mercies of enemies whom we had justly counted barbarous in respect to the motives of the war they precipitated and are needlessly waging. The fates of many seem desperate. How many of this long line of Unionists will return to their Northern homes! How many and who of us will sleep the last sleep in the far South!

We pass two large buildings used as hospitals which appear filled. It was an hour and a half before we reach the cars, a long train of flat and box. I take a seat on the bottom of a flat. At 10 a. m. we start on a new road from Danville, Va., to Greenboro, N. C., 48 miles. A guard near me, a man about 55 years old, ventured to say that he believed the South missed it in going to war; it was not true that they were forced to it. He believed President Lincoln just such a man as Henry Clay in his principles, and he was a Clay man all his life.

"That is so, the South can settle with Abraham Lincoln as easily as with any living man," I replied. He said:

"I believe it."

"Then why do we find you with your gun in the Rebel service?"

"Because I had to be somewhere; I enlisted in the militia, rather be here than fighting. Had I not gone in they'd 'scripted me and sent me to the front; but being pretty old and willing, they have me to do such duty as this."

"How do you expect to come out with this war and how long will it last?"

"There's no telling, not right away; there will be some right smart fights before you get Richmond."

"Will they give up then?"

"Well, no; I reckon—it's the hardest place we've got; I reckon it can't be taken."

"Clinging to Richmond will only continue the war until we completely besiege it; the shortest way to end it, unless the whole South lay down their arms."

"You are divided in the North; we think you will get sick of fighting. Heaps o' people believe you to be a hard race; they want to get rid of you. This is what we people are told."

"If the South wants to settle as it is claimed they do, why don't they lay down their arms and ask for terms?"

"That's it; they no more want peace than they did when they commenced."

Looking about him, he said: "Plenty of men have been put in prison and hung for saying what they believed; they'd send me to the front sure for what I have said."

"We must have Union and liberty as the ultimate result of this war, or there is no salvation for North or South. The triumph of the South would be the greatest calamity that could befall; our triumph the blessing of both."

"You're right."

"Then as a Union man whose election do you prefer this fall?"

"I think Lincoln is a good man."

This was an interesting conversation; I am really in the Confederacy in conversation with a Union man but a Rebel soldier. After going 25 miles we were ordered off the train, there being a piece of road six miles not completed. We moved off across the plantation till we came to a road. Long trains loaded with army supplies driven by the raggedest negroes I ever saw, began to meet us as we went on the road. It was amusing to hear their answers as to the distance to the railroad, which the men were frequently asking. It was very hot several men died on this short march. We reached the road about 4 p. m. and waited for the train. I was here introduced to James B. Hawks of the 7th Michigan, by Thompson, which was the beginning of a new friendship. Hawks had the advantage of a collegiate education, and pleased us with several declamations still fresh in his memory although he had endured the hardships of the peninsular campaign. A pile of supplies lay beside the road. A group of ladies and men came to look at us though there was few houses in sight. Just dark the train backed up with several hundred soldiers for Lee's army. Here as at Charlotteville a few contemplated escape if possible, should we remain after dark. But by dark we were all driven on board. The order was "Shoot every man that tries to get out," so Boodger and I were again flanked. It was midnight before we started. As to the mode of our lodging we were like the Dutchman's hen that stood up and set.

Friday, May 20th.—As it grew daylight we arrived at Greenboro, N. C., a pleasant place, appropriately named, I judge, for

the beauty of the scene cheered and made me forget I was not on a pleasure trip. The village is full of green trees and flower gardens, splendidly located in a slightly undulating, but not hilly region. Away to the west the Blue Ridge appeared like a panorama. We stopped near a large, thickly wooded park charming as the original forest. The wide streets, rows of green trees glistening with dew as the sun shone on them, the morning songs of birds, and the people on the street and those that came to look at us as though we were a caravan of strange animals again made us think of lost liberty. The people appeared anxious to talk but were prevented. The soldiers said a strong Union feeling existed. I judge they are tolerable compromisers. We left Greenboro at 8 p. m.; while there I traded by hat cord for three biscuits with a Rebel soldier going to the front. Thompson and I call it breakfast. From here to Salisbury we halted at three stations; the people appeared kindly disposed, mannerly, our folks like. At one station a citizen gave the boys a few cakes. I find human nature is the same everywhere. Men may differ widely in opinion, still they are alike. Today we can forgive or embrace what yesterday we fought. Whoever we meet and wherever we meet them, we see something of ourselves reflected. This is consoling in circumstances like these; so if we love ourselves we must love our enemies. Man is a curious compound of many animate beings with an additional quality higher and better.
"His nature none can o'errate, and none
Can under rate his merit."

At Salisbury we stopped two hours. Men and women came out to talk but were not freely allowed. One family inquired for Pennsylvanians, stated that they formerly lived in that State, and sent two little negro girls to bring us water, but were finally forbidden intercourse. Here is a prison where many Union officers and Union citizens and newspaper correspondents are confined. At 6:30 p. m. we reach Charlotte, 93 miles south of Greenboro and were marched a mile and camped. After dark we drew a day's ration of hard bread and bacon; had had nothing for 36 hours.

Saturday, May 21st.—We were awakened at 3 o'clock this morning to get ready to go, but remained until 4 p. m. During the day a train arrived with officers who were captured with us and elsewhere. Among the officers of my regiment were Major John W. Young, Captains Swan and Clyde, Lieutenants Buchanan, Homer Call and Cahill, also Lieutenant Cheeseman of General Rice's staff. Among the other officers were Brigadier Generals Shaler and Seymour who belonged to the 6th corp and were taken in the battle of May 6th with portions of their command in the Wilderness, when Longstreet's corp overlapped the Union lines in the crisis of that engagement that threatened decisive disaster to the Rebel army. General Shaler, speaking of the battle of the 6th, says the practical result of Longstreet's arrival simply prevented our victory and saved the Rebel army from decisive defeat, and will simply prolong the fighting before Lee can be forcd back on Richmond. Longstreet's arrival on the field was unanticipated and unprepared for so early in the day. Had it not been for this desperate attack the Rebel army would have found what Pickett got at Gettysburg and Lee's retreat to Richmond would have been hastened. "The battles of May 5th and 6th," said Gen. Shaler, "have put Lee on the defensive, but he is in shape to put up a hard fight. All the fields fought over are ours; success is simply postponed. Both armies are moving on Richmond, Lee because he has to, Grant because he wants to." This made us happy.

Groups of ladies come to look at us but are kept at a distance. At 4:30 p. m. the train moves off and fourteen miles bring us into South Carolina.

### IN SLAVEDOM.

If "Jove fixed it certain that whatever day
Makes man a slave takes half his worth away,"
'Tis no less certain that the galling cord
That binds the slave perverts his haughty lord.
Corroding links his better nature rive
From spiritual touch of his enslaving gyve.
'Tis plain as stars that in the heavens lie,
As plain as sun that burns through lofty sky,
That in a land where men their slaves do count,
That interest rises always paramount.
All else is smothered like flowers overrun
By poisonous weeds that thrive in rain and sun,
While freest men are shackled to their grave;
And cannot rise where masters stern enslave.
Freest souls are but subaltern tools;
The truth is silenced wherever slavery rules.
Men's thoughts grow dormant, their passions turn to hate,
As waters in a silent pool stagnate;
Its merits, or demerits, none debate;
The mass may vote, but must not rule a State.
Public squares, feigned to adorn a town,
Where struts the driver like a Pagan clown,
Are where grave masters sell their slaves for cash;
The press and pulpit help them wield the lash.

The ruling spirit is a demon fraught
With hellish wrath, where men are sold and bought,
And raised like mules for service, and for gain,
For market like steers upon a Texas plain,
Or swine for bacon, that root in Southern wood;
So Sambo's bred sole for his master's good.
He must know but little, never much;
To teach him more no saint may touch;
His innate sense that he, too, is a man,
The breath of Freedom shall ne'er to action fan.
So it has grown a cancer on the heart
Of this Republic the master's sword would part—
Who knows no freedom but to enslave at will—
The North must yield or human blood shall spill!
They claimed for slavery, indeed, the foremost chance
In all the realm where Freedom's hosts advance;
But this denied, a raving spirit rash,
Now lifts the sword to supplant the lash,
And good men rush, enamored for a cause
Where wrong is foremost in their social laws!
And so I muse as on this way we wend
To be enslaved—in some damned prison penned!

## AT SOUTH CAROLINA CAPITAL AND ONWARD.

Saturday, May 22nd.—Arrive at Columbia, S. C., at dawn. The night passed disagreeably. Although our destiny is prison, men are impatient at delays, growl at "such engineering" though the best we have had, a negro at that. I ate my last bread yesterday morning; hoped for rations here; none came. We picked up corn scattered in the cars which served some purpose. We are mingling freely with our officers, sitting beside the track some ways from the city. This is the capitol of South Carolina; population 8,000. A paper I saw today says of the armies in Georgia that Johnston had retreated from Dalton towards Rome, Hooker and Thomas pressing him. Details are given of skirmishes and glaring headlines of great disasters to Yankees; but in important movements they concede failure, then attempt to distort facts. Lincoln has issued a proclamation for thanksgiving. It looks as well for us as we ought to expect; we have had to contend against disadvantages; a hard struggle is before. Some gentlemen engaged in conversation with us. They evinced a spirit narrowed to mere State pride all for slavery. The bane of State right had been so profusely imbibed, that they had forgotten what Edmund Randolph termed the "rock of our salvation" which gave "safety, respectability and happiness to the American people," namely, "The Union of the States," and plunged into that which brings destruction. Particularly was this addressed to the South; nevertheless we are cursed for loving the Union. They ask us to give it up, to give up principles for which we would preserve the Union.

Gen. Seymour had his buttons cut off by Rebels while asleep. He has no hat, it having been lost in battle; he seems very disconsolate. General Shaler sits beside him with one arm about his waist trying to console him.

Rebel officers have been here and offer $5 to $15 Confederate for $1 in greenbacks. They have a curious faith in success. At noon we left the junction for the South. Kingsville is a junction of two roads, one for Charleston, the other north to Wilmington. Four or five miles below we cross the Santee River, or one of its branches, and an extensive swamp on a tressle, seemingly two miles long. Here I saw several live alligators. We reached Branchville at dark and switched to the west. Country is level, woody and in poor cultivation. On much of the cotton lands trees are standing dead. Fields look like vast swamps. Land is worked in this way wholly by slaves with little knowledge how to improve land, with neither facilities or encouragement to do so, and when exhausted, it is left. We could see the salves toiling in "the cotton and the cane."

Monday, May 23d.—Arrived at Augusta, Ga., at daylight, one of the nicest towns of its size in the South; the home of Alexander H. Stephens, long celebrated as one of the ablest Southern men, now the Vice President of this so-colled Confederacy. Business appeared dull. Trains from Savannah had troops to reinforce Johnston beyond Atlanta. After an hour we run out of town and changed trains. We have had no rations since the 20th, resort to various means to obtain bread. Brass buttons, pocket books, knives, any Yankee trinket are in good demand; bread is scarce, prices enormous when we find it. They like Yankee notions emblazoned in brass and gutta percha, but they are too supercilious to adopt Northern principles. I succeeded in trading a silk necktie and an ink stand for a loaf of bread. These fellows are the queerest traffickers I ever saw. The Esquimaux and native Indians have no greater hankering for a ten-penny nail than these people have for brass ornaments. A good jack knife counted in their cash, is worth about $25; a wooden inkstand $3 to $15; brass buttons from $3 to $10 per dozen. The country around Augusta looks nice; it is on the Savannah River; population about 8,300. In the afternoon we drew rations for a day; moved on at 3 o'clock.

On, on, on we go down to the Rebel jail;
I reckon this is rather rough a riding on a rail.
Oh, here are boys from many a hearth,
Dear to many a breast,
Many a mothers heart is dearth,
Many a wife with woe is press'd;
And many a kin and many a friend
Will long to know their fate;
Bnt many a precious life will end
Within that prison gate;
And many a day ere we can see
That dear old home again,
And rest beneath that banner free
That traitors now disdain.
Many a long, long weary day,
Many a dismal night,
Our hope and strength may waste away
By hunger, pain and blight;
And many a vow may be forgot,
But we shall not forget
The glorious truths for which we fought.
The cause that triumphs yet.
But we hear their vauntings everywhere;
They never can prove true;
And yet what devils ever dare
These Rebels dare to do;
And matters look a little rough,
Things look a little blue,
You bet it is a little tough,
Going down to Rebel jail;
'Tis not so very pleasant, though,
This riding on a rail!

## ARRIVE AT ANDERSONVILLE.

Tuesday, May 24th, 1864.—Another night cramped up on the cars; another night of painful nipping at napping amidst the roar, the heat and jogging of the train. Everybody wanted to lie down, but everybody was in the way; everybody wanted to straighten out, but no one could. Once in a while one lifts his aching legs over heads and bodies, or stands up to straighten them. Oh, the weary night, the sweat, the heated air of the car, wherein were jammed 80 men till no more could get in, with the doors closed. It is sickening to endure! Not a drop of water to cool thirst, not a moment of ease for weary bodies; no rest for aching heads; not an overdose of patience for one another. Morning came and we were still rolling on through the pine, the barren waste, the plantation, with its mansion aloof, and slave huts; the thatched roof shanty of poor white, and now and then halting at small stations "to feed the hoss."

Villages of any account are far apart. At all these places the negro is chief; Nig does the work, eats the poorest victuals, is an all around man. At every depot, every shed, wood pile and water tank, the darky "am de man." He engineers, fires, he brakes. This animal runs the Confederacy. Everything is very unlike our Northern routes, in wood, in field, in civilization. It appears to me like "Reducing the white man to the level of the negro"—indeed it does, Jeff!" These motley crowds, these black white faces, these white black faces, look like amalgamation, you conservators of an oligarchial, doomed institution upon which you seek to rear an oligarchy!

At 6 a. m. the whistle blows at Macon, Ga., and we stop. The doors open and a few slide to the ground to straighten out, to limber up and to try and get a drink; but few succeeded in getting out, however. A citizen told me the population of Macon was 20,500. It is located in a basin formed by sloping hills around it, near the Ocmulgee River. At 7:30 a. m. we start southward towards Americus about 70 miles south. The country is more thickly inhabited, is a richer region. Fort Valley is 30 miles south of Macon. Here were plenty of customers for anything we had to sell. Men came out with corn bread to exchange for wallets and it didn't take them long to "get shut on't"; both sexes, all colors, all grades. We were not the first load of "hyenas" that had gone down, so they did not come out to see the show, but wanted to know "Whar you'ns all from" and to traffic. It began to be hinted that we were not going to Americus, where the guard had told us our prisoners are; that it is a splendid camp, greensward, beautiful shade trees, nice tents and a right smart river, those that had "been thar a heep o' times with you'ns fellers." We had hoped that such might be our lot; but now everyone was wonderfully ignorant. When asked they would say, "can't tell you sar." At Oglethorpe I asked a citizen how far it was to Americus.

"Oh, right smart, I reckon; you'ns not going thar though."
"Where are we going?" I asked another.
"Oh, just down thar where all o' you'ns fellers goes."
"How far?"
"Right smart bit, I reckon."
"Well, how many miles?"
"Good bit, fo' mile, reckon—you'ns got any rings?"
"What place?"

"Andersonville, they call it I reckon."
"How do they fare?"
"Right good—don't know; die mighty fast, I har."
A gentleman of leisure said, "You bet they do."
"It is a hard place, is it?"
"You will see all you want to see before long"
"Have shelter, of course?"
"Guess so—you'll see, pretty soon."

Heaving a long sigh we cursed their blasted Confederacy and black infamous cause, then took it cool. In 30 minutes the train halted again. There was a newly built storehouse consisting of pine slabs set up on end, and appearances of a hastlily constructed military station. Preparations were made to disimbark. I looked out, saw but one house in the place, country looked barren, uninviting. About half a mile east was a large pen filled with men. At a glance I caught a view of thousands of prisoners; ragged, rusty blankets put up in all conceivable modes to break the blistering sun rays. It was a great mass of grim visages, a multitude of untold miseries. It reminded me first of a lately seared fallow, then a foul ulcer on the face of nature, then of a vast ant hill alive with thousands of degraded insects. The degradation that pervades the lowest and meanest beings in nature struck me as beneficent compared with the desperately barbarous conditions imposed upon the inmates of those roofless walls. Not a shed or a sheltering tree was in the place. Some whose senses were not benumbed, exclaimed, "My God that is the place, see the prisoners; they will not put us in there, there is no room! By this time men were getting off and straggling along the sandy road to the prison. About half way we halted to form and an officer on horseback met us heading a new guard. "Git into fo's thar," was the order. We moved to the right near the south side of the prison near Captain Wirz's headquarters, and formed into detachments of 270 in charge of sergeants. We were suffering from thirst, heat, hunger, fatigue. Presently the commandant of the prison with a lieutenant and sergeant came down the line. I asked to go to the creek and fill some canteens, pleading our suffering condition. In a passion, pistol in hand, the officer turned with a ferocious oath, putting the pistol to my nose saying, "I'll shoot you if you say dot again." Stepping back he yelled:

"If another man ask for water I shoot him."

To the left a poor fellow had squat in the ranks. This officer whom I found to be Captain Wirz, rushed upon him with an oath kicking him severely and yelled savagely, "Standt up in ter ranks!"

The ground was covered with small bushes. While waiting

some worked industriously pulling and packing in bundles to carry in for shelter. After two hours we started, but all were forced by bayonets to drop the bushes. As the column was pouring through the gate, a comrade said 'Take a long breath North; it is the last free air we shall breath soon." Oh, how many lingering looks and despondent sighs were cast, as we were driven like brutes into a worse than brutish pen!

We entered the south gate. A narrow street runs nearly through the prison from east to west, the narrowest way. I had reached nearly midway when the column halted. Old prisoners gathered frantically about, begging for hardtack, or something else. The air was suffocating, the sights beheld are not to be described. The outside view was appalling; contact a thousand times more horrible!

On my right, as we entered, I saw men without a thread of clothing upon their dirty skeletons, some panting under old rags, or blankets raised above them. One was trying to raise himself; getting upon his hands and feet, his joints gave way; he pitched like a lifeless thing in a heap, uttering the most wailful cry I ever heard. Such things are frequent. The simile strikes me that they are like beings scarce conscious of life, moved by a low instinct, wallowing in the filth and garbage where they happen to be. On the left the scene was equally sickening. The ground for several yards from the gate was wet with excrement, diarrhoea being the disease wasting the bodies of men scarce able to move. Need I speak of the odor? Then the wounds of eight months were visible and disgusting! We dare not look around! At a halt we asked where are we to go? Why do they not take us on?

"You can't get no further; as much room here as anywhere," said an Ohio man.

"For God's sake," I said to the anxious gazers that thronged around asking to be given something—"Give me just one hardtack," begged starved creatures—"stand back and give us a chance! We have no hardtack."

Finding a spot eight of us deposited our luggage and claimed it by right of squatter sovereignty." Eight of us are so fortunate as to have five woolen blankets, our party consisting of Orderly Sergeant G. W. Mattison, Second Sergeant O. W. Burton, W. Boodger, Stephen Axtel, Waldo Pinchen, H. B. Griffith, Lloyd G. Thompson and myself. Here we took up our abode together. I obtained three sticks split from pine, saved at the time the stockade was opened, four and six feet long, upon which we erected three of the blankets in the form of a tent. For these I paid 50c. each.

Nothing of the rules and regulations of the prison were announced by the authorities, in consequence of which, I learned after, many a man lost his life by being shot. Soon after arriving I went to the stream to drink and wash. Being ignorant of the supposed existence of a dead line, and, to escape the crowd, I stepped over where it was supposed to be. Immediately I was caught by a man who drew me back shouting: "Come out, they will shoot you!" Looking up I saw the sentries, one on each side with their pieces fixed upon me. I then learned that the order was to shoot any man, without a word, who steps beyond the line, or where it should be. I was partly forced, by the crowding, into that vacancy, and partly tempted by the clear water which was pouring through the stockade a few feet to the west, the water in the stream appearing very filthy. With feelings of thankfulness towards the strangers who frightened that rule into me, I shall ever remember. I thought of the maxim in Seneca, "Let every man make the best of his lot," and prepare for for the worst. So I determined to do what I could to inform new men of the danger at this point, for I soon learned that nearly every day, since new prisoners had been coming in, men had been shot at this place under the same circumstances.

After being settled Thompson and I took a stroll to find, if possible, a better place, without avail. Passing down the older settled and thickly crowded part where there are small dirt huts which were early erected, I observed a man sitting under an old tent with a book. This was unexpected. "Here is a book of poems," I said to Thompson, halting.

"Yes, sir, Milton's 'Paradise Lost,'" said he, handing it to me. He was an old prisoner from Rosecrans army, having wintered at Danville, Va., a prisoner since Chickamauga. He told us freely all he knew about our new world, appeared a perfect gentleman, manifested very friendly feeling, urged us to accept his book and call often. The mellow beam of a genial nature shone in his face. Although we did not learn his name that day, we felt him to be a friend. I had a paper, purchased at Augusta, having accounts of Johnston's run before Sherman, how one of Johnston's men cried, "General, we are marching too fast; we don't want to retreat, had rather fight." "We are not retreating, boys, we are only falling back so Sherman won't get round our flank," said Johnston, which I gave him.

The stockade is made from pine trees cut, from the prison ground, into 25 feet lengthts, 5 feet of which is set into the ground, and the timbers are strongly pinned together. Until last winter this was primeval forest, heavily timbered with pine. The sentry boxes are six to eight rods apart near the top of the wall, each box having a roof, the platform being reached by stairs. The ground is said to contain 13 acres, including the lagoon of about two acres, which cannot be occupied except a few islands in the midst. A small stream runs through from west to east. The water is nearly as black as the mud of its mirey banks, and tastes of it, and nearly divides the camp equally, both the north and south parts sloping towards it. There are some log huts built by the first prisoners when the stockade was opened, from the waste timber left on the ground. Now even the stumps have been dug up for wood. Two large tall pines are left standing in the southeast corner; otherwise there is not a green thing in sight. The dead line is a board laid and nailed on tops of posts, four feet high, about six yards from the stockade. There are two gates on the west side, north and south of the brook. Sinks are dug on the bank near the swamp on the east side, but not sufficient to accommodate a tenth part of the persons on the south side to which it alone is accessible; so the north edge of the swamp, parallel with the stream, is used for the same purpose. Just at dark two mule teams were driven with rations, to be delivered to sergeants in charge of detachments for distribution to their men. We get two ounces of bacon, a piece of corn bread 2x4 inches for one day. There are over 14,000 men here, mostly old prisoners from Belle Isle, Libby and Danville prisons. The bacon is so stale, that a light stroke from the finger knocks it to pieces, leaving the rind in the hand.

### PRISON SCENES, INCIDENTS AND RUMORS.

Wednesday, May 25th.—The air is purified by rain during the night. At first dawn we go to the stream for a bath. Knowing the difficulty to keep clear of lice and dirt, we take the first precaution. Found plenty of the same opinion. Breakfast from our scanty lump of bread and lump of bacon. Roll call at 8 o'clock whereat Rebel sergeants attend. The purpose is to see if all are present. In the event of any being absent, the detachment is deprived of rations for the day whether the missing man appears or not. The bread is of course unsifted meal, mixed without leaven or seasoning, baked in creased cards two feet square. The cry of "raiders" awoke us last night. We were told by old prisoners yesterday, about gangs of thieves composed of brutal men who steal everything that they can use or sell to Rebels; and in some cases they brutally beat and kill. These organizations have grown rapidly since arrival of new prisoners, and act in concert in their nefarious practice. They boldly take blankets from over men's heads, pieces of clothing, anything that can be carried away, standing over men with clubs threatening to kill if they move. They are led by desperate characters said to have been bounty jumpers. They bear the name of raiders. Going among men of our company I found they had not realized their danger; some had lost boots, knapsack with contents, blankets, provisions and other things. In some parts, we hear of pocket picking, assaults with clubs, steel knuckles and knives. This happens every night; in some places at day, especially after new arrivals.

The rumor circulated last night that there was a plot to break out of prison on an extensive plan,has some weight and is the topic of the day. Near the gate an address is posted signed by Henri Wirz, captain commanding prison, saying the plot is discovered; he is fully apprised; warns all to abandon the design; that if any unusual movement is made, the camp will be immediately swept with grape and cannister from the artilery; that all must know what the effect will be on a field so thickly covered with men. Evidently the strictest vigilance is kept over us day and night as shown by the movements of the military posts from the outside.

Inquiring in reference to the matter, I learned that a large number of western men had formed a plan to undermine a section of the stockade from which point the artillery and other arms were most available, and had tunneled along the wall underground, having approachedit from a tunnel from the interior with a view, at a given signal, when the wall is sufficiently weakened, to rush upon it with as much force as could be concentrated, push it down and sieze the guns while the Rebels are sleeping. It was a daring plot, easily discovered and defeated.

Thompson and I go in search of "Paradise Lost" to quaff from the Parnassian springs of Milton. After a long search, for we became bewildered in the crowds, we found our friend who welcomed us. After exchanging addresses and a glance with the mind's eye over his field of philosophy, we bore away the prize. Could that great author, Milton, have thought of a title more appropriate to the place into which the work of his genius has fallen? Foe without, foe within, robbery, murder, sickness, starvation, death, rottenness, brutality and degradation everywhere! Fumes of corruption greet our nostrils; the air is impregnated with morbific effluvium. It seems impossible that fearful epidemic can be stayed. A few weeks hence but few may be left to tell the tale of misery. The sacred realm of nature and its virgin purity have been invaded by the crushing power of tyranny and ravished by the cruel hand of false ambition. Where but lately the songs of happy birds rang from lofty pines through heavenly air, today we hear the groans of men in unrestrained agony. On the foul atmosphere is wafted the expiring breath of men wasted and wasting in their prime. Daily they sink as if their feet were planted on a thinly crusted marsh, and, as they sink, there is nothing to which their hands can cling; no power can reach that would save, while around hisses the foe who madly thrust us into this worse than den of lions.

W. H. Harriman, Zanesville, Ohio, 15tht U. S. Infantry, our new acquaintance, is a finely organized man, possessing a calm, genial nature, of sterling intelligence. He has patience, faith, hope, and enjoys their blessed fruits. He has a fine sense of things, takes a comprehensive view of the crisis, how results one way or another, will affect the interests of mankind. The right is clear to him; he has faith it will triumph; regrets that any doubt. His knowledge of things common to schools and men of thought, proves him of a reflective mind; his candor, brotherly conduct, render him a noble companion.

We are camped in the midst of Ohio boys belonging to the 7th cavalry. Thirteen were taken, only seven alive. One has a malignant sore on his arm caused by vaccination. It has eaten to the bone, nearly around the arm; gangrene is spreading. He is very poor; soon must die. (Note—June 13th, he died. He had a wife and comfortable possesions in Ohio.)

A sergeant of the same company is afflicted with scurvy in the feet. They are terribly swollen, nearly black, give almost unendurable pain; still he is kind, cheerfully sings for our diversion in the inimitable tone the western country boys have in their songs, "The Battle of Mill Spring," "Putting on Airs," etc., accompanied by his brother whose limb is contracted from the same disease. (Note—He became helpless, was carried to the hospital in a hopeless condition in June.)

I speak of this as a few incidents among hundreds all over the camp, illustrative of patient suffering of as noble young men as grace family households, under circumstances that have no parallel in affliction.

At 8 o'clock this evening a sentinel fired. Going to the vicinity I learned a man who came in today, knowing nothing of the dead lines, lay down near it, was shot in the side and borne away by friends.

Tuesday, May 26th.—At 7 o'clock, another man had been shot, lay near the creek. Brisk showers in the night; the day is steadily hot. Rumor that 4,000 are to be sent to Cahawba, Ala. Some of Siegel's men arrived reporting a fight with Breckenridge, in the Shenandoah Valley, in which we got the worst. Another sentinel fires into camp this morning with what effect I do not learn.

About 125 negroes are here who were taken in the battle of Oolustee, Fla. When brought here there were 200, 75 of whom have died since March. Five hundred white Union soldiers were taken at the same time. The white officers commanding the negroes were not allowed the usual courtesies of war and were turned in here. The most prominent of these was Albert Bogle, a major in the 8th U. S. colored regiment to which they belonged. He was severely wounded. No attention was paid to the wound by Confederate surgeons who claimed to be acting under military orders. While on his way, between here and Macon in a box car, suffering from his wound, at one of the stations a Confederate officer fired two shots into the car seemingly designed for him. He is an intelligent young man and bears these abuses with a dignified composure; is still suffering from his wound, but is now improving. He regards their attitude towards him as a fair exhibition of the insane vindicativeness of some Southerners and their extreme rashness on the negro question. These 200 colored men were put into squads and put under charge of white Unionists taken at the same time and had been doing Rebel work outside, which, it is claimed, was to keep up the prison, but some of which is said to be on fortifications. Major Oberly says that none of the negroes who were wounded when taken, received medical attention, and died rapidly after being put in. The Confederates boast a fine rifle battery planted on the ridge commanding this prison, captured at the same time. A few days ago a white sergeant, while waiting at the gate to go out with a squad of negroes on Rebel detail, was shot by the guard, and immediately killed, the guard pressing his gun against his victim's breast, there being no apparent provocation for the outrage.

This Southern insanity on the color question is their sole reason for refusing exchange of prisoners. These negroes appear to have an intelligent understanding of the issues involved in this contest, often more so than some of our own people; for I must confess that here are men of every type of ignorance, vicious and innocent, that can exist under Northern civilization, as well as the better class; some of the meanest outlaws found in our cities, renegades from Canada, a plenty who are fit tools in the hands of scoundrels at the head of raiding gangs who seek to perpetuate damnable careers; some who are naturally good but are easily duped, under existing conditions, to join in evil pursuits. In an assemblage like this, promiscuously drawn from a large country, if all were honest men it would be strange indeed. But as I have thus spoken I will say that in no community of like number is there more patriotic zeal, manhood, virtue and intelligence than exist here.

The raiders are out tonight before dark; assaulted a man near the gate and robbed him, it is said, of a $100. Others interfere in his behalf and a desperate fight ensues which is checked by the guard who threatened to fire into the crowd and the thieves got away with the cash. Another hub-bub soon occurs. A fellow is caught stealing a pair of shoes and after a squabble, is tied up. No rations today.

## STORIES OF FOUR DAYS.

Friday, May 27th.—Water in the stream is very foul from so many using, and the refuse thrown in it from Rebel cook houses and camps that floats down, and drainage from offal that covers portions of the banks. Notwithstanding we practice bathing before sunrise, we always find the water foul. Men with blotches, putrid sores, gnawed by lice and worms, squalid from weakness, scurvy and wasting diseases go there to drink, wash clothing and bathe. They are obliged to step into the stream the banks being two to three feet high, slippery, nasty. Daily lice are seen floating while clothing is being washed.

Excitement this morning is about a fellow caught last night and cut loose by a fellow raider; retaken, knocked down three times, sopped in the filthy swamp, then marched about camp as a warning, after which he is given seven lashes on his bare back that brings blood. Mob law is our only recourse. Neither friends or foes outside protect us. He is an inferior looking man. A search follows among known thieves for articles lost. Several things have been found when a dozen savage fellows came with clubs. A few fought them with their hands, were badly beaten and forced to yield.

A rally was made to release one who had been knocked down, and one raider was captured, who was administered a course of punishment to exact promises of better conduct. Raiders are on the good side of our keepers. They sell articles they steal, or exchange them for food and things which help to keep them in strong physical condition. They are allowed favors not accorded others, are continually fawning to Wirz and his subordinates.

Some are excited over a report of the fall of Atlanta, Richmond and Charleston, which I see no reason to credit. Considerable excitement manifested in the Rebel garrison; troops being arrayed for a show, or a fight for two hours this afternoon. I learn that three tunnels have been found which led to the belief that an outbreak was contemplated. Every day squads of men explore the ground inside and outside of the stockade with feeling rods which they punch into the ground.

As a contrast to the scenes of the day Thompson and I have been reading Milton's description of Eden in the days of Adam and Eve's primal purity. No rations granted today. The stench from the lagoon is very disagreeable every night in the south part of the stockade.

Saturday, May 28th.—In consequence of the damp nights I cough badly. Nights are cool, compared with the heat of the day, the sun being terrible, in consequence of which I have suffered with headache. Going about camp I find several wells 20 and 25 feet deep. In company with twenty others our mess have commenced digging today. Pinchen is whittling staves out of sticks of pine rations for a bucket with a small jack-knife, to use in pulling up the dirt. Prison managers are against this enterprise; but the jealousy is being overcome happily, through the influence of surgeons and military officers who occasionally come inside and we have shown them the condition of the stream. As yet no spades are allowed for this work, although these officers have kindly suggested that they could be trusted to us under restriction. So they have been dug with case knives, pieces of canteens, or any piece of iron or stick convertible for such use. As digging proceeds men go down on poles, where one can be obtained, bracing against the bank and ascending the same way. The earth is a red sand, packs hard, needs no stoning. After several feet a fine layer of clay is struck, smooth and soft which is a curiosity to some, who smooth it and whittle it into fancy articles, among which are pipes. Tin pails are attached to whatever we can create for ropes for drawing up dirt and water.

Yesterday I noticed a dead-line board laying on the ground inside, one end about three feet from the post, blown, I suppose, by the wind. We have been troubled about getting in and out of the well we are digging, and cannot find anything to put down to climb on. I conceived the idea of capturing it to obviate the trouble. It got pretty dark near midnight. I approached the place cautiously, and lay flat and crawled to the board and tied a string to the end farthest in and sitting on the ground 25 feet away, drew it cautiously until out of danger from being shot by sentinels, when I picked it up and brought it to our place. We covered it with sand when Rebel sergeants came in the morning, and after the well was finished, broke it up for wood to cook our rations of meal. The Rebels missed the board, but never found it. Thompson watched the guard while I pulled it away, to warn me if they were likely to shoot, but the other boys didn't know when I stole the "dead line."

Seven hundred men taken at Spottslvania come in; report Grant at Mechanicsville, Johnston falling back on Atlanta. Those who have razors shave for 5c., cut hair for 10c. Sweat boards or dice appear in camp where men can stake 5c. a throw, if he wishes to try his luck at gaming. I have known some to win quite often, but hear of more who lose. A few things have been worked into camp by men who get out on duty or by Rebel sergeants. A fair sized onion goes for $1, apples 10c to 40c, dry hog peas 40c. per pint, plug tobacco $1.50. There is one commodity never had in any market. It is ahead of any Dutch brewery extant; it is meal beer made by letting corn meal sour in water. Molasses can be had for 5c. a teaspoonful; a little is added to give it a twang and sassafras roots can be had by digging, the tea of which is often added to give it flavor. Those who have money, pay ten and fifteen cents for half a pint and drink it with a relish. Men crave something sour, and poor fellows with feverish lips and scabious tendency, without money, beg and whine for it childishly. The vender cries, "Here is your nice meal beer, right sour, well seasoned with sassafras."

Sunday, May 29th.—The incident at the creek, where I nearly drew the fire of two sentries, led me to inquire as to methods prison authorities have for informing new arrivals, of their rules in reference to the dead line, especially where no line is visible, which is the case for 60 yards at the point mentioned, parallel with the crossing from south to north. I learned they never published their rules, every man learns at his peril, just as I did, or by hearsay. Old prisoners say there never has been a visible line at this creek crossing; that no man knows where it is except as he judges the distance from the stockade, or guesses where it would come by looking at the line where it stops north and south of the creek. The sentry is left to guess when a man gets over the line, that is not there and shoots according to his guess. It involves upon the prisoners to post new men, as much as possible, but comparatively few think to do so. It is a serious matter as new arrivals nearly every day are apt to transgress the rule ignorantly and innocently, and if shot they have been murdered in cold blood. During new arrivals this happens often, as guards are mostly young fellows whose chief education is to despise Yankees whom it is a Southern virtue to kill, and to perform this patriotic duty he has been trained to shoot well, and to watch for a chance. At this point he finds opportunity. Guards are composed of Alabama and Georgia youths reared under the fire-eating doctrines of Yancey, Cobb and Toombs, and to believe in the infallibility of the chivalric South, its institutions, peculiar rights, as superior to all else, whose leaders have led the Southern mass to engage in a bad war for a bad cause. Probably these shooting imps know nothing of this, are ignorant of the crime they every day commit. Not a single instance, so far, were men who were shot seeking to escape. They were ignorant of any rule and unhindered in their approach to the stockade by a visible dead line at this point. Hence the shooting has been unjustifiable by ordinnary prison discipline prescribed by treaties or laws of war.

It is one continuous, irksome every day recurrence of unpleasant scenes. But one event is looked for with hopeful pleasure, that is the issuing of rations which never lacks serious, if not total disappointment. After roll call the sick are helped to the gates; those ready to die are put on stretchers and carried to the hospital outside near the south end of the stockade. Of all the grim and ghastly sights imagination ever depicted, those we see at this hour far excel in horror. Poor, squalid, yellow faces, eyes sunken and glassy, cheeks hollow or swollen with scurvy, fevered lips drawn tightly across the teeth, the mouth agape to breathe or let escape fetid breath, some borne by comrades, others tottering by the help of staffs or supported by friends; some without half a suit to cover them, some with terribly swollen limbs, putrid sores, dropsical distensions and bent forms. One holds his breath to look at them, nay turns away! Men walk about whom we would call bad corpses if seen in coffins anywhere else. Such a pitiful look as they give I never saw; their voices are as if the dead speak.

Two rods to the rear of us I witnessed the death of a Tennesseean, the last of three brothers who died on the same spot since March. All were Belle Isle victims. He had laid all day in the heat and will not be carried out till morning. He gradually wasted and died without a struggle. It is more remarkable than anything I ever read, how men lose their sense of life; imperceptibly degree by degree, it goes out leaving only a latent consciousness of what they have been, what they are, and a vague, unintelligent hope. Even that departs and his mind ranges in the narrowest sphere the human spirit can. For weeks he is robbed of himself; an infant is not more childish or weak; age not so whimsical or broken. He is a mere human worm! Another singular phase of these conditions: We frequently see men unable to arise from the sand, threatening to knock down strong men for trivial things they deem insulting. Men of skeleton forms lock in each others puny arms in a rage, falling on the ground unable to rise, they still boast of what they can do. So long bereft of comfort, so long have they only hoped for bread and liberty from day to day at the hands of merciless authorities, that reason is extinguished in many, and the lowest, blindest, selfish passion clings to the rotten thread of life. The phases which life assumes in this degraded condition, is inconceivable. Some retain the tenderest affection and the broadest faith, as long as consciousness remains.

I saw a man today in the last stages of starvation having sickened of his scanty food. His cry was bread, but when offered that given us, his stomach heaved; he turned his face with expressions of hopeless agony and exclaimed: "They can get me something else! could I be at home!" There are many cases which doctors might term chronic innutrition, where they eat with avidity all they get and still starve, the food doing no good. Doctors have been made acquainted with many of these cases, but will not admit to the hospital. Bell Isle boys tell me they have often dreamed of eating and woke up to go through the motions frothing at the mouth. In one instance they begged the guard to throw over pieces of a cow that had been delivered of a calf three days before, some of which they devoured raw. They exhibit some rings claimed to have been made from the bones of a dog, eaten at Belle Isle, kept as a memento.

Monday, May 30th.—What a night! In addition to scent from the fearful swamp, we had that of dead men in our rear. At our feet lay one begging for water groaning with pain. It was conjectured, because of his hoarse cough, that he had mumps, or measles or small pox, by some persons. Some dare venture but little here to aid suffering strangers when it is all one can do to keep alive. All the assistance we could offer was to give a cup of water. This I gave at arms length. He lay close at our feet but when we woke in the morning he was gone.

Prisoners from Butler report having helped tear up the Petersburg railroad. The stockade is to be enlarged. There has been a call for men to go outside to work on the timber. The old pen is so densely crowded that we are willing to help enlarge the prison. The Rebels are much hurried, being fearful of the reported raid from Kilpatrick. It is said some who went out in the squad to work are put on fortifications, refuse and are sent in. Some may be willing to do this for more grub, but we understand they were parolled on honor and then ordered to work by the commandant as he pleased. It is shameful if men assent to work on Rebel works, that they should be ordered to do so, is more shameful, and outside the laws of war.

Rations are cut down one-half; barely enough for two meals a day. We could eat all at one. Steward Brown has been out to the hospital a day or two. He tells me that 31 died yesterday, 39 today in the so-called hospital, saying nothing of the prison. He says they are miserable mockeries of hospitals, a discredit to the medical profession; but that the doctors are seemingly powerless in the matter, being under orders and practically destitute of medicines. All medical supplies, he says, furnished by the Rebel commissaries at Richmond, are sent to the military posts and are very scant and held by the physicians having charge of that department for use among their own soldiers. Brown is lately from England, pretty well versed in medicine, having had 30 years' study and practice in British hospitals and in military service. He professes neutrality, but was taken while helping care for our wounded in the Battle of the Wilderness, May 5th.

He is allowed more liberty than a Yankee. He says a bunch, that is still quite sore on my forehead, was caused by a spent bullet.

Hiram Morse of Co. F, 76th regiment, admitted to the hospital today. He sickened on corn bread, lost appetite, became helpless from diarrhoea and attendant fever; has wasted rapidly to a skeleton, helpless in body, crazed in mind. He has been kept alive by crust coffee and a little black tea we happened to have, since he got here. Many are becoming so homesick and downhearted, that they believe any report, good or bad. It is no place to get sick; courage must be kept up though rations go down.

## IS THIS PARADISE LOST?

Tuesday, May 31st.—A good work designed to remedy somewhat the unwholesomeness of the place, began today. A squad of men are furnished spades, hand barrows, which they themselves constructed, and carpenter tools, and voluntarily go to work burying the filth and sinks that have overflowed, and cover several yards and is in terrible ferment and alive with vermin. The plan is to cover a portion of the swamp near the east part each side of the stream, about five rods wide by 10 long, with dirt from the banks and erect a framework over the stream for a privy. This will partially supply the wants for the south side, but the north is separated by an impassable marsh. This project is set on foot by persistent pleading of our men with physicians and officers of the military post, as chances have been offered, to get the means for doing it. Through them Wirz has been induced to acquiesce, but like all internal improvements, humane influence has to be brought to bear upon Wirz. He was persuaded by the argument that prison insobordination was more likely to occur under unsanitary conditions, that there was great libality of epidemic that would sweep both the prison and military post. A colonel of the post was inside this morning and talked with some of us. His opinion is that we will soon be exchanged; but I do not indulge in hopes likely to be deferred, which "maketh the heart sick." A day ration was shown him. He said more was allowed; that there was no reason why rations are so small; that more is provided under the regulations; expressed a belief that someone is speculating to our injury and, though he had no authority, he would inquire into the matter.

Weather intensely hot, the sick badly affected and are multiplying. Every day men die, every morning are carried out. The average number of deaths now is said to be 40, although 70 have died some days, the principal disorder being diarrhoea, induced by the nature of the food; it has become chronic. Scurvy which affects mouths and limbs, sometimes back and bowels, is increasing. One doctor speaks of an affection of the spleen. In many homesickness may hasten disease and loss of strength. It seems as inevitable as bodily ailments under these conditions. When men fall hopeless and helpless, griping with pain, it is not unnatural that nostalgia be added to the scale of misery. When these complaints unite, the days of victims are being numbered.

Prisoners come in from Florida captured on the 18th. They were engaged in collecting horses and cattle for the army. I spoke with a man, prisoner since Gettysburg, who attracts attention, though thin and yellow, he is remarkably smart. His clothing is all worn out. On the way from Richmond a woman gave him a petticoat which reaches just below his knees that whops about his legs as he strolls characteristically through the camp, a sailor's cap on his head, and not another rag on his person.

Two wells near us are finished which we assisted to dig; the water is excellent. Pinchen has finished his bucket whittled from rations of wood, and hooped with knapsack straps, and it is used to draw water. Griffith and I have sold four tin plates for $1 each. This money helps us live.

Wednesday, June 1st.—Scalding heat during forenoon; heavy showers follow. Water is running through camp like a flood. Prisoners reported missing, rations suspended; Rebels are making a stir on the outside.

Finished "Paradise Lost"; called on Harriman. He supplied us with Pollock's "Course of Time." We had read this, but it is now more acceptable. In our view it is a work of more natural thought and imbibes less of the unnatural. Milton has soul-stirring passages, alive with truth, significant expression and beautiful simplicity. Then he goes deeply into themes beyond most conceptions; we don't wish to follow him, or cannot, have not, unless this is "Paradise Lost." Did he mean the Southern Confederacy when he said:

"Devils with devils damned firm concord hold."

Did he mean the North when he wrote:

"Men only disagree of creatures rational,
Though under hope of heavenly grace"

how they should save the Union?

The following lines express a truth in human experience:

"God proclaiming peace,
Yet men live in hatred, enmity and strife
Among themselves, and levy cruel wars
Wasting the earth, each other to destroy,

As if man had not hellish foes enough besides,
That day and night for his destruction wait."

Milton seems to have designed to impress the thought that man had hellish foes distinct from his race, awaiting his destruction, which originated through rebellious war in heaven. I think the causes of our troubles lie in our lack of knowledge and misconception of our social relations, wicked ambition, foolish pride, and that these lines better fit an earthly than a heavenly realm.

The usual monotony except an unusual amount of firing by sentry. Prisoners arrive daily from both our great armies. Men crowd near them to get news and hardtack; occasionally old friends meet. About half the camp draw raw meal; we are of that half this week; have the trouble of cooking it without salt or seasoning or wood, half the time. We stir it in water, bake it on plates held over a splinter fire with a stiff stick, or boil it into mush or dumplings, baking or boiling as long as fuel lasts. ,, ,

Tuesday, June 2nd.—Heavy showers all day to near evening. The ground is soaked; thousands walk or lay in mud without covering unless they are among those who have some frail shelter, the latter being but a small percentage of the whole. I feel fortunate to share the frail shelter of worthy comrades. It does much to ward off sun and storm; but our bed in the sand is exposed. We dig trenches to prevent water from running over it, still it soaks through. Water comes from the upper part in swift brooklets, sweeping every pool of foulness below. I will record, and hope I may not refer to it again, this fact: Men unable to go to the swamp sinks, have holes dug close by where they lay. The rains wash these away or overflow them, and the filthy contents are carried into our resting places. These violent storms render the condition of the sick more sad. I met J. B. Hawks of Michigan, and Peter Shaffer, 22nd N. Y. cavalry, who resides in Nelson, N. Y., today. Shaffer was taken May 8th on a cavalry raid, was robbed of everything except his clothes, including $50.

Friday, June 3rd.—A cold rain continued during the night. What would the good folks at home say could they see this camp this cool, wet morning—men lying in the wet sand? Could they have heard the coughing of thousands as I heard it when I walked the camp to shake off the cold that chilled wet clothing, would they not say: Now that so much has been imperiled for the country, let us make it a glory and a blessing to ages, an honor to ourselves, our institutions the abode of liberty, a beacon that shall light the world and silence the wrath of treason? There are 20,000 within a space so small that a strangling cough can be heard from one side to the other.

Report that nine men tuneled out and one guard escaped with them. The tunnel is found and being filled. Col. Parsons was inside; he thinks exchange is agreed upon, but can't be effected for our forces cover the point in the cartel. Were that all we should soon be relieved. He is quite familiar with a few of us and expressed a feeling that he would resign his command were it possible. He was sent for duty here because the most of his command are prisoners. Earlier in the war he was twice a prisoner, captured by Burnside's men, and was well treated. He says men are sent here without any provision made for shelter, and he has no orders or means to furnish it; that it is not the fault of the local commissary that we are left to suffer. Wirz is the jailor, a morose, inclement tempered man. It requires but little to get him in a rage. He is called "the old Dutch Captain"; is generally hated. Men caught in attempting escape are unreasonably punished by wearing ball and chain, bucking and gagging, putting in stocks, hanging by thumbs, by lash and close confinement.

Prisoners in today report the two armies on to Richmond, Lee with his right, Grant with his left; Kilpatrick 25 miles in the rear of Atlanta tearing up roads.

Saturday, June 4th.—Wirz, Gen. John H. Winder, commissary general of prisoners, Howell Cobb and several minor personages came inside on horseback and rode partly through the prison and along the stockade over the dead line as far as possible. Winder is said to be invested with full authority over prison matters. Howell Cobb was the Secretary of the United States Treasury under Buchanan, just prior to the secession of Georgia, and was the provisional president of the so-called Confederacy, before Davis.

Monday, June 6th.—The impression is growing that the situation is more and more unfavorable every day. Hospitals are overflowing with sick and no more admittance, though crowds throng at the gate daily; deaths are rapidly increasing. The numbers laying about, helpless and speechless, are growing daily. Thompson reported a particular case to the gate, asking help, and got the answer: "You Yanks help yourselves." Sergeants of detachments have reported so many cases of insane, helpless and entirely naked men, and got no satisfaction, that they ceased to do so.

A much worn Atlantic Monthly of 1861, fell into my hands which I read with interest; "Concerning Veal," by the author of "Recreations of a Country Parson," and "Nat Turner, the Slave Insurrectionist of 1831," who aroused all Virginia to defend slavery. I noticed today a man with the whole lower part of his body buried in dirt as a remedy for scurvy.

Tuesday, June 7th.—A week of rain. Five hundred more prisoners, twenty being marines, captured as late as May 27th. Since yesterday morning the number of deaths are put at 110 inside the prison. They are being carried out on wagons six at a time, for burial. They are thrown on as if they were logs of wood; the driver takes a stand between them and as he moves, the limpsy bodies bump and knock about.

A wreckless tempered man struck one of his companions with a club, inflicting a fatal wound on the back of his head, fracturing his skull. The quarrel arose over which should have the first right to the fire for cooking. The man is insensible. A crowd gathered around the assailant and gave him a course of buck and gag, the same club being used for the gag. Thirty of us go to the gate and ask permission to go out under guard to get poles and brush to build shelter for the sick laying on the streets and in the swamp in deplorable condition. We were refused, harshly cursed and ordered away by Capt. Wirz. The opinion is strong that it is the Confederate policy to destroy as many of us as possible, but in a way to evade the censure of the world. There seems to be a studied disregard of the rights of prisoners. It is said that Gen. Winder boasted exultingly that his prison policy would kill as many men as Joe Johnston would in his opposition to Sherman. The hot headed leadership of the South, the mad spirit with which they plunged into war, the unholy purpose for which it is waged, furnish precedents for such belief. The means is justified by the end, assuming that the end were justifiable. At best the better instincts of humanity, or fear of the power of civilization, seems to be all there is in our favor to save us from butchery or utter starvation. The foulness of this physical corruption and the fiendish conduct by which it is produced, fitly represent the animus of their cause. No men were ever more implicitly trusted by the masses than the leaders of the South; no people were ever more treacherously led to trouble. We can now see how foolish and infernal human nature can be, how perverted man's sense of right may be! We also see how men can be degraded, pressed to the very dust and filth with worms, and still retain a sense of justice! Our hearts are void of malice.

## FACTS AND RUMORS JOURNALIZED.—A REBEL SUTLER SHOP.

Sunday, June 12.—Four days I have been ill. Among new men bloody flux and dysentery prevail; this is my trouble. I am better today; a fine breeze lifts me. From last date it has rained every day. We have news from my regiment. Adjutant Carpenter was killed in a charge, both Col. Grover and Lieut. Col. Cook are disabled; Capt. J. L. Goddard, of my company, in command. The movement of trains toward Americus is on account of wounded Confederates being taken to Americus from battlefields about Atlanta. All doctors absent; no sick call for a week. The dead are daily drawn out by wagon loads.

On the 8th a Catholic priest said to us he supposed we were badly treated, but there are as kind hearted people about here as anywhere; that officers have it their own way; thought our government unwilling to exchange, but if better provisions could not be made for us, something ought to be done. Priests, though frequently in, have little to say. They are said to be using their doctrinal influence to get men to swear allegiance to the Confederacy. I do not accept this as true, though one of Erin's sons frequently visited, who said to me that he refused to renounce Uncle Sam, yesterday went out with the priest and has not returned.

I am out of conceit with many reports which originate in camp. I have no faith in innocent liars who tell so much news. For instance: Lincoln is going to give two for one to get us out; "is going to throw the nigger overboard to please Rebels"; that Secretary Stanton has said that "none but dead beats and coffee boilers are taken prisoners, and the army is better off without them." Likely some Rebel started this story, but it had weight among some. Indignant crowds gather and vent their curses on Stanton. Grant is cursed by some, so is the President and the Cabinet; for these gossipers have but little depth of thought and are easily moved by groundless rumors. It is cheering to know many on whose eyes are no scales, logically rebutting these stories and laying the blame of our abuse on the Rebel authorities, where it belongs. A small ration of rice today.

Monday, June 14th.—Northeast storm badly affects weak men. I know of twenty who since yesterday have sunk to utter helplessness; others have died within a few hours. Their clothes are besmeared with wet sand and soaked with water. The sand where we lay is wet as dough. Our rations are so insufficient that we are continually hungry. Got boiled rice again at night, totally unfit to eat. Several bushels are poured into large kettles, greasy and nasty, and cooked with less care than if it were hog feed. I believe hogs would loathe it. If it is merely economy to feed us so, it is crowding them down closely to the provision line. Rumors of the renomination of Lincoln and the nomination of Fremont on a side line. It is a Rebel lie or a Yankee blunder, much talked about. If it is so, the action of the Fremont wing is disapproved. I never strongly believed in Fremont, but the cause he essayed to represent, he will not see sacrificed for per-

Monday, June 14th.—Northeast storm. Badly affects weak ultra anti-slavery men add themselves to the pro-slavery party North, and defeat the policy of the government? They cannot succeed; they can only defeat. The feeling here is for Lincoln. Twelve men escape; it is reported six guards are gone. Tunnels are found and being filled. Rice and meal rations.

Wednesday, June 15th.—Last night "raiders" attempted to profit by their vile practices. "Moseby's" (this name is given one of the chiefs) whistles blew and was responded to by the sub-leaders. Suspicious-looking chaps move through parts of the prison. Presently the cry of "thief," "raiders," and suppressed voices are heard, like men in a struggle. Again cries of "catch him," "murder," "Oh, God, they've killed me!" Now and then one is caught, and cries, and begs dolefully. Then a squad of twenty strong savage-looking men ran through the streets with clubs; soon there is a desperate fight. Blows are plainly heard, and savage oaths and cries of fright and distress. For a time the desperadoes vanish, then reappear. The disturbance kept up all night; we did not feel safe to lie down unless someone of our tent watched. I hear of two watches and other things being lost; have seen some men who got hit. Some Massachusetts boys near us had their blanket seized. Luckily one awoke as the last corner was drawn from him. He sprang up and so closely pursued the thief that he dropped it. This morning a fellow had his head shaved for stealing rations. Toward noon excitement attracted attention to the north side. Going thither we found a fellow had been seized and was being shorn of one-half of his hair and whiskers. He had been outside shoemaking and had been commissioned by the Confederates to come in and take the names of others, of the same trade, with the view that they might be induced or impressed into the service, for Rebels are in need of men of all trades; especially men are wanted to make "government shoes." I saw a man playing the same treasonable game yesterday and a group of us resolved he should not go unnoticed. Shame on those men who are willing to sell their birthright for a loathsome crust! Turn their hands against the cause for which they fought, and virtually balance the power of brothers in the field! The blood of our brothers would cry out against us. For a Southerner to do this is treason; for one of our own men to do it, what is it?

Twice, the first in two days, has the sun appeared today, but it is still rainy. Several hundred men arrive from our army in Virginia, the majority of whom are stripped of blankets and tents. The number of deaths within 24 hours ending at 9 a. m. today is stated at 160.

A hermit wrote of his situation in solitude as "a horrible

place"; "Better dwell in the midst of alarms." But we have no choice; we both—
"Dwell in the midst of alarms,"
And "reign in this horrible place."
It was not poetical to call Nature's solitude horrible; nothing is so horrible as subverted, debased, cruelized, distorted, dying human nature.

Thursday, June 16th.—The man who was deprived of his hair yesterday had taken the oath of allegiance to the "C. S. A." He wished to get 200 names—had about 50—to make army shoes. His papers were taken and he was forced to swear not to assist the Rebels any more. The affair soon reached Capt. Wirz who sent a guard to escort the ex-Unionist outside and to arrest his assailants. He also ordered that no rations be issued until the man who shaved his head was apprehended. All honor to the brave man who shaved the Judas head.

Rather than that thousands of comrades be deprived of scanty rations for day, he bade farewell to friends and calmly reported at the gate, was taken out by the guard and locked up, refusing to divulge another name. After a thorough search for the others, rations were issued.

Friday, June 17th.—The night of the 11th a well caved in; two men asleep slid in; one was killed. Soon after coming in, we learned that one of the dealers, or "raiders" bore the name of Cary. He was at Belle Isle and is charged with being the cause of several deaths. Today he was pointed out to us and we recognized Sullivan of our company (76th N. Y.) who deserted October 10, 1863, near the Rapidan River south of Mitchell, Va. He was a substitute from Buffalo, a "gambling, fighting, bad tempered fellow, feared in the company. He thinks we suspect him, and tonight sends word by Mooney, who knew him in Canada, that if we do not expose him, Company F shall never be disturbed by raiders.

Monday, June 20th.—Yesterday a sentry fired on a man who was attempting to kill a snake near the dead line, but missed him, the shot taking effect on four others; wounding one in the face, one in the thigh, both lying under their blankets, and grazed two others. Gen. Sturgis has blundered in a fight with Forrest in Tennessee; lost 900 men. Sigel has been relieved by Hunter for fighting Breckenridge with an inferior force, less than at his command. These seeming disasters fill Rebels with bombast and are not encouraging to us.

These little triumphs seem to raise their wind;
But great defeats they never seem to find;
They cut loops, but not the ropes that bind.
We look at them, then coolly turn aside,

Annoyed that Jonnies have such narrow pride,
That it should never enter in the mind,
'Tis but a wave blown up against the tide,
For surely Forrest breaks not the comet's tail,
And Joe E. Johnston goes down before it pale;
While flirting in Virginia are but attempts to rise
When U. S. Grant rolls Lee upon his thighs.

Robbers more desperate and bold. Two men have lately been murdered, and a number hurt and robbed. We watch nightly, fearing attack. Two guards are reported hung for attempting to escape with prisoners a few nights ago. The old guard leave this morning, probably for the front; we have a new set on.

Passing up from the creek this morning I saw a crowd standing around a dying negro boy about one-fourth white. A white man stood over him holding in his hand a stick, to one end of which was attached a stiff paper, with which he brushed the swarming flies from his face and fanned his dying breath. He was emaciated and bruised. Presently the feeble breath stopped the man bent and lay his bony hands on his breast. Again there was a faint heaving of the breast, the eyes brightened and glanced meaningly at him, then rolled back, and he breathed no more. I cannot tell why I forgot every thing for the time—

And intense interest took in him,
When hourly almost, each day, I see the dead
Of my own race, far loftier brows
And comelier forms, pass by.

Involuntarily, almost, my face turned towards the skies, my forehead and temples felt the soft, thrilling, intangible pressure of an electric band; my left arm and shoulder, for a moment, electrified. Then I looked at those about, and wondered what they thought. Turning to one, I remarked:

"I should have thought he had a soul, were he not a negro." He replied: "I know, if the human is immortal, he had a soul. I almost felt it when it departed."

This is what is going the rounds tonight: "They say Davis has sued for peace." Too sensible to be true!

Tuesday, June 21st.—At 9 o'clock another man was shot. He was crossing the swamp in the east part to go to his lodging. Attempting to clear the mud, he leaped to a root near the dead line, but not up to it. The ball entered above the hip, and passed to the intestines. His groans and shouts are pitiable.

Wednesday, June 22nd.—The first day of the month that it has not rained. The man shot last night is carried out dead this morning. By trading some, we are enabled to increase our rations to about half we could eat under normal conditions.

Selden, the Rebel quartermaster, has set up a sutler shop

on main street on the north side, with a view of absorbing Yankee money men are starved to spend. The fact that some of the stuff on sale is the same as that issued to prisoners justifies suspicion that he had a reason for cutting down our rations. He attempts to whitewash this matter by putting two prisoners in charge, Charles Huckleby, of the 8th Tennessee, and Ira Beverly, of the 100th Ohio. Nevertheless we are told by Rebel sergeants that he has a commission from Richmond. He only appears, however, once every day. These boys expect to live better while in his service, but admit that the profits are "gobbled" by Selden; that he furnishes the stuff and fixes prices. It seems an unlikely place to make money, but the few who have any spend it fast and pay high prices. While exchange in Federal money is prohibited by Rebel law, it is openly done everywhere by Rebels, and in this case by a "C. S. A." military officer. Articles in stock consist of flour, molasses, small sticks of wood, plug tobacco, a vicious sort of whisky made from sorghum. These things appeal to starved appetites of thousands; and those who have money cannot resist the temptation to let it go. Though this is poor stuff, it is better than the scant rations irregularly issued. We have to pay from 25c to $1 for an onion, 10c to 40c for miserable apples, 25c a pint for meal, 40c for wormy hog peas, 40c for ½ pint of flour, 10c for small piece of wood. With the advent of this institution rations grow less in quantity and quality. It is simply a scheme of this Rebel quartermaster to catch greenbacks, watches, rings, and things of value which men eagerly put up. It is not instituted with a view to benefit us. If such were the object, why do they extort such prices, why are rations cut down, why are we cheated out of one day in five by not getting rations?

### THE PRISON CLEANED OF RAIDERS.—CANDIDATES FOR HEMP.

Thursday, June 23rd.—With the passing June storms, hot weather begins. Spent the afternoon with Harriman. He has been nine months a prisoner and has the first symptoms of scurvy in one leg. He was a very sound man and is vigorously resisting the disorder by use of water and rubbing. He has a work on stenography, the art of which he practices with some success. He urges me to visit Ohio with him, should we be released together, and speaks highly of the people, especially of Ohio girls. This is tempting; but I indulge no dreams, not even of home. Sleep is blank, waking a horrible dream, which I try to break by pencilling some of the horrors and by raising my thoughts to better things, occasionally.

A number of brutal fights today among the rowdyish, strong, sour, crafty fellows, not blessed with reason, but well endowed with bulldog strength and bravery; fighting hard while up, but not hitting a man when down. They are the pugilistic champions of this kingdom and enforce their rules. One man was knocked down eleven times before he left the ring. God knows I am sick of such sights; seldom get out to look at them. There is a lower grade who go in rough and tumble, clubs and fists, on the least provocation, or misunderstanding. Peacable men occasionally get "chucked in the mug" as they call it, for attempting a friendly interference. There are men here whom nothing but clubs, or something more severe, will quell, when they put decent men on the defensive. The necessity of law restraint can never be doubted by those who here witness the rage and mad fury of these vile passions let loose with impunity, if they are reasonable. Poor, sick men are sometimes kicked by these brute-like sons of excess.

Bloodhounds this evening are heard circling the prison in search of a trail of men who escaped from a wood squad today. Men caught by these hounds are brought back and punished and forced to promise obedience. I saw two men who had been bitten by these hounds, while the wounds were fresh. Capt. Wirz came inside and rode around outside the dead line with an orderly. One man complained to him of hard fare, and was threatened with shooting and marched outside and put in the stocks. A piece of raw beef, about three ounces to a man, was issued to about one-fourth of the camp today.

Tuesday, June 28th.—The days have been continually hot since last date; rain at noon. Every day we see the extreme, nameless misery, feel that awful helplessness of languor creeping over us. We weary of observing and noting. Nobly nature struggles against the noisome corruption and economizes her wasting resources. Nights are dreaded for reason of murderous raiders getting bolder, robbing men by force as well as by stealth; pounding with clubs, cutting with knives, even in day time. It is dangerous to sleep; not a night passes but the camp is disturbed; cries of murder are heard; somebody is hurt and robbed. Three nights ago three men near us were attacked while asleep, one was stripped of clothing; but before we could rally to assist, the scoundrels fled. Last night twelve of the murderous wretches rushed up to where we sleep with the intention of smothering us with blankets; and being armed with clubs and knives could have done us harm. Thompson and I were watching, awakened the boys and were ready. Seeing this they got up a sham fight. One says, "It's not here, I will show you, come," and they ran away. We have a watch and $26 amongst us.

Sullivan has denied, to Mattison, having any connection with the "raiders"; but knowing that we know he lies, he tells Mooney that he controls the gang, being a chief we need not fear. It was by accident Mattison met him as he evades us. But the wicked shall not go unpunished. He will find the truth of this text.

A few nights since Mooney's blanket was stolen. He appealed to Sullivan with threats and promises. Sullivan brought him the identical blanket. A man was attacked this afternoon but the raiders were beaten. Prisoners come in so fast that we are terribly crowded. At night when we lay down every passage, every space is covered, thousands sleeping without the least covering or shelter.

Wednesday, June 29th.—More brutality and robbery. Half asleep I heard blows, groans of distress, and voices that combine the savage tones of ruffianism. One man badly injured; two reported missing. Steps are taken to organize a police force. We are doing the little we can to assist. The safety of the camp requires it; our lives are every day in jeopardy. We are in greater immediate peril from these villains than from the atrocities of our keepers. At 3 p. m. a man was violently assailed in the street, while asleep, and robbed, he said, of $85 and a watch. He had arrived that day among others of Sherman's soldiers. With blood streaming down his face from a gash on his forehead, I saw him hasten to the gate where he reported the affair. A number went forward, among them several sergeants of detachments, and an earnest, but respectful appeal was made for assistance, or that we might be allowed to protect ourselves, or for some encouragement that the matter should have a hearing. Meantime the robbers, not intimidated, thinking that our appeal would avail nothing, gave out certain threats, and three of them visited the tent of an elderly man whom they knew to have money, and presenting knives, demanded it without one word, or they would kill him on the spot. The man handed out a portion, less than the amount, (about $40); but they were not permitted to prolong their visit. About 5 p. m. an order came from Capt Wirz that if we wished to take them outside, he would furnish a guard, we to point them out, and he would "clear the stockade." Exciting scenes followed. Shouts went up from thousands; the whole camp swarmed like a bee-hive. The gates open. Sergeants with revolvers, guards with bayonets fixed, enter, and Rebel and Union soldiers walk side by side in a good work. Our boys lead the way to the den of thieves, murderers and traitors, point them out, and put them under their charge as fast as found. Outside the gate was another strong guard who received them and they returned for more. There was a rush in every part of the camp, the raiders trying to skulk, the boys hunting them. Toward night the leaders began to resist, but under the clubs of our police they quailed. Near us one of the leaders, a strong man, was overtaken, but swore he would never be taken alive. He fought desperately, but one of our men struck him with a stake, knocking him senseless. One or two others were badly hurt. We saw Sullivan marching under three bayonets, and as he turned his eyes towards us, so full of guilt, we almost pitied him. Still we rejoiced; our only fear was he and some of his troop would be turned in again. At dark the work ceased; nearly sixty had been taken out, and a few, no doubt led astray, sent in. The boys shouted, "Bully for the Captain," for the men who took the initiatory step, and for the guard. With the work of catching raiders began a search for money and lost property. In one place two stockings filled with greenbacks, another with watches (two gold), and other things were found buried, preparatory to being sold to the Rebels. Two men were found buried near the southwest corner. One had his throat cut, the other had the appearance of having been beaten and strangled. Bones of others were reported found.

The real organizer of this body, known as regulators, that led in apprehending the raiders, is Sergeant Leroy L. Key, of an Illinois regiment, evidently a good, brave, astute man, very choice in choosing his adherents. The organization was made up of western men, from Illinois, Iowa, Indiana and Ohio; comparatively few from each of these states. He seemed to have some distrust of laying his plans before eastern men generally, but with no valid reason other than that precaution was necessary until these organized, savage gangs could be suppressed. We New Yorkers felt galled, at first, by this manifest distrust on the part of some western brothers who seemed to desire credit for the move. The fact that the chiefs were from eastern regiments, had its effect. We thought best to watch and wait and aid when needed, realizing the necessity of curbing the outrages of this murderous bandit, and hailed the movement with joy, perfectly willing they should have the credit if they succeeded. Sergeant Keys had an instinct for choosing his men and, though a self constituted leader, none better could have been chosen for the terrible and unique duty imposed, which is not a task ordinary men have an ambition for; for it was known from the start, by intelligent men, that extraordinary means would be necessary to put an end to the leaders, even if death were required. Hence the admiration of all lovers of men in the prison, is accorded Sergeant Keys and his efficient aids.

Thursday, June 30th.—Men lay down last night feeling more secure of their lives. Hunting for raiders continued, this time without assistance from Rebel guards, except a lieutenant and guard at the gate. The formidable resistance of yesterday was not repeated; the combined efforts of the raiders having so signally failed yesterday. Our men are armed with clubs; when one is found he is hustled to the gates, often with a kick or a punch in the back, amid the sneering and shouting from lookers on, and goes sneaking out. Lieutenant Davis gave me permission to go out with witnesses to take evidence when the trial proceeds, which is to be conducted by thirteen men recently in from the western army, as it is the design of Sergeant Keys that the hearing shall be before intelligent and impartial men, with a view of giving them a fair trial; but feeling so badly, having been sick several days, I was obliged to return, Baldwin of my regiment goes out against Sullivan. The greater part of those taken out are returned on promises of good behavior and on the plea that they have been decoyed. Some of these Keys had strong evidence against but the place where they were kept, just outside of the gate, was overcrowded and Wirz insisted upon them being returned. A few were sentenced to wear a ball and chain. The abuse inflicted on those turned in, by the crowd, as they were forced to run the gauntlet, is almost cruel, two lines being formed from the dead line towards the center of the prison through which they are forced to pass. Many were severely pounded and one, a sailor, was struck by a fellow who had just come in from outside, with a rail, knocking him down, and he died from the effects of this and other blows.

### MOVE TO PRISON ANNEX—HOW WE CELEBRATE.

Friday, July 1st.—The addition to the stockade is finished. An aperture, ten feet wide, is left in the old wall at the north of the old ground. Thirteen thousand are ordered to move through (my detachment is one designated) in three hours. The weather is very hot and that mass of men moving without order over ground already crowded with those who are to remain, is horribly fatiguing. This time is given us to get on the ground or no rations will be given these detachments; so we strove at the walls like a crowded flock of sheep escaping through a hole in a fence, being obliged to jump a trench five feet deep, three wide with a bank of dirt on the opposite side. Never did men work more earnestly for a prize than we for a little course Indian meal to appease our terrible hunger. But it smelt so good, the green stuff that had been growing, that we felt rejoiced and thrilled at the sight of Nature's face yet undefiled, but soon to be desecrated by the foulness of disease and decay. A score of men fell into the trench in clambering through the stockade, and had to be helped. Fragments of trees lay about over which men strove to obtain fuel and shelter. The average number of deaths per day is estimated at 70.

Sunday, July 3rd.—New prisoners report favorable progress by our armies. Yesterday there was a powerful rain lasting ten hours. In this part the soil is red and hard, surface flat, and water stood from two to four inches deep. We stood up all night to keep out of it. Those too feeble to do this, were drenched and drowned. It was with great physical and mental effort that I was able to endure the strain as I have been feeble several days.

Four crazy men have been wandering through camp several days. I noticed one today without any clothing, having been naked for two weeks. He lay within four rods of the south gate, arms extended, exposed to the sun, in full view of everybody. His whole body was blistered, his countenance frightfully distorted, giving utterance to unintelligible sounds, frothy matter oozing from his mouth and nostrils, his eyes appearing blind. Another prisoner shot through the hips last night by a guard. One lay near the brook delirious, burning with fever; another near him was unable to speak; one-half buried in the swamp, covered by a mass of maggots and flies. Those who brought him out said his eyes, ears, nose and mouth were filled. Near the sink, in almost every passage, lay half-rotting skeletons, evincing all the signs of deprivation and symptoms of pestilence, and yet alive. All of this and I have not been out of my usual course. Neither do I mention those who have a slight covering to turn the sun. There are hundreds who would require the best treatment to be saved, and perhaps could not be saved. In this absence of medical treatment we resort to simple means to cure ourselves. A very limited supply of red root and white gum bark can be found, on our new lot, and pine bark, which are used to check the almost universal complaints, diarrhoea, dysentery and urinary troubles. I observed several men today had buried their limbs to the knees, as a remedy for scurvy. But the truth is there is no remedy for this condition under the circumstances. Never could we imagine anything so horrible! We might write volumes, and fail to describe the horrible reality. Our people would disbelieve it, and "pooh" as if it were a fabulous tale. Tonight some have a season of prayer near us. One or two most excellent prayers were offered, prayers that would grace pulpits, bearing an earnestness of the soul's devotion. It seemed so much like home, like steadfast faith and adoration, a reflex of the all-reaching Providence, that we felt it good to be there; that hearts are still alive, the finer sympathies not entirely stifled. How much better to see men in such communion, seeking consolation from heaven, than to see them worse than brutes, or fighting demons! No rations today.

,Monday, July 4th.—Eighty-eight years this day since our fathers gave to the world that important document setting forth the immortal truth that all men are born free with equal rights to life, liberty and the pursuit of happiness, and declaring the independence of these states from foreign domination—the Declaration of American Independence. On these great truths they founded a Republic. Today their posterity are in mourning for the loss of sons. In painful expectations, in earnest hope and fear, their eyes are turned toward two mighty armies contending on the same soil,—one for those principles and that Republic, the other battling to maintain a dying rebellion inaugurated to overthrow the work of their hands, and to found a government on principles the reverse. Nothing was ever more plainly asserted in both words and deeds than this. Here within the scope of my vision, are 26,000 men suffering for the great sin that has cursed our people, offered a living sacrifice that it may not be destroyed but saved free from the contaminating influence that has stained our fair emblem—the boasted emblem of liberty; that the Union of the States shall not be broken by the hands of Treason; the foul assassin of Liberty! O, that the day of glorious triumph may soon come and with it the right, and stop the horrid evil of war! Let the demon that actuated it be destroyed! Apropos to the day are these beautiful lines from Longfellow, which Thompson recited:

    \* \* \* Sail on, O Ship of State!
   Sail on, O, Union, strong and great!
   Humanity with all its fears,
   With all the hopes of future years,
   Is hanging breathless on thy fate!
   We know what Master laid thy keel,
   What Workman wrought thy ribs of steel,
   Who made each mast, and sail, and rope,
   What anvils rang, what hammers beat,
   In what a forge and what a heat
   Were shaped the anchors of thy hope!
   Fear not each sudden sound and shock,
   'Tis of the wave and not the rock;
   'Tis but the flapping of the sail,
   And not a rent made by the gale!
   In spite of rock and tempest's roar,
   In spite of false lights on the shore,
   Sail on, nor fear to breast the sea;
   Our hearts, our hopes, are all with thee,
   Our hearts, our hopes, our prayers, our tears
   Our faith triumphant o'er our fears,
   Are all with thee—are all with thee!

Have had but little rest for two nights, owing to the storm and severity of my complaints. No rations since the 2nd. Two hours of terrible thunder storm. At the Sutler's "Shebang" I purchased a small wheat biscuit for 35 cents. This is my feast (after two days' fast) for July 4th, 1864.

Tuesday, July 5th.—We moved back to the old side, five of us, unbeknown to Rebs, it being improved by the removal of so many to the new part, and to get near the well we dug, for we were fifty rods from water. About 3 p. m. the mule teams came to the north gate; the boys cry "rations," the first issued for over sixty hours. I know no other reason for this than that the first night after the new part of the prison was occupied men carried off timbers of the old north wall for wood or for huts. On July 2nd Capt. Wirz directed that no rations be issued until every stick was replaced. He was heard to say on the 3rd, at the gate, that he would "learn the G——d d——n Yankees that he was in command and if the sons of b——s died like hell ,there would be enough left." I paid ten cents for a small rotting apple; it was good. The 6th, Sherman's men report Johnston whipped at all points; the 8th, behind the Chattahoochee, Sherman crossing on his flank; Grant's, Richmond in danger; Lee's cornbread line troubled. The Southern slave empire must come down. Billy Decker, prisoner since October, a Belle Islander, "Pinch's" old playmate, is stopping with us. He belongs to the 1st U. S. dragoons; is from Steuben county, New York.

Thursday, July 7th.—Cool nights, hot days. My complaint not so bad. I have a painful cough. From three to six shots fired nightly by sentries, so common as not to be of note.

Friday, July 8th.—Prisoners arrive, 300, taken at James Island, S. C., the 3rd, belonging to the 52nd Pennsylvania, also a squad from Virginia. Fierce lightning and thunder in the middle of the day, the sun shining brightly, and scarce a cloud in the sky. A Rebel paper admits the country open to Grant, and Lee in a strait. "All we want is to be left alone," said Jeff Davis at his inaugural. His wants will grow, like "bull pen" lice.

## SCENES AMONG SICK.—RAIDERS CONVICTED.

Strong these men had been;
In vast army camps had duty done;
Had useful service'in field and fort performed,
Some also on the sea and river fleets.
Strong on marches and in battles' strife;

> Strong in perilous trenches behind belching guns
> On skirmish lines at opening frays,
> And bravely stood the shock of charging lines
> That brought the battle's final test.
>                    From The Vision of North.

Saturday, July 9th.—More than a week since a sick call. The Doctor came to the gate this morning; and many sick go forward. Crowds are carried who cannot walk and are laid over a large space. Still in a bad state and quite weak, I go, hoping to get a prescription, for "camphor pills," which sergeants of "nineties" draw, after the examination. Doctor comes in and looks them over hastily, going among them some, touching a few as though he felt squeamish. Two hours would be required, at least, to get along with the "nasty job," the doctors think, and only wink at them at that. I could not endure the hot sun, the awful stench, the sight of those sickening objects. I soon lost faith, if I had any, that I should be healed by a slight hem touch. I came to doubt, upon viewing the condition of so many others, whether I needed anything. More curious than charitable—charity is a cripple here, begins and ends at home. I looked them over, and was not curious.

> "Here pity doth most show herself alive
>    When she is dead."—Dante.

There were stronger forms and more robust constitutions than mine, weaker than infants; more loathsome than if they were dead; so they soon must be—once a part of the bone and sinew of the Union army! What ten times worse than ghastly expressions! What pitiful complaints! What peevish, unmanly cries, calling for the doctor to "Come quick, for Christ's sake, quick!" constantly begging for water! Aghast, I stepped hurriedly, shamblingly, but carefully over those wasted, corrupted bodies, once beautiful caskets of immortal spirits, and hastened here and sit down with the boys under the shade of the blanket, my heart sinking,—is it not hardening with gloom? I shudder while I write lest my fate shall be like theirs.

"What did you get, North?" they asked.

"Nothing; didn't try."

"You ought to."

"It wouldn't amount to shucks."

"Perhaps it would; at any rate, get all you can out of the Confederacy."

"That would do."

"Then go back and try."

"That makes me think of a man standing all night in the cold to freeze an ugly dog. The soundest man in the bull-pen would be sick to stand in that dying crowd an hour."

"That's what's the matter."

Tonight some of the sick are still at the gate; no attention paid, but ordered left till sent back. Many of the worst cases were admitted to hospital, a large number carried back by friends. Out of those who remain, six have died during the day; others on the verge of death. Doctors claim they have no means to care for the sick, therefore neglect them, let them rot rather than parole and send them to our lines. They are not admitted to the hospital, which is little better than this den, until in a condition of death; nor are we allowed to go out for brush and timber to build shelter here though thousands would volunteer for that service and the timber is all about us.

Sunday, July 10th.—Hot, showery day, renders the condition of the sick more appalling. It is believed that more than two-thirds of the 700 men at the gate in response to the sick call, are victims of starvation. Healthful action of the stomach and other organs of the body is destroyed; the food supplied imparts no nutriment though appetite craves it. Men eat whole rations ravenously, while unable to walk, which is not retained, sometime two minutes,—if it is, it is an internal fire and blood and decayed flesh come with temporary relief. Others loathe it, strain to vomit at sight, and so remain till death. Those not so afflicted are more or less infected with scurvy, dropsy, urinary disorders or these combined.

It is announced tonight that six raiders have been convicted and condemned to death and are to be hanged tomorrow in the prison shortly after noon. The names of these convicts are Cary Sullivan, of 76th N. Y. regiment; William Collins, alias Moseby, 88th Pennsylvania; Charles Curtis, 5th Rhode Island artillery; John Sarsfield, 144th N. Y.; Patrick Delaney, 83rd Pennsylvania; A. Muir, alias Jack the Sailor, U. S. navy. Sullivan's given name, announced by the regulators as Terrence, was carried on the company roll as Cary. It is understood that these men were professional bounty jumpers, going out for the money they could get, and were captured outside of the line of duty. **We know Sullivan** deserted our regiment while it was forming for expected battle, on the night of October 10th, 1863, and was captured by Rebel cavalry that was flanking our infantry a few hours prior to the beginning of Meade's great retreat to Centerville, Va. To carry out this grim project Sergeant Keys and immediate assistants have got the use of timbers and tools and secured a few carpenters to build a scaffold.

## HANGING THE CHIEF RAIDERS.—SCENES AT THE EXECUTION.

Monday, July 11th, 1864.—Building the scaffold for executing the principal raiders, began at 9 a. m. a few yards within the dead line near the south gate. By 1 p. m. it was finished and the crowd assembled everywhere a footing could be had in view of the scaffold. Looking from my position near the scaffold to the north on the sloping ground I beheld the most densely packed crowd I had ever seen. The south side if possible was more densely packed. They came from every extreme portion of the stockade until they could get no further. Evidently every man that could be was on his taps. A multitude of probably 30,000, all astir on so small an area is seldom if ever seen. The regulator squads, armed, with clubs, formed a square around the scaffold to keep back the crowd. It was feared by leaders that an attempt would be made, by associates of the doomed, to destroy the scaffold and release them. Sometime was employed in attaching halters to the beam and adjusting nooses, then all was ready. Shortly after, the gate opened and Capt. Wirz, dressed in a white duck suit, upon his gray horse, accompanied by a Catholic priest, followed by the guard with the doubly doomed war prisoners. They were six dressed only in undershirts and drawers and heads uncovered. Capt. Wirz addressed us in broken Swiss nearly as follows:

"Prisoners, I deliver these men to you in as good condition as I found them. I have had nothing to do in convicting them of crime of which they are accused, except to lend my assistance for their and your protection; nor do I charge them or believe them guilty, and shall have nothing to do with the execution of your sentence. You have tried them; I have permitted it. You have convicted and sentenced them; if they are hung, you, not I, will be responsible for it. I deliver them to you; do with them as you please, and may God be with them and you. Guards about face; forward march."

All but the priest moved out and the gate closed. This address was delivered from a paper in his hand said to have been prepared by Lieut. Davis or some officer of the post.

The prisoners had doubted the earnestness of the proceedings up to the moment of the egress of Wirz and the guard. However, their arms had been pinioned, and when they looked at the gallows the dreadful truth struck terror to their hearts. Their executioners were in position and without the least delay pressed each man to ascend the scaffold, Curtis, a strong man, shouted in a strong, rough voice, "By God, boys, we will never go up there!" At the same time fiercely wrenching away, loosing his arms and throwing them about his head, dashed madly through the regulators' lines rushed through the weak crowd to the stream, plunged into the swamp, sometimes to his hips, but was retaken by two pursuers before reaching solid ground. Meantime the crowd took panic, supposing the rescue of the condemned was attempted and in the confusion jostled and trampled one another down. Their fright was greatly increased on seeing the Rebels fly to their guns. The crowd surged back like a heavy sea, trampling hundreds of the weaker under feet and leveling flimsy tents in the rush, which had hardly ceased before the fugitive was brought back trembling and cowering with fear. The others had been left standing, but now all were pushed up the steps to the trap by the executioner, talking and wailing unintelligibly while the priest begged fervently for them to be spared. As the nooses were put over their necks, and the bags, used for caps, were ready to be drawn over their faces, with what awful woe they crouched and pleaded for life. The priest, at their request essayed to address, not only those in charge but the vast crowd as well, uttering an appeal and urging that the final disposition of the matter be left to the crowd. Alas, of no avail. The witnesses of their crimes by thousands, as well as their condemners stood before them and their clamor for the execution to proceed overwhelmed the frantic effort of the priest. They believed them guilty of direct murder, the means of suffering and death of many by depriving them of scanty clothing and fare; by theft and in having cruelly beaten them. The guilty clamored for mercy that they had denied to innocent, helpless men. Yet willingly would most of us spared them to be dealt with by law, but with their lives we knew no safety.

Who has seen the soul's anguish pouring out in tears? This was the agony of guilt. It fired in the wild eye, flashed on the cowering cheek, darkened on the crazed brow and poured in frenzied tones from quivering lips. If the executioners were moved by these appeals they knew their duty and performed it. The firm answer was, "No you must die." Then said Collins, to the priest:

"Then do pray for us, pray long and hard!"

He prays but Collins breaks in vehemently.

"I am guilty, but not of this; I have been an awful man! I have not had a fair trial," and many other sentences, and all shout together, "Yes, yes!" Sullivan broke in:

"Neither am I guilty, but"—and he groaned, "I did not expect ever to come to this." "Nor I," all shouted in concert.

Their exclamations were so loud, continuous and distressing, that I heard nothing of the prayer. Several times the sack was removed from their heads as they feelingly urged to be prayed for, until the executioners had decided not to repeat it, when

Curtis asked for one moment. Speaking loudly, he asked:
"Have I a friend within hearing?"
A voice answers, "Yes, it is me, Curtis."
"Is it you, Tony Ryan? Come up here."
Executioner—"No, he can't come up."
Curtis—"Then I have one request, Tony, it is my dying request. I want you to keep my watch and send it back to my father-in-law in New York City."
Tony—"I will do it, Curtis."
Curtis—"I am ready. This is a hard sight, boys," and he groaned.
Sullivan and Muir both said: "May God bless our souls!"
The executioners stepped from the platform, the props were pulled, the traps fell. As I looked upon the scene I saw that Collins had snapped his rope, and fallen to the ground. He was restored to consciousness, and though he plead that as God had saved his life once, he should be spared. But he was forced upon the raised trap, the noose readjusted while the other five were in the throes of death before his eyes, and swung off, partially kneeling, an impulsive movement all made. It was indeed a hard sight; six strong men sent from life for crimes against fellow prisoners. I almost think I am hardened because I looked upon them with the composure that I did. This is the breaking up of a gang organized in the Richmond prisons.

But there were interested spectators outside the prison, the soldiers standing in their rifle pits with arms ready; the artillerymen standing at their pieces ready to pull the ledyard cord at command; and from 1,500 to 2,000 people, composed of old men and women of both sexes and all colors, from several miles about, who in their anxiety to see, had edged from positions assigned them, in front of the artillery and infantry lines, and were thrown into panic as they supposed they were to fire upon the prisoners.

It is told of Muir that he was acquitted of a crime in Dublin, Ireland, though he had confessed guilt to his priest. Since conviction here he told the story to an Irish friend, adding that after acquittal the priest told him that death by hanging would be his doom; that the priest's words had always haunted him; though he sought to avoid acts tending to their fulfillment, he often lost self-control and went wrong. To him he confessed complicity in crimes charged and proved against raiders.

## DREADFUL DAYS DRAG ON—NIGGER IN THE EXCHANGE FENCE.

Tuesday, July 12th.—A man shot through the body and killed

while dipping water from the stream several feet inside the dead line. Two sentries fired.

Wednesday, July 13th.—Corn bread, as served here, is to me what a single feather was to Paddy's head on a rock and what he thought more would be if supplied. Irrepressible conflict is brewing between hunger and filling up. Putting plenty of water in the mush is common with some who want something to fill up. We get nothing but rice tonight.

I find Harriman and tent mate Phillips bad off with scurvy, it having assumed malignant form and the flesh of their limbs has become lifeless. Harriman was looking at photographs of home friends and spoke of them with tenderness and a tone keyed to despair. He has ever before been cheerful and quickly responded to expressions of hope and cheer. We find a word of cheer comes not amiss. I trust that "each does well in his degree." But time comes when condolence takes its place and when that cannot remove the fact. How little of either have we now! The downcast soul is robbed of the blessings of consolation from kindred when wafted from this den of sin to the realm beyond. Are its celestial features tainted with this morbid air; is it enfeebled by this languor? God's unbounded provision is the universal remedy for every woe. This we must feel as never before, or be insensible to ourselves. Harriman then related his strange dream which, to him, was extraordinary, in which he beheld immediate conditions, and the blackness and terror of the supposed "river of death" which soon brightened into a bordering stream, before which all misery, terror and darkness vanished, and he beheld the mystic world. He regarded this as a prophecy of a change soon to come to him and said he had no terror of what might come; it had given him strength ineffable. He then briefly sketched his life, his aspirations and disappointments, which are of so much interest to me that I carefully noted them for future writing.

Saw a paper of July 1st; most notable item: Democrats postpone their convention to be held in Chicago, August 29th. Made the acquaintance of a namesake, John H. Northrop, a nephew of the celebrated lawyer, Henry Northrop, of New York; a prisoner nine months, clothes nearly gone, is lively though he has symptoms of scurvy. The evenings are beautiful; religious meetings are being held in various parts. There are some remarkable singers who attract the attention of outsiders.

Thursday, July 14th.—Report that Lee is moving forces northward; Ewell at Harper's Ferry; and a cavalry raid into Maryland. Whether this is to attract attention for political effect, or is a military movement is a question. While writing, sergeants of detachments have been called by Capt. Wirz and notified that he has if attempted he will kill every man in camp. Reports of two cannon startled the prisoners this afternoon, and we turned out to see Rebel soldiers pouring into line double quick. It was soon evident that it was practice. They formed on the hill, deployed skirmishers who indulged in a vigorous fire, interspersed with several volleys of musketry from a brigade, showing how they would do if Kilpatrick came, or if prisoners break out.

July 21st.—A weak and disagreeable state of body since last date has waived my practice of noting; but everything has been as now—"hell upon earth." We have a few dottings of this kind: the Rebel quartermaster is from Baltimore, and to counteract some suspicions of his speculating in rations, makes lots of promises when he comes in of late. One of our fellows got thick with him and told him where to find a tunnel, for a plug of tobacco. Soon after he came with a squad of negroes armed with feeling rods and spades, found and filled it. It had baffled their scrutiny for three days. The man who revealed the secret betrayed himself and that evening was hunted out, given a clean shave of his head and on his forehead was tattooed the word "Traitor." Next day rations were ordered withheld till those who did the job reported at the gate. I don't know that anyone reported but rations came the day after leaving us a vacuum of one day.

Petitions have been circulating praying our government for relief. I did not sign. They are sanctioned by Rebel authority, intended to produce political effect and to leave the impression in the North that the prisoners condemn government policy in reference to exchange, therefore to serve a purpose of its enemies. It abounds in dictation and censure, suppressing facts.

Reports of movements in north Virginia are true. Sherman is up to Atlanta; Johnston relieved by Hood. They think Johnston fights on the principle that "He who fights and runs away will live to fight another day." Federal cavalry at Montgomery and Taladega, Ala., and at Macon, Ga., only 60 miles away, which causes great excitement here. The Rebels are fortifying. Droves of negroes are brought here from plantations and put to work. Troops and citizens, all sexes and sizes, flock in and quarters are being built, making a ville of the place. We look over to it from high ground and reflect that it is one of the new born of Secessia. A man near the stream cut his own throat today. Several hundred Rebel soldiers are shipped by rail for Macon. Three men brought in whom the Rebels suspect were scouts. They were put in the stocks several hours, but gave no information. James English of our company, of New York City, died July 17th.

Wednesday, July 23rd.—Weather severely hot as it has been learned that a break by the prisoners is planned, and warns them for three weeks. A supply of sumach buds must have arrived and are given out freely to be steeped and drank for scurvy. A sergeant belonging to a work squad outside was shot by a guard, wounding him in the arm and hip and wounding another man. He took hold of the guard's gun. Some on parole get too intimate with Rebels; value principles less than extra rations. That such men have to be shot to remind them that they are dealing with traitors does not so much matter. While washing my shirt at the creek this afternoon the centry fired, the shot whizzing by my head as I stooped, striking in the bank and spattering mud in the faces of four of us. Lots of shooting has been done by guards for over a week and several men have been killed and wounded. Limbs are amputated at the hospital for slight injuries. The arm of one of our men hit by a sentry a few days ago was promptly sawed off. Another tunnel found; dogs are seeking a trail. New forts are plainly to be seen. Negroes work all night. Reported fighting at Atlanta and that some of our forces are expected at Macon.

Thursday, July 24th.—Before day the dog horn and the yelping of hounds was heard. Men on parole about the depot had attempted to escape. Two trains of wounded from Hood's army passed here. Rebels report a victory, then admit a loss. Frederick, of my Company, died this afternoon. He has been ailing but we did not think him dangerously ill. He was carried out at 5 o'clock and is the 51st man who has died since 7 a. m. in prison.

Sunday, July 26th.—Attended meeting this morning near the big pine trees in the southeast part of the pen, preaching by Sergeant B. N. Waddle, of 126th Ohio. Some of those active in carrying on the meetings are Rev. T. J. Sheppard, B. N. Waddle, M. H. Miller, 22nd Mich. Cavalry, and Robert H. Kellogg, of 16th Connecticut Regt., Thomas A. Cord, U. S. Infantry, also Boston Corbett. Some who show extraordinary talent as singers, are J. O. Turner, David Atherton, 65th N. Y., John W. Kerr, L. H. Cummings, Massachusetts; G. W. Pomeroy and others. There is often a chorus of nearly a hundred voices, some evenings, of fine singers.

Called on W. H. Harriman in the afternoon. He is so affected with scurvy that he cannot stand. The doctor tells him that they have no medicine that will cure; he is expecting to go to the hospital tomorrow; bade us good-bye, grasping our hands, in tears. He said: "Ever hoping for the best I shall not forget you and Thompson. We shall not meet again; I hope I shall have better treatment, at least better fare. If I am exchanged I will write your people, you do the same." (I heard nothing definite from Harriman until July, 1865, when his sister, Anna E. Harriman, wrote me from Zanesville, Ohio, that he died in October, 1864).

Monday, July 27th.—Prostrated with severe pains, chills and fever which lasted most of the night. Getting a small piece of beef and rice in lieu of meal we have a fine dish. Griffith has sold a three quart tin pail, given us in Virginia by Wesley Norwood, for $5 U. S. currency.

Tuesday, July 28th—News from Atlanta conflicting; papers, so far as we know, admit the repulse of Hood, then claim a victory. Later statements rather choke victorious editors. Hood feels compelled to fight and not leave the town. Sherman intends to give him the whipping Johnston has all summer been running away from, if he makes the stand.

My complaints are unabated; are attended with weakening pains which at times prostrate me. Rations irregular; often missing a day or two.

Wednesday, July 29th.—Had Job greater patience? Here are men of true mettle or we might see them knocking at the gate to swear fidelity to foes. To lie down is to submit to be eaten by lice and rot. When strength fails, such is the lot of all. "All that a man hath will he give for his life." But what have we to give? A great deal of money will get a little flour from Rebels, such is their love of money. But their lack of love for humanity feeds us husks and loathsome things. We are in prison and they visit us with torments and reproaches; we are athirst and they give us to drink of water tainted with filth and excrement; sick and afflicted and they torture us; weak and weary and they give us to rest on the sand filthy and full of breeding vermin; shelterless and they give us no roof; lacking raiment and they take much that we have.

A man shot dead, the ball passing directly through his head back of the ears, while kneeling near the dead line innocently looking at something. He had just come in and was unwarned.

I bought an egg for 20 cents, a small biscuit for 25 cents for supper with proceeds from the tin kettle sold.

Thursday, July 30th.—Breakfasted on half of a small biscuit and an onion. Prisoners arrive; a crowd gathered when a cannon was fired over the camp.

Friday, July 31st.—Several shots fired during the night, one from a cannon, the shot screaming overhead. Yesterday and to-day's arrival of prisoners is about 1,200. White flags are put in the center of the prison to designate ground on which crowds must not assemble. If they do they will be fired upon. Accordingly men are constantly at the guns.

Saturday, August 1st.—Fresh calls for shoemakers. A few weak ones give their names but are not accepted. Negroes have begun additional fortifications working all night and Sundays, falling trees and making the night air ring. Last night my mind was filled with thoughts of the misery of this place; I could not sleep. One poor boy near cried all night and wished to die and suffer no longer; he is an awful object; his clothing is gone but a rag of a shirt; his body is a mere frame, his hair has fallen from his head; his scurvy ankles and feet are as large as his waist. I never saw a sight more appalling. Then the awful thought that he is a man, somebody's darling boy, dead and yet breathing. And he is but a sample of many. To think of it blunts one's faith in men as brothers.

This forenoon a priest came in saying he had great news; we are to be exchanged. He read his news; it stated nothing definite, a mere if-so-to-be-perhaps, and yet he tried to make us believe it did. Then he preached about the blessed apostles and dealt out hell-fire in big rations unless we accepted certain theories. It was not consoling. It is true Fremont and Lincoln are both nominated. I visted an Ohio 100-day man taken in Maryland since the nomination. He thinks the Fremont ticket will be withdrawn.

Sunday, August 2nd.—The policy of enlisting negroes renders it harder for prisoners. So does the emancipation proclamation. The government having enlisted negroes, it is bound by laws of war and all honorable considerations to protect them as soldiers. To do otherwise would be dishonorable, cowardly, pernicious. Their enlistment more excited the unreasonable hatred of Southerners toward the North. The only way they can punish the North for what they deem insulting, is through their military prisons and they open their vials of wrath on "Lincoln hirelings," as they call us, who are wholly in their power. But the ever present fear of retaliation, man for man, men would be slain by hundreds, lined up and shot after being brought beyond the seat of war. As it is they come as near as they dare without displaying the black flag. Exchange was blocked last fall because Rebel authority disregards the negro as a man. That has long been a civil code of Slavedom. They adhere to it with a vengeance when he appears in arms against slavery. He is saved from slaughter if captured, on the theory that he is property, a theory in practice here for 100 years, or more. If any are escaped slaves they are to be returned to masters or used for war purposes indefinitely. If free they are appropriated as laborers, never exchanged, and if their war succeeds he can be sold. Hence the case of a white man is worse than that of a colored. He is deemed deserving of death because his government puts whites and blacks on an equality. The slave codes of the South, written and unwritten are in force, emphasized by the war power. This cruel and absurd animus of "Southern civilization," this unrighteous despotism, is of long standing. It is unquestioned by Southerners; woe be to him who disregarded it during the long arbitrary reign of Slave Kings. The mass accept it as right which is equivalent to thinking it right, and as men think so they are. Hence the critical situation of the white war prisoners at this time. We are wholly at the mercy of this cruel spirit which has transformed the South into a foe of everybody antagonistic to their customs and laws

Shall Lincoln recall his emancipation proclamation for the reason which as surely exists as we are at war? It makes it the deadliest war of any century. Nor should the policy of allowing negroes to fight for liberty be recalled. Shall free men cower and longer concede the injustices of this hell-born slave power? Indeed not. That is the issue—deadly issue—to be fought to death. How well do I remember the word passed along the lines at Mine Run and other places last fall and winter: "No exchange of prisoners, men, remember." The same word sounded along the lines in the fiery ordeals in the Wilderness. The die was cast. We fought with it before our eyes. Who does not now realize its import? Davis seeks to supercede the laws of war with his old slave code. Soon after Lincoln's emancipation Davis notified his Congress that he proposed to turn commissioned officers thereafter over to State authorities in States where captured to be punished under State laws providing for criminals engaged in inciting civil insurrection. That is his disposition, overlooking the fact that codes made to hang "abolition fanatics" can not be safely applied to war prisons in a state of war, where the States he represents are belligerents fighting for independence and asking for foreign recognition. Davis' blood-thirsty fanaticism for slavery, supercedes the intelligence he has been supposed to have and displays his savage inhumanity, thus seeking excuse to hang all U. S. officers.

[Note.—January 12, 1863, Davis, in a message to the Confederate Congress, said: "I shall, unless you, in your wisdom, deem some other course more expedient, deliver to the several State authorities all commissioned officers of the United States that may hereafter be captured by our forces in any of the States embraced in the proclamation, that they may be dealt with in accordance with the laws of those States providing for the punishment of criminals engaged in inciting servile insurrection."— Confederate War Records now at Washington.

The same records show that in May, 1863, the Confederate Congress in its "wisdom," passed a law embodying the above suggestion, but confining its operation to commissioned officers of negro regiments. Negro soldiers, when captured, by its provisions were to be delivered to authorities of States where captured, to be disposed of according to the laws of those States. This law was never repealed, so that, as a legal proposition, any officer of a negro regiment who became a prisoner was liable to be hanged, as John Brown was at Harper's Ferry. The records also show that the prisoner problem was much discussed early in the war. A Yankee caught in slave States to "free niggers" prior to the war could be safely hanged under slave codes. Shallow minds, like Davis, assumed that it could still be done, others saw that having gone to war in the spirit that enacted the codes, they had barred themselves from exercising that sacred function. Some said make Uncle Sam feed them at his own expense though they be kept in the South. Others said starve them; others give them poor bread and water; others, break their legs and turn them loose. Some said make them build railroads or work in other ways to boost the Slave Confederacy.]

### BUERILLA SHOWS PLUCK—GEORGIA PATRIOTISM.

Tuesday, August 4th.—Several men of our regiment are failing fast. H. D. Merritt is an object of pity and getting worse. We have cut his hair close to keep the myriads of lice out. He has lost all disposition to try to save himself. About 400 of Gen. Stoneman's command captured in the vicinity of Macon, were turned in here today. They report Maj. Gen. Stoneman captured. His expedition to that point with the intention of coming here has proved disastrous. Rations suspended. Sick ordered to the gate at night; and ordered to be brought again in the morning. None to go who can walk.

Wednesday, August 5th.—Sick come to the south gate in horrible crowds. Every inch of ground covered. What sights, what groans! Nine hundred admitted outside, the remainder carried groaning back about noon to be returned in the morning. Oh, for the Messiah, the hem of whose garment they might touch and be healed!

Thursday, August 6th.—At daylight a man shot and instantly killed. He had no particular stopping place, had become partially crazed; in the night had crept beyond the dead line and fell asleep. As soon as seen, the guard shot him while yet asleep. He had just been seen by two of our men who were calling him to come out. He lay until "dead call" and was carried out. Those who have helpless friends are eager to get them out. So at an early hour this morning they are crowded forward. Regulators are clearing every passage to make room for the sick. The main street on which I stop from the gate to the east, is filled with prostrate men. There is a greater number than yesterday. The doctors are making special efforts and one said yesterday, "The sick must all come out. The condition of the prison will breed pestilence that will spread through the country." It is through their importunity that this movement is made. They appear frightened. I heard another say, "Conditions are shameful." Long have doctors complained that their government furnishes neither medicine nor decent quarters; that men can not be successfully treated on such fare and in these quarters. One told Steward Brown that men could not live long on the rations given us; that well men will soon be sick. They have some new tents up; some are being carried thither in army wagons. The Rebel sergeant who counted us today said:

"Captain don't care how many Yankees die; he says he has killed more men than Joe Johnston," then added: "What did you'ns come down heah for if you'ns didn't want tough fare? But we can't help it."

After two hours laying in a crowd, "no sick call," is announced. The sick are being returned to all parts of the prison. I am living on rice alone, draw some, trade meal for some.

Report is rife that our government has offered the Richmond dignitaries to accept a parole of all prisoners, especially sick, and take care of prisoners of both parties. Undoubtedly this is the disposition of our government. This evening I met an intelligent talker who knows what he sees more than most men. Having frequently met him, I inquired his name. "Buerila," he replied; "I am from Illinois, have been a prisoner ten months, came here from Florida; I will stay ten more, I will be eaten up by lice and maggots before I will ask our government to get on its marrow bones to these Rebels. I am glad to see Lincoln stand square on his feet. I was a Douglas man, not that he was a better man, but had had more experience. I knew both personally and now believe Lincoln the best man for the place. If I can get into God's country in time he will get my vote." I referred to the report; he said:

"I asked the old Dutch if that thing was true myself. The old bummer looked mad, but answered more than I expected: 'Py Cot ve vills to no such ting! Py Cot, ve vill starf every son of a pitch! Now, I tells you, you vills all tie pefore ve vills parole ye—an pefore exchange. Py Cot, your Covment is too tevilment. Ve cot you foul!' Turning his horse around to go away, he said: 'Py Cot, you as vell pe schoot as stay here, and ve no trust damn Yankees.'"

Friday, August 7th.—The sick carried early to the gates but not received; ordered to be brought at 2 p. m. Doctors have got it into their heads that some system is necessary, and so much crowding at the gate was unnecessary and detrimental; so they ordered all back but the sick of eleven detachments and that none come tomorrow but those designated. Many are taken out. It gives hope that they are going to try to help us. Men persist in flattering themselves that we are soon to be relieved. I guard against disappointment and defer hope while action is deferred. The wolf at the door will not go away bloodthirsty until driven. They brought us to Georgia according to a decision of powers that be, that no shelter should be furnished Yankee prisoners. They will not release us for our sake, have disregarded our rights and purposely wronged us. Their cause is desperate; they fight for unprovoked revenge. They fiercely kill with bullets and designedly and half disguisedly plot our lingering death, seeking to profit their cause by our suffering. They began the war in hasty spite; it will end in hellish revenge. If they believe in their cause, need we hope for mercy? Has the government raised its hand to strike out one right the North claims for itself? Have we not compromised our sense of justice to appease unreasoning wrath, and have they not placed the dagger to our hearts? Now shall we be delivered by the murderers from the hands of their agents? Not till the last pillar has been broken and the hell-born spirit that incited this war shall rule no more, will their nefarious plotting cease. Yet we have hope which all of this surmounts,—they must fail.

### A PRISONER'S SONG.

Strident, yet more strident,
Sound the notes of war.
In our hearts confident
Behold the end afar.
Patient, yet more patient,
We'll bear the pains of fate.
Awake, oh, spirits latent,
And ward the blows of hate!
Higher, and yet higher,
Raise the hope of love;
Let faith new strength inspire
And make us stalwart prove.
Calmer, and yet calmer,
Wait we for the light,
Through savage din and clamor,
The passing of this night.
Freedom, on forever,
O, swiftly onward stride,
Enslaving bonds to sever,
And in this land abide!
Steady, and more steady,
Let our armies go;
They are strong and ready,
They move—it seems so slow!

Starving, we are starving!
We are sinking in distress;
Disease is gnawing—carving;
Our foes do sore oppress.
Help us to see the sunlight
Of victory and feel
Treason's bane has ceased to blight,
E'er death our eyes shall seal.

There is no danger from robbers and Thompson and I walk in the cool of the evening and talk about these things. A sensible companion in tribulation, is worth a thousand fools in peace if one appreciates him. The happiest man I ever saw was a man happy under miserable circumstances; the most miserable man is one wretched when surrounded with the benefits of life, with a vacant heart, a volcanic head, an iceberg and a fiery furnace freezing and burning his nature at the same time. To be contented, to be happy here, in one sense, is a mysterious art, yet the plainest fact.

"There is a Divinity that shapes our ends,
Rough hew them as we will."

We know now how to appreciate a man who is a living statue, not a human straw, a weed, jostled by every breeze, whipped about by adverse winds. We feel like him, believe in him; we are encased in steel. He is one, at least, who appreciates us. He has not only got the poetry of our best poets, but he has the heart, and the head; not only the rhyme but the sentiment.

Recently an interesting episode occurred, but it was not devoid of cruelties incident to this place. It reveals qualities of noble patriotism and keen foresight with a tinge of stern romance. A Georgian is a prisoner here. Early in 1861 when the war-spirit had become rampant and Georgia was swayed by men like Toombs a man whose name is said to be Hirst, probably assumed, lived not many miles from this prison, who resolved for the Union. He went North, leaving his wife at home, and joined a Western regiment. In a battle between Sherman and Johnston's armies he was captured. He was recognized by a Georgia Reserve, while carrying a sick man out, who in peaceful days lived near him. The recognition was mutual and friendly. From him he got some news of his wife, the first in three years. It was arranged to get a note to her, telling of his imprisonment. In a few days the guard was on duty and tossed the wife's letter over the dead-line in a ball of clay. Two days later the woman came before Wirz and asked an interview. It was granted, the lady to stand outside the gate thirty paces, the man at the gate, neither to speak. At sight of each other they spoke each other's names endearingly. The interview was abruptly ended, the woman ordered away, the man driven into prison. The next day she came again bringing clothing and provisions which she begged Wirz to send him. Wirz promptly ordered her away, warning her never to come again, and sent soldiers to escort her off the ground. The husband was then brought before him and an effort made to enlist him in the Rebel service. This was resented, when he was bucked and gagged and locked in the dungeon, being brought out and maliciously punished at intervals for several days. Failing to impress him into the service, by advice of doctors he was turned into the stockade. [Note.—After leaving Andersonville I learn he escaped from a train conveying prisoners from there, after Atlanta fell. He probably visited his family and later joined Sherman's forces.]

## STACK ARMS.

See, an officer in quest of men,
To do some work the Rebels need;
Invites us from this prison pen
To work for them while brothers bleed!
Foreswear our country, Southron? No!
For its cause is true and high!
Join the hosts of Freedom's foe?
Far better starve; in prison die!
We fight for section, Southron? No;
We fight that liberty may spread
O'er all the land that freemen know,
Where, too long, the slave had tread.
We fight for justice in the land
Where freeman's voice has been suppressed;
It shall be heard, from strand to strand,
And every wrong shall be redressed.
Patriotic to fight for wrong
Because 'tis in your section built?
To fight this evil to prolong
Does but enhance the master's guilt.
Patriotism knows no line
That shall Freedom's law restrain;
The die is cast, 'tis God's design
That slavery shall no more remain.
Ah, heed the call of destiny!
The black and white shall both be free;
And stack your arms, for liberty
O'er North and South alike shall be.
Stack arms, brave Southrons, and repent
You ever raised them 'gainst the right.
You know the force of brave dissent;
'Tis murder now to longer fight!
The "Stars and Bars" pull down, pull down;

They lead you wrong, in Slavery's ways,
More hateful than King George's crown
Our fathers spurned in other days.

## RAIN KNOCKS THE STOCKADE—A NATURE STUDY.

Saturday, August 8th.—No sick call; the poor fellows are disappointed. Well dressed officers ride out the street and back. Passing near us they inquire of a fellow who is whittling a bone:

"What State you from, young man?"

"Massachusetts."

"Do you rather live here than in Massachusetts?"

"No, sir."

"Well, you'll be apt to live out your days here, for there'll be no exchange till the war closes and that won't be in ten years if Lincoln is your next President."

"There'll not be a corporal's guard left of this crowd before that time, Colonel," remarked the other.

Before they reached the gate they halted to buy a watch, and a few of us followed up and I asked:

"Colonel, will you come back into the Union if Lincoln is not elected?"

"Ho, ho! You Yankees are not fighting for the Union; that's your mistake. It's the nigger you want."

"If McClellan is elected will the South come into the Union?" I repeated.

"Ah, the Union! The Union's gone up!"

By this time the Major had got the watch by paying $100 in "Confed" and they spurred up. We are often taunted by the slur that we are no better than niggers. They say:

"You fight with niggers; you think it's all right to fight us with niggers."

We retort by saying that it is no worse for a nigger to fight with us than to work for them, and that they would put a gun in his hands if they dared. It is not so bad for them to be hunted by niggers as it is for us to be hunted helpless and half starved, by blood hounds.

A little after noon a man shot and killed. I hastened and learned that he was dipping water from the brook. The sentinel had been observed to be closely watching. The ball passed through the forehead, tearing out his brains. The guard was immediately relieved by the officer of the day as they all are when they make a sure fire. It is a story never denied that for every Yankee killed a furlough is granted. In a few minutes a stretcher smeared with blood and brains bore another Yankee to the dead house.

Tuesday, August 9th.—Terrible rain; it swelled the stream to a river. The stockade fell in several places. On the east side through the swamp about eight rods fell. One place on the west a sentry box fell carrying the sentry in it. Soon as it occurred the sentinels fired and two cannon shots over the camp succeeded, to warn us to be quiet or shot would be rained on us. Meantime we were amused to see the Rebls get out of their quarters and double quick to the weak points. The camp was in a hurrah to see the Rebs getting drenched as well as ourselves. Some prisoners plunged into the flood to bring out floating timber or pieces of boards that came down as if they were a God-send, for we would not be allowed to pick them up if we were outside. At these places the Rebels stood in line of battle for more than an hour and when the rain ceased, they had only time to temporarily repair the damage before night; so fires were built and a strong guard kept out all night.

Wednesday, August 10th.—Soldiers and negroes are rebuilding the fallen wall. Prisoners stand at a distance often shouting: "That is good for you, Rebs"; "That's the way your Confederacy will fall; Grant and Sherman are making bigger holes than these." "Ho, Reb, what are you doing with dat nigger dar; 'pears to us you're reduced to the level of the nigger." "It's hard enough to starve on cob-meal and be hunted by dogs, but when you come to build bull-pens for us with niggers, working by your sides, you are hyenas, you are black abolitionists, you are barbarians." Plenty of other taunts are indulged till men get sick of it.

Two new walls are being built outside of the main one. The most hopeful believers in immediate exchange, are puzzled as to what it means. Tunnelling cannot be successfully done more than sixty or eighty feet horizontally, the air becoming insufferable. The vacuity is necessarily small, just admitting a man as he draws himself along. It cannot be larger for fear of exposure, besides the dirt is dug with hands, sticks, etc., and passed to the opening to be carried to the swamp, or whereever it can be concealed. It cannot be ventilated for that might be a key to discovery. Likely these new walls are to obstruct the digging of tunnels.

For several days barracks have been in course of erection in the north part, the work being done by our men on parole who bring the lumber in on their shoulders. They are allowed an extra ration and occasionally opportunities to trade for their benefit. What do these barracks mean? Are we to stay here all winter? men asked. At the rate they go up, I think we will, if we wait for them. Some say they are for hospitals.

Steward Brown, who is an Englishman and not a soldier, on

parole, expresses the belief that it was fortunate for prisoners that Stoneman's expedition failed, for it was the intention of Gen. Winder to use the Florida battery on the prison had any considerable Union force approached Andersonville within seven miles, and had so ordered in the regular way in writing, on July 27th.

[Note—Here is the order. It was found on file among the records at the Confederate War Department at Richmond, and is with other records in possession of the government, so it is plain Steward Brown knew his statement was true. This is the diabolical order:

Headquarters Military Prison,<br>Andersonville, Ga., July 27, 1864.

Order No 13.

The officers on duty and in charge of the Battery of Florida Artillery at the time will, upon receiving notice that the enemy has approached within seven miles of this post, open upon the stockade with grapeshot, without reference to the situation beyond these lines of defense.     JOHN H. WINDER,

Brigadier General Commanding.]

Five men sunstruck and reported dead; most of us are stupefied by heat. For more than a month it has been almost unbearable. The dazzling rays reflected by sand flash through us like flames of fire. The stench of the filthy earth rises hot and vapory to our nostrils. Oh, that I might feel the shade of the beautiful forest yonder, whose green trees look pityingly over upon us! How relieved we would be by an hour of repose on the fresh earth beneath them!

Go to the gate to help William Kline. A number of the sick are carried through the gate and laid in the yard by the stockade. A Rebel sergeant soon ordered us back, no doctors appearing. The sick had been notified at roll call to go for treatment, and their feeble spirits were animated with hope. Some wept bitterly and sank into despair at the disappointment. The Confederate sergeant, in answer to questions, remarked, "They might as well go to hell as to the hospital. It is a right hard place; the doctors can do nothing."

Naturally we believe the word hospital means something. In this horrid distress men long for its benign influence; many are consoled with the thought of being admitted, even when we know it is a cruel, wicked mockery.

Near the sinks a sentry fired tonight, the ball grazing a man's thigh, near where I walked, and whizzed by into the swamp. No rations today; nothing to eat. Men have loitered near the gate since noon hoping for something but in vain. We lay down tonight hungry, sick and sad. Not a crumb of anything all night, all day and all night again, with no certainty of anything tomorrow.

## ODE TO WIRZ.

Cheating them who truly trust
Is a coward's villainy;
But when we yield to whom we must,
We suffer viler tyranny;
If venom doth full license wield
To feed the vengeance and the hates
No virtue has for years concealed,
And which a misled South elates.
A brutal knave were he who slay
A child that slumbered on his knee;
But we are thrown within his sway
Who lacks sense and magnanimity,
And glories in a brutal way
Toward men who fight 'gainst slavery.

Looking at the swamp with its deposit of ordure, intensely alive with billions of flies and maggots, today, it came to me that not only the early but the late bird can catch worms and catch them continually, if fool enough to visit the place. But no bird have I yet seen in this foul realm. Mingled with a sense of disgust, I am prone to wonder. Out of this mass I see a new creation, an emerging of animate life of low order. The flies that feed on the excreta, deposit germs from which, in connection with the deposit, when operated on by solar energy, the sun being the battery, these lives germinate in form of maggots totally unlike the fly, unlike any worm I ever noticed. These millions of loathsome things, squirming in roasting sun, in a few days develop into winged insects larger and darker than maggots, an inch long. From among a cloud of flies and acres of worms I see them rise and fly from the filthy bed of their inception, seemingly seeking existence elsewhere. Interest was first incited in these low fledglings, when they appeared on ground bordering the swamp, where they fell in the mush when men were at repast. Indeed there is life, or principles of life in matter dead. Here is a low order of exhibition of Nature's power to evolve and produce phases of animation degrees above their physical source.

## A FEW DAY'S DOINGS—TENNESSEEANS.

Thursday, August 11—Recent improvements in camp are timbers laid across the swamp on the west side north of the stream for 20 rods, this will help escape the filth in passing from north to south. A flume and bridge has been made which improves washing facilities; also a road from the north to the stream in the east part. We have more variety of food but scanty allowance, to-wit: corn bread, rice, a curious kind of bean, old and wormy. For several days a small piece of poor beef has come with cooked rations, hardly a mouthful, and in lieu a little sorghum molasses. We have built bake ovens of sand and clay. When several of us have raw meal, we club together to bake it, it being sweeter baked than smoked on a small fire. It economizes fuel, encourages the hope it will not have to be eaten raw. There are five very sick men within a few feet, groaning day and night. It is remarkable with what tenacity life clings to emaciated, corrupted frames.

Williams of the 111th N. Y., of Lyons, N. Y., a boy of education, talent and refinement, a nephew of Hon. Alex. Williams, visited us. He is declining rapidly and engages our sympathy It is a joy to cheer such a sweet spirit. He showed us the likeness of a beautiful girl, remarking that he never expected to see her again, and wept bitterly. We all parted with him regretfully. (He died in September).

I was again struck today by one of the daily duties of men. Passing from north to south through camp I see them stripped, examining clothing for lice. Immediately after roll call they "have a louse," or a "skirmish" or a "peeling off" as they express it from head to heels to give the "gray backs" a cleaning out. These pestering varmints infest clothing, sticking along the seams. Where the torments come from, how they grow in a day, or an hour, is a mystery. Drawing our minds down to hunting lice is humiliating; but the man who don't isn't respectable; we feel disgraced in his company Once a day is tolerable, twice better, three times makes a man of the first order. Neglect this, and he is soon over run, pitied, loathed, hated, sneered and snarled at. Lice polute and sap his blood, he loathes himself and dies. They crawl in droves over the sick, herd in his ears, gnaw him, shade in his hair deep as the hair is long. Talk about "gophers" in the army, no name for this! They sap the life of the strongest. Men who fight their lice effectually every day are brave, meritorious. But wouldn't we be pretty guests for parlor bedrooms! Trousers under the pillow! What would the tidy chambermaid say at Hotel Eagle? , Charming guests for ladies, lousy, brown, yellowed bloated, dirt-eating, wallowing Yankees! And we do laugh though it is not a laughing matter. But I am the only bachelor in our notable family of eight; should we be wafted to Northland from Dixie tonight, no one would be obliged to submit to my embraces. Poor, indeed!

Saturday, August 20th.—For nine days I have been prevented from making usual notes. Little passed I care to recall; I force myself to write today. I know no one who takes a general note of things; it is with hesitancy as well as difficulty, that I do. I cannot say that mine is more than meager penciling. They are samples of the best and some of the worst things that I note.

Two of the sick mentioned the 11th, died the 13th; the others on the 15th. One had turned gray since I first saw him. He had money but could not save himself. His was the common complaint. He died within four feet of me suddenly falling; was from Pennsylvania. Another old prisoner died today of squalor within a few feet of us. The mortality, notwithstanding the removal of so many of the worst cases, has increased. The average is over 100 per day this month. On the 15th, 140; the 17th, 128 died.. I am told by a man who is on duty at the hospital. The sick again admitted to the gate for prescription; but three taken to the hospital out of several hundred applicants. It is the most disagreeable task one ever had to do, to cary a sick man before the doctor and then it amounts to nothing.

H. D. Merritt of our company was taken out in an awful condition on the 14th. He is from Sodus, Wayne county, N. Y. Fourteen of Company F have died; eleven more are in bad condition. (This does not include myself.) Madison hurt his foot a few days ago; his blood is so weak that it does not heal. Gangrene set in; it has eaten to the bone. The limbs of others are so affected as to be unable to walk. Most of them were strong heavy men, but we have to carry them to sick call. Gangrene is one of the frightful phases of these diseases. W. M. Townsend of the 111th N. Y. received a slight scratch on his thigh which has spread to a large and painful sore. It is by great precaution it is kept from being maggoty. The 12th I accidentally found Hanson, a young German of our company whom I had not seen for a long time, he belonged to another detachment. He was helpless but could talk; had fallen in the swamp, was completely daubed. His gums are rotted with scurvy; the backs of his hands and feet raw from sunburn; maggots actually crawling in his flesh. I got Sergeant Burton and went to the gate begging aid. At last got the answer, "You Yanks do something for your ownselves." We returned to Hanson, lifted and gave him water, cleansed his wounds, found his detachment sergeant, borrowed a ragged blanket to cover him; could do no more. He died August 16th.

Tunnel was discovered not long since this way: It had been completed to the point where they wished to come out. The head man was pulling down the dirt when suddenly it broke away covering him, and down came a gray jacket with a Rebel in it, gun and all. The relief guards were just being mounted and one of them stepped upon the exact spot where they were to escape.

A Rebel paper I saw today spoke of Major Currill, Commissioner of Exchange, visiting our fleet in Mobile Bay, having reference to sending packages. Fighting at Richmond and other places, and close work at Atlanta. They abound in speculations on the Presidential campaign, and in extracts from the New York World, Herald, News and Albany Argus and from their view argue the South's success. The World has an article on "The Failure of Grant," denouncing his whole course; and claims that "Grant is played out," though he has punched Lee back into his Richmond ditches and is still operating. Southern Rebels do not claim Grant is a failure. They keep up a bold front which they consider a political as well as a military necessity; but their own admissions, in general tones, are evidences of their strait. To me it seems they have ceased to hope for that degree of success from their armies that can save the little prestige they have abroad, much less secure their recognition, so turning to political bickerings, presenting their armies in the feigned attitude of triumph and strength but base their hope on the election. They believe that a party that could expiate their crimes in the past, would do even more in the future, if raised to power to look down on a forest of Rebel bayonets instead of threatening, sophistical politicians to whom they had succumbed. But they are a mere shell full of dead and rotting strength that has passed its zenith. The Southern heart is burning to ashes; they would negotiate for a respite to replenish the flame, not for Union. Oh, let the North be true in this crisis! Rebels would despair of success before January.

They do not give wood enough to ten men for one. Men go to extremes to obtain it, stealing dead men from their friends to carry out with the hope of getting it. Four men are permitted to go and can bring in quite a jag. Then some will trade half of their scanty rations for a stick to cook the other half. A few will trade a day's rations for a ten cent bit of tobacco. A few so far lose their reason as to throw clothing away, becoming disgusted with lice; add themselves to disgusting sights by going naked. All capable of being degraded so as to lose self respect, become so. God only knows the wickedness and woe of such a state!

I wandered to a locality new to me, a few days ago. I came to a quartet of Tennesseeans who told their war experiences; of persecutions their people suffered for being Unionists; how they fled from home to escape Rebels who were savage against all who refused to support secession. Their madness knew neither law nor friendship; their frenzy neither justice nor mercy. They, with a hundred others, armed themselves and one day cut their way through an armed mob claimed to have been sent by Governor Isham Harris, who designed to massacre or capture them. They marched many miles to join Buell's army;, and had several fights with gorillas. They were captured in Rosecrans' operations near Chattanooga, in 1863; wintered at Danville, Va.; came here in March, seven stopping together. Three have died. Prison hardships affect them severely. The character of these sturdy mountain people, their honest, intelligent patriotism in connection with this crisis, also their general history, inspire these lines:

## THE MEN OF TENNESSEE.

God save from woes of Anderson
    The men who bravely stayed
By Lincoln's flag, for country one,
    Where slavery's power had swayed;
Eschewed the leaders of the South,
    Of low and high degree,
And deemed the flag ensign of truth,
    Brave men of Tennessee.

They lived upon their native soil;
    They loved it well and true;
They lived by faithful, honest toil;
    They loved the peace they knew.
But they were those who weighed events
    As they should pondered be;
They saw conflicting sentiments
    Distracting Tennessee.

And when the Union of the States
    Was threatened by its foes,
With the Union they allied their fates
    Secession to oppose.
When driven from their homes away,
    By the powers of slavery,
They joined the Union's armed array,
    Grand men of Tennessee.

They spurned the rule that would disrupt
    The Nation's life they loved;
They spurned the rule, wrong and corrupt,
    As patriots true behooved,
And leaving homes they loved behind,
    Engulfed in war's red sea,
They showed great strength of heart and mind,
    These men of Tenneessee,

They nobly tendered strength and life,
  If human blood must shed,
Against secession's valorous strife
  By Southrons madly led,
And side by side with Northern men
  They fought most valiantly—
Here brook the ills of prison pen
  Brave men of Tennessee.

Behold them suffer here and die
  Within dark Sumter's walls!
The earth their bed, the roof the sky,
  Where woes their hearts appal!
And yet all offers they resent
  That promise them to free;
By loyalty invite torment—
  True men of Tennessee.

O, hail the men who know the right
  And for it stand and fall;
Who will not swerve at Treason's might
  Though death may claim them all;
And here in prison pine and rot,
  Though today they could be free!
No truer men have ever fought,
  Than men of Tennessee.

The valor of some Spartan band
  From ancient time men laud;
But the acts of these, of Jackson's land,
  Who will their deeds applaud?
I see them dying day by day
  'Mid scenes of misery;
No voice to praise, where death has sway,
  These men of Tennessee.

## HOSPITALS, THEIR HISTORY.

Noting the indisposition or inability of doctors to clear the stockade of sick—victims conspicuous for their wretchedness—I have applied my mind to learn facts regarding so-called hospitals. It is no mystery that men sicken in the stockade. Coarse, unpalatable food, a mixture of meal containing cob and bran—doctors call it meal and husk—often musty and bitter, stirred in filthy water in large batches, often souring before baking or while baking with green wood, no salt, no yeast, no soda, often partially raw, often over-roasted with a crust hard and tasteless. If changed to rice, that is colored with the dirty water and often uncooked. Exposed to all weather and until some wells were dug, all drank and washed in the same small stream, always roiled and more and more, night and day, being poisoned by drainage from without and within. Thirst becomes feverish, unbearable; to drink is to pollute our bodies with the offal intermixed, made more stenchful and rotten by heat and rain. Nothing could be more unsanitary, more conducive to disease. What are the hospital facilities to cope with rapidly developing conditions absolutely adverse to health in strongest men? I find these facts, attested by appearances and results. No Confederate doctor or officer pretends to dispute.

This is the history of so-called hospitals here to date and they must continually grow worse. When the prison was built most of its early prisoners were from prisons farther north, Danville and about Richmond, where they were under roofs. Coming here in February and March they readily chilled through. Some refuse of the timber from which the stockade was built was appropriated by prisoners for fuel and shelter, and before hot weather and an increase of prisoners, both air and water might have been an improvement on their former abode. But old prisoners broke down and the first hospital was erected inside of poles and brush. This was the best hospital the place has ever had. The poles or logs were left several inches apart, and as sickly men were put in them the place became as odious and no more commodious than a backwoods hog-pen. A portion had a lose floor, no beds, no bunks, no blankets, no straw. The storm and wind beat through the space between the logs and rendered patients that retained sensitiveness or desire to live, uncomfortable. A few prisoners had threadbare blankets, or remnants, with the U. S. brand, but no other was provided whether prisoners had a U. S. rag or not.

This was the original provision and remained the only hospital until the middle of May, or a few days later, when prisoners began to come from the spring campaigns and were so packed about this hospital pen that the air was infected and it was removed to its present locality to make room. We arrived here from the Wilderness fields in Virginia just two days after this change; but even then the place where it had been, was covered with men fresh from our armies little heeding that the very earth which they had been forced to accept as their abode, was soaked with the filth of the lately removed wards of death, for, then as now, there was no means of disposal of excreta of men who were slowly wasting and unable to seek the swamp or stream, except in illy provided open excavations within the "hospital" or death-pen. The hospitals now simply consist of old canvas appropriated from other use, ragged or patched, open at the sides, without floors, beds, bunks, stoves or straw. Men lay on the earth in ghastly rows. The ground where they lay is saturated with offal of wasting bodies. The sickening exhalation is constant. Patients have no clothing except that worn during their imprisonment and in active service, never but a single suit, in many cases not much of that, no blankets, except where prisoners happened to retain them on coming to prison. Patients are sickly visages of squalor, decaying bodies, while yet their minds retain dreary existences. There are fleshless skeletons with skin drawn over them; on some bones have broken or worn through the skin. Limbs of others whose flesh has not vanished, are swollen with dropsy and scurvy, discolored, yellow and brown. In many cases ulcers appear—sores from wounds that never heal, and gangrene is having an unchecked if not undisputed reign. Myriads of lice and flies swarm over helpless men; maggots infest gangrenous sores that may have originated from a scratch, a sunburn or from ulcerous eruption caused by corrupted blood.

These matters, seemingly, have reached an uncontrollable stage. There is scarcity of medicine, scarcity of physicians. Nurses are dumbfounded; if they have any sense of the situation they are in despair; can do little to comfort and it seems that those detailed have no adaptation for the work. Except now and then one, would they be retained and for just that reason, in a hospital well ordered for work. From first to last there is nothing provided, nothing arranged, nothing expected but death, and the quicker the better. If doctors had ordinary skill, and nurses had any idea of sanitation, some police regulations would be visible. If this were so and the Richmond government had meant to do anything but murder, better facilities would be provided. I have met a doctor or two apparently of skill, good sense, and humane intent; but they seemed to have despaired of doing justice to their profession or to patients, lacking means and having to contend against conditions which no skill and no medical supplies can meet until conditions change. They have no hope of that. There are some bunglers in charge with a slight knowledge of surgery ready to improve their quack skill by revolting practice. Amputation has been performed where no hope was possible or expected, and in cases where there was a lingering hope, yet the bodily condition of patients did not justify amputation. In no case as I can hear, has gangrene been cured by amputation. Slight wounds are not healable owing to weak blood. Some of these fellows are perfectly brutal, and enlisted in this capacity rather than be conscripted and carry a musket. These conditions are known at Richmond. The prison has been inspected by military and civil officials of high rank. Reports of surgeons, Drs.

Reeves, Pelot and Thomburg in preceding months expressly stated not only general conditions but that there were men that were living masses of putrifaction; hospitals without bunks, beds or straw; as above stated, speaking of corn bread raw and sour and the effects of such diet on sick and well that they could not practice successfully, that sickness could not be prevented nor patients cured until made comfortable; appealing for "beds if any in Dixie." All was unanswered. Confidentially these facts are told me by a doctor.

### WOMEN PRISONERS.—PROVIDENCE SPRING.

Sunday, August 21st.—Rainy. A man with gray hair has just died within six feet of us; another is dying within twenty; another within forty. The dead are almost continually being borne past, more than usual today. We walk, sleep, eat and drink among sick, dying, dead. We pass them on our way, meet them sinking with fell disease, turn to pity, but languishing with weakness bethink ourselves; shut sympathy in our breasts; nerve ourselves, pass on.

Of our detachment of 270 but 123 are able today to appear in ilne. Any man able to be about can consume the day's ration at once. Man never looked on scenes more horrible! Oh, God, assist us; on thee alone our hopes must rest for strength!

I saw by a Rebel sergeant's book that Harvey Deyo Merritt died the 16th inst. I learn he died laying in the sand outside the hospital having been carried out owing to the crowd. All knew him as Deyo in my company where he was a favorite. He often entertained the boys with songs. He had a melodious voice, was a good singer, a pleasant young man, a faithful soldier. I have composed the following lines in his honor:

### DEYO.

Dead he lay upon the sand,
Breathless lips and pulseless hand.
Dead he lay, appalling sight;
In those eyes there is no light;
Dead 'mid living, dying, dead,
And we have no tears to shed!
Death is but a common sight,
Dying round us day and night.
Scores are dying every day
And by comrades borne away,
Under gleaming Rebel guns
To cemet'ry for Northern sons.
Rolled in ditches by the score—

Ay, thousands—paroled forevermore!
No more his voice in song is heard
That sweetly once his comrades stirred;
Dead within this dreadful place,
The peace of God upon his face.
Nevermore the ration spare
Of prison pen with him we share.
He stood with us in fighting line;
Alas, together here we pine;
We sat with him in camp at night
Cheered by the Union firelight;
On weary marches night and day,
And with him in embattled fray;
On picket when the camp did sleep;
In wood, and field, and trenches deep;
When as skirmishers we creep,
And here where foes their vigils keep!
But now he sleeps in Dixie's soil,
No more, no more with us to toil;
Sleeps in the land he helped to free
From the bane of Slavery;—
No more to languish with us here;—
Dead, without coffin, shroud, or bier.
Deyo, good boy, farewell, farewell!
Who your wretched fate will tell?
Sadly you were heard to speak
"Mother, mother," faint and weak,
Until your starved and fetid breath
Was silent in this squalid death.
Thank God, your face she could not see;
Your soul from this damned pit is free!
No more your lips will songs repeat
We heard so fondly and so sweet.
O, lifeless body, let it rest,
Wasted in this place opprest!
He is gone who was its guest;
We who stay are still unblest.
Lying dead in Georgia's sand
He obeys the last command.
Deyo, rest, your service is done;
Turned in your knapsack and your gun.
Rise, Deyo, genial soul, arise;
Soul of Deyo never dies!
Soldier, in what realm now?
Whose command obeyest thou?
Freed from this place of pest and blight,

Where rests your spirit, calm, to-night?
In camps with comrades gone before
Where fearful war you know no more;
In peaceful gardens of delight
Rest, Deyo, in peace, tonight!

Sergeant Bourne of the 58th Massachusetts favored me with the reading of a book entitled "Isabelle," devoted to the subject of home influence. It contains suggestions lovers of home ought to heed and practice. Although from the American Tract Society, it speaks of the visitation of spirits to "Quiet and influence and lead us in the way of heavenly things." Says the writer, "How much a word or a sentence may do to influence our associates!" I have been thinking that if these things be true, may not unseen influences buoy us up, inspire us with hope and strength to survive these ills. I have often asked they might, and felt perceptibly an inner delight; a joyous confidence. Spencer wrote of angels—

"They come to succor us, who succor want,
They for us fight, they watch and duly ward,
And their bright squadrons round about us plant,
And all for love, and nothing for reward."

Milton expressed similar ideas, putting these words into the mouth of Adam in one of his happy talks with Eve, which likely expressed the views of the poet on this topic—

"Millions of spiritual creatures walk the Earth
Unseen, both when we wake, and when we sleep;
All these with ceaseless praise his works behold
Both day and night. How often from the steep
Of echoing hill or thicket, have we heard
Celestial voices to the midnight air,
Sole, or responsive each to other note,
Singing their Great Creator! Oft in bands
While they keep watch, or nightly rounding walk,
With heavenly touch of instrumental sounds
In full harmonic number join'd, their songs
Divide the night, and lift our thoughts to Heaven."

I have been thinking, too, that I ought to mend in everyday talk and demeanor; have made slight effort; but everything around is hard. The temper is all the time worked upon; there is nothing pleasant but hope, good thoughts and desires. God and Nature are no less great, friends no less dear, liberty no less sweet, principles I attempt to defend no less sacred. I will not cease to defend them against rash, thoughtless men. Two men die across the street as I write this.

Monday, August 22nd.—Most important reports are from Virginia. Grant's movements a mystery. Sheridan met Early in the Shenandoah with a heavy force, but whipped him to pieces. Flag of truce boat off Charleston. The boys talk this news over with satisfaction. Once in awhile there is one who says, "I don't care how they do if I can get home." We draw rations of rice and molasses only, tonight. It is a change and "change of pasture makes fat calves."

Capt. Wirz has not appeared for two weeks. It turns out he is sick; the boys hope he will die. Lieut. Davis commands the prison; we ascribe improvements to him. We could not account for how "Old Dutch" had become so enterprising. It is his custom to ride about like a pompous chief; to devise ways to punish offenders, as he calls men who attempt escape; watch them groaning in the stocks where he has kept them all day and all night with hands and feet outstretched to their utmost, and grinned as he saw them hanging by the thumbs. While suffering this punishment, two have died we know. If more have not, it is not to his credit. Neither has every little pretext to deprive us of rations from 24 to 60 hours, been so readily caught up. Nevertheless our principal ration has been bad, sour bread and hungry as we might be, some has been thrown away.

Tuesday, August 23rd.—An interesting gossip was afloat when I came here that there were two women in prison disguised as Union soldiers. It was accepted as a fact by many who gave plenty of reasons for believing it, and it was a topic for talk among them which I was curious to hear. In June two sprightly persons were shown me as the alleged women. Many times after I saw them, always together, always by themselves. There was nothing in their appearance to discredit the story except male attire; nothing to suggest to me, under the circumstances, that they were women, in the absence of the story that they were women. They looked like beardless boys, feminine of stature and of features, with an air of shyness. The story could not be traced to an origin, nor was it denied except by ridicule. Its believers said their appearance was prima facie evidence, and accounted for their presence in several ways. For three weeks they have not been seen. This morning believers in the rumor are on to the fact that three weeks ago they left their dugout at sunset and passed the south gate. Where they went, how and why, is a mystery, but the story is now more than ever believed. They were called by some, "camp angels."

A. hints whimsically, he shall take his duds and leave because we disagree with him on important questions discussed. Steve is a rough, disagreeable talker on many things, reviles our cause, slanders Lincoln and his advisers. "We don't want a Union; that dog is dead. If we whip the South we had better give them independence. " Nonsense; yet he was all right in the ranks. Prison deprivations disturb his equanimity.

A mere professional patriot, if weighed, is found wanting. Principles defended through superstition, selfish pride, blind party habit, or hatred, will ultimately be cursed by such defenders. That pride degenerates in its grossness; the man is "the wretch concentrated all in self," and obscures the self he really is. He who submits to be a mere tool in the relations of life, or exerts his power to the injury of others for rash and sordid reasons, is worse than inertia even when unused. The man without sentiment, strikes no spiritual goal.

As I passed the gate this morning I saw seven dead and met several on the way. Corpses are being carried to the burying ground in army wagons, loaded in like wood. The fellow who enjoys funerals ought to get satisfaction out of all he might see here.

During a terrific storm a spring burst out on the north of the swamp close to the dead line on the west side, below the north gate from a dry, sandy knoll, and now flows profusely; is pure, clear, soft and sweet as any water I ever drank We consider it remarkable, almost marvelous. It is difficult on the north side to reach water by wells. Men there, 20,000, perhaps more, have been obliged to get their water from the filthy run which catches the drainage from the Rebel camp, the cook house, and from excrement deposited on either side covering at least an acre, in places a foot thick, and filth from other sources. The south side, had, several weeks ago, reached water by digging 20 to 30 feet. In the 36th detachment, on the north side, they have sunk 80 feet and the water is red, hard and impure. A board spout is made conveying the water from this spring about 30 feet down the hill and out of danger of the dead line, where men flock by thousands daily to drink and fill their little buckets. Falling into files of four, a column is often formed which it takes two hours to pass the end of the spout. It runs a stream as large as my arm, white and clear, from the end of that spout.

Wednesday, August 24th.—Three months today since I entered this prison. How much has been seen and suffered none can tell. One-third of our company of 47 men have died; we wonder that more have not.

Gold is quoted in the Rebel papers at $2.86 greenbacks in New York. Not so many dead today. One fellow was just carried past who died, it is said, with symptoms of cholera. I saw two cases thought to be yellow fever. I was near one man when he was suddenly taken with black vomit. One of the doctors was asked by a sick man if more would not be admitted to the hospital soon. He answered: "Likely, they are dying off right smart out there." How consoling! There have been commissioned officers in the prison. Today eighteen were taken out to be sent to Charleston. I know of two who have not gone: Colby, of a New Hampshire regiment and one of a regiment in the 6th corp. Another day is closing. I feel that God's blessing is with us even here.

Not all the dreary intercourse of this daily life,
Nor all the dreary instances of this daily death,
Nor Starvation's threatening visage gaunt,
Nor guards that shoot on vile pretexts,
Nor pangs of pain and heavy languor
That press and sickening fill
My body, thin my blood, shade my brain
With clouds of squalid gloom, like miasmatic mists
That haunt befevered vales;
Or like this stench that thickens prison air,
Night and day up-steaming from polluted
Swamp that bisects the prison ground, a sea
Of foulness dead, yet maggoty with life to rottenness germane,
Within the frowning walls of this huge pen,
Nor all these certain deaths that seize
Strong men and they are gone,
Shall e'er prevail against, or disturb
The cheerful faith that beyond all here beheld—
Even in these very woes—are blessings
Which in time shall gloriously unfold
And sometime bless our people, bless the world,
Ay, bless the foes from whom offenses come!

There never was a curse inflicted
On men for sins of others, or their own,
But blazed the way for blessings new.
So bear, as we must, unto the end,
Trusting firmly, howe'er that end may be!
As in this mortal life seeds of death are set,
So in all death the germs of spiritual life
Uprise and bloom and bear ten thousandfold.

Men honor martyrs slain in high renown,
But martyrs here who by thousands fall,
No tongues of eloquence may praise;
But they who die in duty's strenuous path,
Howe'er devious its unwelcome course.
Missing the good things of the present life,
Can ne'er be barred by massive walls,
Or foes in arms, from good things in the life to be.

## INTERESTING RECORDS AND COMMENTS.

Thursday, August 25th.—Henry Broader of our company, died last night. He joined our regiment last winter fresh from

## CHRONICLES OF A WAR PRISONER. 119

Germany and died a victim to barbarity in Southern United States. A man was struck with a club and nearly killed, by one who helps unload rations. Assailant has the name of being a rough fellow, as many do who get work.

Friday, August 26th.—Tried to get Reuben Ellis to hospital again today, but failed. It was a hard task as four had to carry him to the north part of the stockade in our arms or on a stick. He is unable to care for himself; his dirty clothing is filled with vermin which crawled on us as we bore him along. The man who was struck yesterday is dead. The murderer is sentenced by the chief of the regulators, to wear a ball and chain here and to our lines.

An insane man went over the dead line last night; was ordered to come back by our men but refused. The guard shot three times, the third shot striking the top of the head, passing out at the collar bone. He was alive this morning, but a frightful sight. Mosquitoes are troublesome nights, more than previously. They pick us like vultures when we lay down, our faces, arms, breasts and bare feet are blotched and itchy.

Saturday, August 27th.—Tobacco scarce, prices high; men will as surely have it as they can get it. This proves the strength of the habit of its use; but the use of it does not prove the theory propagated by users, that it prevents scurvy in the mouth. It is extensively used, but I notice that scurvy in the mouth is as common among chewers as non-chewers. Eight out of ten of my company who use tobacco, have scurvy. Most of those who have died used it; several of those alive are toothless because of diseased gums. I know of an inveterate chewer whose cheeks are badly swollen who still munches it, if he can get it, and expectorates blood and matter and tobacco juice. In these cases it may only irritate parts affected and add poison to disease. Smoking is more consistent; the fumes of burning tobacco are more preferable than diseased atmosphere. I think it tends to purify it from pestilence. Smokers resort to gathering quids that have been chewed, dry them in the sun, pulverize, then burn it in their pipes.

I am forced again to depend entirely upon the prison ration, having run out of money, and go hungry constantly. Reuben Ellis died last evening. Conscious to the last he called the boys about and bade them good-bye tenderly, perefctly reconciled. Ellis was an honest fellow, a faithful soldier. Pinchen has possession of his papers and the likeness of his wife. He was drafted from Steuben county, N. Y. William Grennels died yesterday afternoon on his way to the stream. Frederick Shultz died August 22nd. All are of my company, the latter two eGrman.

Sunday, August 28th.—At 11 o'clock a. m. I counted 30 dead

men at the gate to be carried out, 36 had already gone out, making 66 since sundown last night. The bodies were exposed to the hot sun; some were putrified.

The Macon Telegraph of the 25th has something in reference to exchange from a Richmond correspondent to the Savannah Republican. It says: "The exchange will probably be consummated in this way: Man for man, officer for officer, either side to keep excess; probably the onfederate government will have no objection to exchange freeborn Northern negroes, as French and English enlist them in their armies the same as white men and they are exchanged the same; but slaves, or negroes seduced from Southern homes will be returned to their masters, if any; if not, sold."

Monday, August 29th.—My hat is worn out; I buy a cap for 15 cents, probably a dead man's. Democratic convention at Chicago today. As Rebels desire McClellan for President it would be "sectional" not to put him up. "Little Mac" will be the honored man. Rebels cry "bully" for him; he is next to "Bobby Lee." Of course, Seymour and Fernando Wood will pledge their friends! All are anxious to see how this Pandora's box will open. Juggle, juggle, juggle! Rebels think it the most important event in their nation's history.

Going through camp last night, groping among heavily breathing hundreds, I came to one sitting by a prostrate comrade. The moon shone brightly over the trees, but a few minutes risen, lighting up the camp of thousands who are "waiting." I stopped and crouched over the small pine knot hanging fire near their feet. I saw the prostrate man was dying, as his friend held a piece of blazing pitch pine near his face, no longer conscious of the sad scenes about him. He who was by his side was his brother, watching the going out of life. He said he was an old prisoner, and five weeks ago the dying brother came. The sudden change and treatment threw him into a fever, attended with diarrhoea. The meeting which, in his hard fortune, gladdened his heart a short time ago, sadly ends. This morning the brother was carried out a lifeless, faded picture, and laid among the squalid dead. But he who mourned was not permitted to mark the spot where he should be laid, nor shed one tear of sorrow over the grave of a brother. No tears of kindred mingle with his grief; they know it not. He feels the agony alone, unheard of for months, by those who watch and wait in the far off home. Oh! how much can the poor heart bear! How many times can the silken web of affection be broken, and reason not despair!

Tuesday, August 30th.—Common talk since June, that Kilpatrick was coming to release us. Many think it strange he does not come, almost curse the seeming inattention. Perhaps he might come here, but he would be unable to hold the place, or even if he could he could not be supplied. To move us to our lines would required to start with, a train sufficient to transport 5,000 to 7,000 men. Many who could go a few miles would perish by the way, unless put in ambulances. The column would incur the risk of attacks from Wheeler's cavalry for 150 miles; to attempt the daring feat with our lines at Atlanta, would not be good generalship, would not be common sense. We have only to hope that Gen. Sherman, with his noble boys, will come on as he has, and if they hold us here, he will do the best thing for us, he will shake the old flag over us, and we will be free! Far better than exchange.

Wednesday, August 31st.—Summer gone—gone! As if we were brutes, convicts, or worse, it has been nothing to us. Languishing in prison, all is unnatural, asleep or awake. Oh, spiritless life! We do not live, we do not refresh; we do not sleep, we languish; we wake to a dreaming existence, but a sorrowful reality. We do not hunger, we faint. Our joy is, that surest prospects of increased miseries, may in part fail. Our blood is vapid; a feeling more stiffening and stupid than age stifles us. Which do we covet, life or death! Standing between the two we struggle and hope for the one while we are drifted on to the other as if borne by a stygian billow. The air we breathe is a cloud of corruption; the bread for our bodies is deceit and cursing to our breasts. We would sooner die and pay the price of loyalty to a holy cause, than ask for mercy, or pay the price of treason at the Rebel throne and live a slave, or tool of slaveholders!

I know this is the real feeling. Men from 20 or more great States, mingle their patriotic sentiments, their love of truth, and suffer and sink together toward a common grave for a common liberty. Thank God, there are no single martyrs—they die by hundreds! He who is nearest my heart here, clasps my hands when we talk so many things over in the evening hour, again and again, and says. "God bless you North! God only knows the result; but to look out of prison, matters look favorable. We believe proposals of exchange are under consideration."

Complaint continues with singular cutting pains through the back. Rations are more and more unwholesome and scanty. Hounds are out every night; reported escapes from the cook house. A paper contains a dispatch from Mobile stating that the agents of exchange had met and come to an understanding in relation to prisoners. This news is eagerly sought, but I am inclined to think it has reference to prisoners in that department, not to a general exchange.

Thursday, September 1st.—I am faint and weak; am obliged to make a marked effort to raise up when sitting. Men walk about like trembling, palsied, old men. I am continually reminded of the languid feelings of old age (as sometimes pictured, probably over-pictured), so stiff and heavy that I cannot summon my usual manner of walking. Involuntarily I long for a cane to help me about; other poor victims have them. At first it seemed strange to see so many young men moping about with canes. It recurred to me what father used to say, that a cane was a bother to him; but they are needful since bread has ceased to be the staff of life. My voice at times is weak, my lungs oppressed. Some entirely lose their voices, can only whisper. My breakfast, this morning, was a piece of sour bread so coarse that it hurt my mouth, causing it to bleed; those who have scurvy bad, cannot eat it. No rations drawn, but Griff trades for a few peas. Though wormy, and taste strongly of bugs and not half cooked,—we know a hog would not touch them,—to keep alive the waning fire of life we eat and are thankful.

In the prison and hospital 3,079 men died in August. God only knows when this calamity to the American people will end! The negroes have been overhauled. Some were slaves; a number have been taken out to be sent to masters. A rport is rife that for fear of retaliation Rebels resort to a dodge and give them a choice to take the oath and work here. Some have been on "parole of honor" all summer. The oath of a negro, even a slave, in spite of slave codes, has come to be regarded in Georgia, and by the Rebellious powers of Slavedom! Verily there is reformation in war! Negroes are men, only nominally slaves, in localities. The thunder of war rolls along, flashing the light of liberty. Because of caste the negro has been denied protection by the United States government. Now he is to be protected in his rights as a man. Revolutions do not move backward. When this is done our calamities end.

Sunday, September 4th.—Have been quite languid; something has thrilled and cheered me. Hope to make my exit yet. Nothing discourages or disappoints me. If I hear a good report I never believe it till all the facts address themselves to my mind; as Old Deny says, "not till I see it in the man's own handwriting." If Winder should tell us we would be exchanged tomorrow I should want to see 'the point"—of exchange. They take all pains to tell us we are abandoned; that we had better enlist, that the C. S. A. is recognized by England and France, or is just "a go'n' to be;" talk real pretty as to how much better off we would be out of this "blamed hole;" "heap o' bisnis for you'ns that don't see alike. As a reward for this abuse, they ask us not only to become non-combatants, but to carry Rebel guns as citizens can work, clerk and write." A clever little sergeant tells me: "You'ns 'd do right smart to take the oath, I reckon." But we of Slavedom are subject to do. They act as though they were special rulers of God's earth, not amenable to anyone, to multiply and subdue. Andersonville is one of their special "rulings;" The old slave system, tne nucleus of the grand constellation in their vagary of vision of a new sort of "free government" founded on slavery! O, jewel of bogus consistency! Elon J. Warren of my company, died August 31st. Nights are damp, chilly; sun rises in a mist, then gets hot.

Papers smuggled in by new arrivals have correspondence between Judge Ould and Major Mulford which indicates that the Federal agent of exchange was not authorized to accept certain proposals. There have been important movements by Sherman, throwing a force on Hood's flank and rear. Atlanta is reported abandoned. Rebels will not own it to us. The event will necessitate our removal. If true we shall soon get orders. There is fighting at Richmond, Grant holds his ground, presses Lee. Rebels talk that McClellan and Pendleton were nominated at Chicago.

Boodger and I are reading Hugo's "Les Miserables." He shows genius, says good things in a good way; holds up opposite characters, good and bad, which, lacking intelligent independence, may become impudent tools. He justly points out and criticises fallacies and foibles of society; the coarseness, licentiousness and materiality of royalty; suggests economy in correcting customary waste in cities, and in disposing of refuse that goes into the sea which should enrich the soil; contends that such methods of sewage disposal is unsanitary and unjust; illustrates good and bad practices in a way proverbial. The work is not sensational, but philosophical; not a "yarn" but a social teacher. Victor Hugo was banished eighteen or twenty years ago for liberal principles expressed in "Little Napoleon." Sergeant Sibley, of Ohio,, owns the book, is choice of it although worn to rags.

## NIGHT OF JUBILEE.—STRANGE SCENES.

Tuesday, September 6th.—Last night one of the sentries cried "Post No. 18, 1 o'clock and all is well; Hood is licked and gone to hell." One shouted, "Good news, Yanks; Atlanta is taken; the Confederacy is played out, bully for you." Some Yank asks, "Anything about exchange?" "The hell, no; Sherman's after you!"

Prisoners were generally soon astir. Cheer after cheer was given from every part of the camp. Men sang patriotic songs; religiously inclined assembled for prayer; a song service of thousands of voices was held, curiously blending with the shouting of other thousands. Chorde and discord expressed joy and thanks.

Early in the morning a few prisoners came in, confirming the news, bearing a paper that said Atlanta was hurridly evactuated August 29th, Hood losing heavily in property and men; that a force of Federals were 90 miles in advance near Jonesboro, Ga.; also a conference of Governors with President Lincoln regarding release of prisoners.

At dusk eighteen detachments were ordered to be ready to move at midnight. Great excitement; loud cheering. It would be interesting for Carlton, fresh from Boston, to note the whys and wherefores of the matter; for Leslie's artist to sketch the squalid picture of huddled groups leaning on canes made of rations of wood, ready to fall in for the grave, our lines, or anywhere else. I feel like taking it quietly. In instances with some, the sudden thrill of joy was like the shock of sorrow in effect. Many fainted. One man who had pined to almost helplessness, on hearing the news leaped to his feet, shouted, clapped his hands and fell dead. Another told his friends: "You are all going home, I cannot go. I wish I had died before; I had no hope or wish to live; but now if I could live a little longer I might get home. Won't they take me? Ask the doctor. It's too bad!" He sank back on the sand, his eyes glared, his lips paled, for a moment was silent; then waved his hand and said in delirious delight: "They say I may go," and died.

Wednesday, September 7th.—Ten detachments went out in the night; six returned this morning for want of transportation. This afternoon more cars arrive and they go. It was hurly burly all night. There are two parties; one full in the belief of exchange; one that we are to be shifted to be imprisoned elsewhere. Excitement runs high. There is a rumor that U. S. transports are off Savannah, loaded with Rebel prisoners. It is believed because all hope it is so. There are two possible cases, viz.: Most probable that they wished to get us out of Sherman's reach; the other is exchange. Soberly it does not come the right time to be exchange;, this change is forced. Rumored that Grant surprised and cut up some of Lee's forces.

I have completed my scrips in pencil for preservation. Among them are poems, "Ruined Homestead," mostly written in Virginia, last winter; "Prisoner's Dream," "War and Peace," "Prison Psalms," and others.

I note an incident of a father and son: The son, about nineteen, had been feeble all summer and the special object of his father's care. They struggled hard to realize the hope of seeing home. The father did every way possible to obtain food adapted to his case, carried him to the sick call in his arms, begged doctors to give him the best treatment possible that they might not be separated. The other morning the boy died, the father kneeling by him fanning his brow and wetting his parched lips. He laid him out as well as possible, went to the gate and begged for lumber and tools that he be permitted to make a coffin. His request was granted. Lumber and tools were placed inside the gate; the coffin was made, the corpse deposited in it, a prayer offered, and the father bade farewell. While paternal affection may not be diminished by hard circumstances, it is indeed notable to see with what cheerfulness the father sought to alleviate his boy's pain and save his life; with what natural fortitude and resignation he bore the grief while suffering the penalty for being a loyal Kentuckian what all Union prisoners know is. My admiration for these noble, loyal Southerners is beyond expression.

Thursday, September 8th.—Rebels make strange guesses; have too much business on hand. They take out more men than they can accommodate and send back half of them. James B. Hawks tells this regarding his young friend, Willie F. Eggleston, the only son of a widow in Kalamazoo county, Michigan, whom Hawks regards as an excellent woman. He left home in '63 and joined the 7th regiment of that State. He was a good boy and a good soldier. May 12th, '64, in the bloody charge of Hancock's corp at Spottsylvania he was taken prisoner. He was stripped of all extra clothing, and being worn by hard service, prison hardships bore heavily and in August he saw his time was short; called Hawks and said, "If anything happens that I don't get home, I want you to take this likeness to mother. Tell her a bright side of a dark story." He then told him of dreaming of being at home, nourished by his mother. The likeness was that of a girl. For a day or two he was cheerful and better; but the storm in August produced a change. With singular coolness he desired his friends to get a pipe and smoke with him; said Hawks need not sell his watch to Rebels to buy food, as he should not need it, and if he would make him crust coffee for supper he would need nothing more, and soon after sank in death. Thus perished a mother's son. The number of men now living here is put at 35,000, making a total of about 45,000 who have been sent here.

Sunday, September 11th.—Streets have been thronged three days and nights by men waiting to get out. The fact that the oldest prisoners go first, is taken as evidence that exchange is in prospect. All unable to walk are being collected in the sheds just built in the north end. Rations are but an excuse for something to eat. Fellows engaged in beer selling have gone out and left their stock and barrels to us whereby we are enabled to get a little money, which helps.

Monday, September 12th.—Our detachment (36th) expects orders; twelve of fifteen thousand have gone out. We have bought meal and are baking pones to take along. We are won derfully lucky; plump full of good cheer; no thanks to Jonnies. If there is a worse place than this Anderson prison we are ready to jump into the fire. The boys are talking about many good things that will come to them when they get to Parole Camp. A bath this afternoon; close attention to toilet in view of a long, tedious journey, be it wheresoever, and a last look at this place of untold suffering, henceforth and forever famous for its infamy.

### GEORGIA GIRLS WITH TRUE SOUTHERN HEARTS.

Seeing too much sadness has congealed your blood
And meloncholy is the nurse of frenzy.
  * * * * * * * *
Frame your mind to mirth and merriment,
Which bars a thousand harms and lengtheds life.

Augusta, Ga., Tuesday, September 13th.—I sit in a cattle car writing my journal. At dark last night a long train came puffing up from Americus, and stopped at Andersonville, and we got orders. In fifteen minutes we were rushing and staggering crazily to the gate; with shouts we struggled out of the jaws of death and hobbled through deep dust nearly breathless to the station. The free air, the sight of that dark wall behind, fire our passions with joy. Several shabby looking men, "crackers," sat about the cars. They asked: "What State you'ns all from?" We answer respectfully and repeat the question, they reply, "We'ns the Georgia State militia. What you'ns come to fight we'ns for?"

"To put down a senseless rebellion against the best government on earth."

If they could not understand the issue in the war by this time, probably they did not comprehend our words. We go right aboard, 60 in a box car, crowded and uncomfortable, but what of that. Once more attached to steam we are soon off, jogging along tolerably from the "bull-pen." Before getting aboard a few huge watermelons beside the track were confiscated and eaten, rinds and all, with avidity.

Although we do not believe as some do that we are going to be exchanged immediately, we have some pleasurable thoughts. Two days, so-called, rations of corn bread, is aboard and was given out after we started. Guards say we are going to Savannah, but appeared so ignorant that we made due allowance. These fellows seem indifferent to the movement or fortunes of their armies. We pass Macon in the night. Instead of switching for Milan we turned north over a long road through bushes, passed gaunt pines, hard looking corn and cotton fields, with girdled, standing trees, large plantations, few houses, wood and water stops and whisky stations, and arrived here late this afternoon much fatigued, much diverted by the change, assuming to be on a pleasure trip through Dixie. I keep my eyes and ears open. The train stands in the streets of Augusta; on one side the doors are closed, on the other rolled back facing a mercantile block, hotel, etc. They are very inviting. I am haunted in mind with peaceful, bustling scenes of days gone of which the present is a wreck. As to business it is dull, closed doors, empty houses. A train from the south is thronged with men in gray with muskets, recently "scripted." In answer to the question, how they were conscripted they said:

"We'ns wus ordered to report to the committee and wus mustered in. Crops wus left to be taken kere on by wimmins and 'oung'ns, till Sherman gits drived back."

Evidently they had no slaves. The guard walked in front of the doors, stray agitators came peeking along with something to say. Among them are high bred fire-eaters, who want to do all the talking. One, after much lip about the uncongeniality of the North, its unfitness to live with the South, the unconstitutionality of invading a State, and desolation we had caused, gave his opinion frankly that, when the war closed the Union would be restored and the slaves freed. He said he rather it would not be so, but it could not be helped. Thus saying, he slipped away as if he had said a fearful thing.

A keen-eyed gentleman, his hair sprinkled with gray, attired in an attractive gray suit, lectured us on Hunkerism in politics. "The South is Hunker, therefore her institution cannot be changed. Slavery should have been nationalized, slave property respected in all the States. Then the Union would have gone along as it was; but the North is in politics as in everything else, dishonest, radical, sectional, infidel, covetous, and the South must seek her own destiny."

"Why sectional?"

"Because the North has grown rich and strong, while the South remains as she always has been, only hates you worse."

He believed in degrees of rights to people according to caste, color and ability. Government belongs to the superior class; the South would never be ruled by "mudsills," referring to Mr. Lincoln, black people and whites, like ourselves.

I alluded to Mr. Stephens as having been a poor boy and as to his famous speech in the Georgia convention against Secession, foretelling the present state of affairs and if the South had followed his foresight he would have been of great service to his people; whereupon he uttered some sharp sentences on inferiority of races, the determination and honor of the South. The boys cried "Hardtack, give us something to eat," and the man turned sullenly away. The curious thing about it is that such a chivalric spirit should consent to reason with the "inferior race" he addressed. He unequivocally said, as I have heard said numberless times, that we came to subjugate the South and deserve no better treatment as prisoners than we had had; that they ought to have "raised the black flag and hung every son of Haman." This is the "fire of the Southern heart," what is the heart?

On the left of the train was a row of handsome dwellings. Just before dark, looking through the cracks of the closed doors, we saw several young ladies in a yard who appeared interested in our behalf. They gave tokens of friendliness, signifying to some of the men in my car that they would come again. We managed to open the door, just after dark; two of the ladies appeared each with a basket of bread in small loaves which were handed into the car, when they immediately vanished and were not seen again. I believe in my soul that these girls more truly manifest the Southern heart than has been expressed through the great leaders of the South, either in peace or war, for thirty years.

> Warm was the love of each maiden's heart
> Who fed a hungering foe,
> Who by word or by gesture sweet hope did impart,
> And tenderly pitied our woe.
> We were looking dirty, poor and hard,
> Scantily clad and fed,
> But dear maidens came from a dainty yard,
> And brought us baskets of bread.
> They watched in the gloaming and when night fell round,
> They came with quick, soft tread,
> For they feared the guards, who watched the ground:
> Oh, blessings on each fair head!

## HOMESEEKER'S EXCURSION IN DIXIE.

Kingsville, S. C., Wednesday, Sept. 14th.—After dark we changed cars at Augusta. I had a hard berth, sitting at a squat, or tailor fashion, all night. So weary at times, however, we lopped on one another and drowsed in spite of aches and itches. We left the Charleston road at Branchville, 50 miles south of this place. During the night a man was shot and left behind, having fallen or jumped off. At Orangeburg a few Yanks were permitted to spend Confederate money for Bourbon at a wayside inn at $2 a drink. We have passed the cotton land, a terpentine region, the alligator swamps and arrived here at 3 o'clock in the afternoon and are waiting our fate. Here is a junction, a South Carolina ville, a few houses and "white trash" shanties scattered about; long rickety storehouses with broad platforms piled with bales of cotton and any quantity of resin, which has waited so long for the blockade that the barrels have burst and scattered it as free as water. The boys eat as much as they please and put as much as they please in their pockets; they pick it up as children gather shells on the shore, for several reasons, first, ravenous hunger; second, as a medicine for urinary difficulties; third it wlil make a fire.

Florence, S. C., Thursday, Sept. 15th.—At Kingsville we got aboard flat bottom train headed for Florence. The guard changed and the all assuming Captain is asked where we are going.

"To Charleston."

"Why, captain, we are right away from Charleston," I said.

"Seventy-five trains are coming up on the direct road tonight, so we go t'other way, just as near," said he.

If I had not had an old map I might have believed him. At 5 o'clock in the afternoon we steamed off again. We had a smart engine, a New Yorker to drive it. After curves, a little up grade and long swamps were passed, we moved lively, the best speed I have seen on Southern roads. Believers in exchange are falling off, while some quote the captain in support, persisting that we are headed for Charleston, notwithstanding we are moving directly north and the peevish fellows get noisy, thinking it a question for argument.

Near night the train stopped in a barren place; not a settlement visible. After half an hour a squad of negroes came out a by-road in the woods, led by an officer, armed with beetle axes with long awkward helves, and make for woods on the other side of the train. An officer and guard came to the train, ordered six prisoners off each car and marched them out to tote the wood the negroes were cutting. I with many others declined to move. After a pile was put on the tender, men were ordered aboard and the train moved. The second time this was performed within a few miles. It occurred to me that this thing called C. S. A. is kept on its haunches in this hand to mouth way. But why did they not call out the "relief guard," instead of going for the negro? They have him in everything; habitually use him as men use whiskey and tobacco. They are out at all times of the night at every switch or station. The Confederacy cannot do without the negro; what the negro will do without the Confederacy is the problem; it is coming to that.

Broad, dreary swamps lay along filled with trees, canebrakes, tangled vines, occasionally clusters of native grapes hung temptingly before our famished crew. The night was delightful, a beautiful moon giving everything a silver hue. Cultivated lands have an ancient aspect; impress me with an idea beyond any romance of the Southern home. Tugging through a dark, dismal, marshy wilderness, pine and hickory forests, then bursting into a vast extent of open country where for miles a single boro (the rich planter's home with its attaches) may be seen. They stand alone in a sequestered, ancient style, presenting an attractive air of homeliness that makes one think of the days of somebody's childhood. Then again into the woods; narrow roads jut off, winding as old roads will, thick trees locking arms over them. Again through an opening to the right or left I see gray mansions shining in the September moonlight. I can liken it to nothing so nearly as an old country in a new, wild world—if such a thing could be—old English plantations two centuries ago spread outing young America; aristocratic planters owning every rod they touch, much they never touched; what they don't own no one does. It awakens traditions; I imagine I am living a hundred years ago; I think of Marion and his men, their sweet potato feast, and almost leap from the car. O, for just one tater, a Confederacy for just one tater!

Till late scenes and thoughts occupied my mind—thoughts of home and friends and a half foolish, half complaining wish that they might see me just as I am, that I might say to them, there is but one way to liberty and peace; that is to fight it out. In silence I prayed that the angel host might waft that message to every hearth in the North, that God would inspire all hearts with fraternal love; that this soil shall not much longer be polluted by the feet of slaves and blighted by despotism. The motion of the car made it breezy; I awoke from my reverie with a chill and a yawn, and doubling in a cramped posture I courted sleep. One can hardly imagine the loathsomeness and discomfort of my position; trying to lie down where there is scant room to sit up; heads and feet together, an old boot in my breast, or other tender places; three or four pairs of heavy legs across me, tired of recoiling, and a pair under me; a nasty old coat tail in my face, elbows in my ribs, a crocky boiling cup whacks my nose; get my heels in somebody's face, get a punch all around; a dozen set to grumbling and scolding; scold myself, apologize, get cursed and wind up with "help ourself." But in spite of hunches and kicks I fell asleep and awoke after the train had stopped some time after midnight. Nearly twelve hundred men, prisoners from three to twelve months, deprived of privileges necessary to tidiness, not having been allowed to wash faces or hands since our journey began, a distance of 350 miles; mixed up with all sorts of men, offers an excellent time to "mix breeds" and our pestilential stock has increased 500 per cent. One feels humiliated, disgusted to think of it. Were it not for such disgust one might be more degraded; lose personal pride which may follow men wherever they go, and suffer themselves to become victims of vermin and lassitude. The best a man can do is very bad. Wives think of your husbands; maids think of your sweethearts; mothers, of your sons, sisters of your brothers! Unfit to lie down on your carpet; would be glad of a place on your lawn with a blanket from the horse barn for a night's repose.

### EX-NORTHERN MAN WANTS UNION DEDICATED TO SLAVERY.

Fully aware the train had stopped, the engine detached, stiff all over I got on the ground by the side of the car. Presently the engineer with an unconcerned air came alongside and planted his bulky physique upon a pine stump. As before mentioned he was once a Northerner, here for business, professing neutrality; talked as such men do about South Carolina and Massachusetts with a heavy leaning in favor of South Carolina, but was more familiar with corn bread, a staple of the South, and State Rights theory, than the fact that there had ever been a National Union; that E Pluribus Unum is the life of our constitution and void a part is voidable in toto. He thought what the South chose to do the North could afford it should. If the slaveholder cared to enlarge his stock of slaves by making a specialty of breeding or buying; if he wished to breed to sell to other States, he didn't see what business it was to New York. He said:

"It's none of the North's business whether the South has four million of slaves or forty millions. The South has the cotton market of the North and of Europe, and of its rice and much of its sugar, and must have slaves to do its work. There is no other way. Why kick about slavery? She has got to have more niggers, more territory; has as good right to raise niggers and sell them as the North has to raise cattle and sell them. They wanted slavery in Kansas, they had a right to have it. Why the hell need we care? I never bother my head about such things; all I want is plenty of business in my line. Then these abolition missionaries with their school ma'ms to try to educate niggers! They need no education; it is incendiary to attempt it. They ought to have been run out." He talked heartily in his way, as a blacksmith smokes at his bellows while heating his rods without inquiring whether his fumes are offensive to his customers. It was suggested that he might favor the restoration of the Union on such a basis. He replied:

"Of course, that's the only basis of continuous Union. On that understanding the Union has been kept together. When a sectional party North broke the constitution by electing a black Republican, the South wouldn't stand it. Black Republicans brought on the war because a few States seceded. If the Union could be restored it would have to be on the plan of perpetual slavery as an indisputable right anywhere. But black Republicans, spawns of abolition nigger stealers, are in power, and would not agree to it if the South'd come back on a fair proposition; so Union's impossible. Maybe, after awhile, it may come around. The Union is busted; I'm sorry as you are about it. The North'll be licked, the South'll grow strong, the North'll grow weak. All old slave states are sure to come to the new nation; they belong there. All Southern territories'll come in clean to the Pacific and California. Looking at the map shows that Kansas belongs to the South, it jines Missouri west; the South'll have it and there'll be no whimpering about the stinkin' niggers in any of the states or territories. The North'll split into factions; states borderin' on slave states'll want to come in. In a few years the slave party North'll be in the majority. Then the South will rule agin, North and South. Jeff Davis, and all the smart men know what they're fightin' for. They're the smartest men on earth, they are. The South alers did rule and alers will; my father alers talked that. The radicals are in the minority and'll be subjugated, or go to Canada to jine the niggers they run off. The country can't be run without slavery. Never has been, never can. My father talked that when I was a boy in New York State. I tell you the country can't be run without slavery any more'n I can pull this train without my locomotive, or run the engine without steam. Niggers ain't good for nothin', without masters. God made them to be slaves. Civilization has raised them from wild beasts to property just like other animals. The Bible says it. The country can't be worked without them, and he won't work unless he's a slave. Abolish slavery and niggers'd murder everybody; or'd have to be 'sterminated. So you can't abolish slavery; God won't let you! Niggers're all right in their place; that is in slavery. We've got to have more slaves to do the work. If they can't be raised fast enough—they'll have to catch 'em and bring 'em here as used to be done; or take free niggers and sell 'em as used to be done until abolitionists got some influence. I've heard my father tell of it. There's money in it. Never ought to have been stopped. The demand for Southern products is growin'; more niggers are wanted to work."

"Why not set the mass of white men to work at wages?"

"White men can't do it; ain't built that way; can't stand the climate; don't know a thing about it; nor they won't work on plantations with niggers. They ain't raised that way. Slave owners won't have 'em. They've other use for 'em; they found it out when war come, and they will need them more and more for armies; every white man will be wanted They'd rather fight to maintain slavery than to be degraded to work with niggers or like niggers. White men in South Carolina who have to grub a patch for a living are low down; thought no more of than niggers; in fact they can get no jobs niggers can do. In the army he's all right; the South worships its soldiers for they are fighting for Soutnern institutions. The poor trash is as good as anybody there. Their wives and daughters are made something of by aristocratic people, when before the war they wouldn't give 'em a smile, or pinch of snuff. You see what the war has done for poor white men. South elevated 'em; some're officers an' they like it, and better fighters never pulled a trigger. There's thousands of men in every slave state that nobody had any use for; didn't seem to have any use for themselves, seemed to me, in years past, an' I've bin South since Polk was president. They shell out brats as fast as a contented herd of niggers, many on 'em. But when the long comin' crisis came which'll make the doctrine of old Jack Calhoun the real thing, the right to git niggers as any property's got, anywhere without interference; to work 'em, to discipline 'em and to raise 'em, to sell 'em; the right of any State to secede, if necessary, to enjoy that right; an' till that's settled every poor white is wanted, every devil of 'em. It'll make a place for 'em and their boys for generations as soldiers to hold down hordes of niggers, incendiary and untrained, the cotton growers and all other growers'll have to have; an' to take care of nigger stealers, cracked brained sentimentalists, fanatics, lunatics and brutes like John Brown that may strike a blow on our borders. It seems to me, since the war, that Providence had jest multiplied the poor trash for the event as foreseen by big men, it might 'apen, a-raisin' 'em up to set up jest such a 'Federacy with slavery for underpinin' as that little midget statesman, Stephens of Georgia said they'd set up. There's Providence in it; so we expect this war had to be. You folks 'ouldn't agree to far-seein' aims of the South—the fight had to be. The South couldn't get satisfaction in the old gov'ment; 'twas gitting wo'se, an' they come out to make a gov'ment for theirselves as they believed they had a right to do. These men bin raised up to protect the South in its rights. Its the sort o' protection the South 'ants for its home industries, an' property in niggers denied by the old gov'ment, an' 'twas gittin' wo'se. The slave owners patiently stood the public burden sometime growin' out of the needs of a great mass of poor whites that lived on the edge of society, paid from profits of slave labor an' slave tradin', havin' faith in great leaders who led the country up to the hour when they should strike loose an' set up for theirselves, an' to set up a free country."

It was suggested that his ideas of a free country to a Northerner were queer, when he said: "Lord, man, don't you know

Northerners, specially New England fellows, make the best Niggar drivers when broke in? They're the best nigger breakers in the South."

His statement of the purpose of the slave power in inaugurating secession, confirmed my own view—freedom to enslave! I thanked him for his frankness and remarked that the evil of secession consists in the objects sought to be attianed, namely: The more absolute establishment of chattel slavery and the rehabilitation of the barbarous practices of arresting and selling into slavery free negroes because of color, for which there would be no legal restraint, and there seems no lack of sentiment, and the erection of a military serfdom, as vicious and abominable as ever cursed mankind; that the war, on our part, is a protest to that kind of protection to the slave breeding, slave working and slave trading "industry" on this continent, or elsewhere. It would always be an "infant industry" if tolerated.

In the matter of exchange he said, "If it means trading niggers for white soldiers of the South, it will be a develish long time coming." We believe it has been; still we believe that the government can not consistently treat its colored soldiers other than it treats its white soldiers which would amount to endorsing the Southern policy of turning negroes captured in our service, over to the States from which they had fled as slaves, back to their masters, or to be sold to other masters. This is the hitch in the exchange problem. We prisoners have to bear the hardships and persecutions of consequent delay.

When this sociable engineer began to amuse the boys by telling what he loved to eat, it was more than I could stand. I crawled back on the car leaving him on the stump, feeling that he is a chip from an old block, shaped to fit his position; a tree in the field of social economy and civic ethics. As to his god that had been "raising up" "brats" to fight for the South against liberty, I ruminated that he has a revelation from the dark aspirations of false leaders; that his specious piety is rank atheism. Stonewall Jackson may have prayed to the same god, might have been honest, but he misconceived. Every Southern soldier may be honest if ignorant, starting from false premises; honestly loyal to a bad cause, bravely contending for its success, never dreaming what success would mean to his country, as we today pray for the achievement of our purpose, believing that it will conduce to the welfare of the South as well as the North. The science of ethics, sociology, and the highest realization of human experience, show that when any people have planted aims athwart the mind of the age, it has brought confusion to that age, confusion and destruction to itself as then constituted. Attempts to give new force to reactionary principles and to obstruct those of progress to broader enlightenment and liberty to all people, have brought back methods

## CHRONICLES OF A WAR PRISONER. 135

and policies of despotism and antagonized both moral and physical forces, against which to contend is crime. In rejecting, as have the leaders of rebellion, the Declaration of Independence regarding the equitable rights of all men to liberty as the cornerstone of the Republic, and seeking to erect a Confederacy upon a foundation of slavery, they assert by their acts that their course is reactionary. They and we, and master and slave, have suffered for this violation of a holy principle.

"The laws of changeless Justice bind
Oppressor with oppressed;
And close as sin and suffering joined
We march to fate abreast."

If we adhere to the right we shall be victorious. The fate to which we march, will be the best possible to our race and our time. Thus meditating, I fell asleep.

### PRISONERS ARRIVE AT FLORENCE.

Unconscious of the movement of the train, I slumbered until the sun was shining, clear and warm. All cars are open; mine is next to the engine, exposed to cinders. We are a smutty, suffering crowd. All are suffering for water, having had none for forty hours. The corn bread, drawn at Andersonville, had generally been consumed by the 13th; all are faint and hungry. At 8 o'clock we were permitted, under guard, to go seventy rods to a swamp, for water, small squads being detailed from each car. The supply was inadequate because no one has more than a quart pail to fill. Thirst and hunger remain to be borne patiently. Griffith and I have a piece of course bread from the Andersonville issue of rations left, owing to extras we secured from the sale of meal beer. This we burned and boiled for coffee, our mouths being too sore with scurvy to use it otherways, which served for breakfast for which we were, indeed, thankful. Prior to our arrival four trains of prisoners had arrived on the Charleston road and were waiting to be disposed of. "Minute men," old and young, had been called to receive us, and they watched us with a frightened look. They are mostly in citizens' dress.

Florence, S. C., is at the junction of four roads; from Columbia, Charleston and Cheraw, S. C., and Wilmington, N. C. It is 100 miles north of Charleston. Were it up North it would be a business center, but there seems little doing here. Things look deserted; woods on every side; clearings near the tracks adorned with decaying brush and stumps. I am told that the country near is noted for savage gangs of marauders who have been known to fight to the death when attempts by civil authorities have been made to break them up.

Three men on horseback rode by and inspected us. Several

ladies on horseback followed. Then came a woman in a cart and six dogs. She had turnips she wanted "to exchange for a ring." At 9 a. m. trains moved down the Charleston road which revived the hope in some that Charleston had been made a point for exchange and that city was to be our destiny. Before noon all were ordered aboard; our train switched to the Charleston road, backed a mile, when we were ordered off and marched out a road through woods for "the old field" where a man said we were to go. Many were unable to walk. A detail was made to carry them. Many who could walk were unable to assist. There was not one in the lot who retained normal strength; few had seen a well day in three months. After half a mile we found ourselves in a field. Tall weeds and long grass stood on portions we passed over, which we pulled and put in heaps where we halted. From a near fence we collected rails, material for shanties. We thought an officer of the guard kind, for when guards cried: "Stop you'ns, sar," bringing muskets down and starting for us, he said: "Oh, let 'em work; they can't carry a big heap," and looked at us smilingly. This awakened in us a grateful, but faint cheer. He might have thought of us as one would of a flock of limping, distempered sheep minus half their wool; but I think his motive merciful.

We found 2,000 prisoners on the ground who left Andersonville before us; had been around by Savannah and Charleston; among them former chums, Wright, Boodger, G. W. Mattison and O. W. Burton. The field is destitute of living water. Details of 100 men go out for each 1,000, once a day, a mile to a stream, consequently our small pails do not contain enough for more than drinking and cooking; no washing. Our hope of using grass, weeds and rails for shanties vanished. Not only did strength prove inadequate, but the need of fire caused our stock of material to vanish.

### PRISONERS OVERRUN GREEN GUARDS.

Monday, Sept. 20th.—It is said 10,000 prisoners have arrived at Florence, from Andersonville, 7,000 since we came. Men have died rapidly. I have been unable to write since the 15th. My health and the effort to care for myself have prevented. The 15th and 16th droves of plantation negroes passed with spades and axes, in charge of drivers, to build a stockade. Griffith, Glover and I are stopping under small trees. Lenity was shown at first. Citizens were allowed to converse and trade through the guard. Had a talk with a group of five women with poor vegetables to exchange, or sell. To my question they said, sadly: "We'nses mens all in Fedrit army." One said, "My ole man kilt long time done gone." She didn't know where, but another said it was at Chancellorville. Another said two of her sons "got kilt", one at Gettysburg, one this year with Gen. Lee. Two others of these familes had been wounded, but were on duty at Richmond. Others were at Charleston and Wilmington. I asked: What did your folks go to war for? Two replied in concert: "Thames hat ter; Yankees were coming to steal all our niggers and everything." They thought Yankees "rich enough to buy niggers if they'ns wanted any."

"Did your people own niggers?" I ask.

We'ns done gone got no niggers, nebber. We'ns poor; no lan', only patches big folks loan. You'ns sees we'ns' mens had to fight for 'em what has to save the South."

"Will it do you any good?"

"Feard it won't, an we'ns 'ill lose our'ns liberty or get kilt off."

I told them I hoped no more of their men would be killed; that the war would end and give them liberty and a better chance than ever before.

On the 16th there was a rush beyond the guard, of several hundred prisoners who brought in a rail fence slick and clean in spite of guards who seemed bewildered by their boldness. There was something comical in their acts. In his excitement one fellow yelled pleadingly: "If you'ns don't stop I git in ga'd 'ouse, sho!"

This was followed by a bigger rush from another part of the field, for the woods seventy rods away, about 500 men going, completely astonishing the stupid guards who had not yet learned they had any power but to "shoot off their mouths," saying: " Har, sar!" "You'ns thar!" "Stop, sar!" "Git in dar you'ns." You'ns can't tote no mo' rails!" "Co'pal g'a'd!" so green were they.

It seems the removal of prisoners had not been anticipated long; little or no provision had been made, and the mass of guards had been picked up by scouring the country, and put on duty without discipline or instructions by officers who had been hurried here with a hundred or so who had seen service. Presently a heavy line of skirmishers, some of whom showed signs of having seen service, deployed and double-quicked to the woods, some parts of the line opening fire. There was quite a sputtering of musketry at intervals. Then our men came straggling in. Most of them, while in the woods, picked up nuts and gathered wild grapes; others skulked away hoping to escape. At the time no rations had been given since we left Andersonville, which was designed for two days.

Before this excitement was over, rations were announced. All got a small piece of Indian pone, a few spoonfuls of corn meal an hour later, largely gathered from citizens. In this raid ten prisoners were shot. Some who wandered away are being brought in. Many of us had designed to try to escape, but lameness, hunger and weakness deterred me. The 17th, scurvy, very pronounced, appeared again in my legs with dropsy. Press the swollen flesh and it does not return to shape. It is yellow, dark in spots. On one ankle the flesh girds tightly about the bone. Every step taken seems like tearing it loose.

Citizens are wild with the idea of getting United States money. Three boys who had been interested in the meal beer deal at Andersonville still had $8 and they divided with Griffith and myself. We buy miserable apples and fine sweet potatoes. I ate them raw. It was the greatest hapiness I had experienced from eating, though blood ran from my gums, inflamed with scurvy, and some of my teeth tore loose.

Since the raid officers have thought best to allow citizens to trade with us. I sold my pocketbook for $5 "Confed" to a Rebel soldier. Bought more sweet potatoes. It don't take many potatoes to smash a "V." The 18th I was detailed to go out to look after sick that had not yet been brought in. Owing to infirmities, I gave the chance to Griffith. He had a better chance to traffic and traded his boots for a pair of shoes of English make, and got $20 "Confed" to boot. This helped us, for the next two weeks; without it I believe we should have famished, for rations did not average one meal a day, poor at that. Thus far they have been less than at Andersonville. Yesterday the issue consisted of three spoonfuls of flour, three onunces fresh beef, one-half pint of meal, the same of brown beans, with the proclamation: "This ration is for two days." Still I hope the transfer from Georgia has prolonged my life—getting purer air and the precious sweet potatoes, rarer than anything I have ever tasted. They have checked the scurvy.

After twenty hours of wind it began raining the 17th, and still rains with prevailing cold wind. The water settles between the knolls in this part of the field, which is crowded, for the reason that the flat part is mostly covered from one to three inches deep, in order to get on the knolls and under trees where we sit and stand as best we can; cling to roots, to trees, to each other, to keep out of the pools which are from three to eighteen inches deep. Of course we are badly drenched from falling rain and more or less chilled all the time. All long for it to clear up.

### NINE DAYS' STORM—SOUTHERNERS WILLING TO STARVE.

Sunday, Sept. 26.—Nine days and nights steady rain, sometimes heavy. This morning it stopped; mists have cleared; we hope, oh, so ardently, the equinoxial storm is over. It does not seem we could endure another day of this awful wet and chill,

Many poor fellows have perished in it. Morning after morning they lay dead in the pools of water among the knolls or in low places. Some too weak to cling to high ground, or crowded off, rolled into the water and drowned, at our feet in the night.

But God's great sun came out today. Chilled, faint, sore in throat, lungs; lame in every joint and muscle; almost hopeless, we drag ourselves from under trees to bask in its thrilling beams. We revive; a thrill of joy comes with it; I hope again. Oh, it is "easy now for the heart to be true." Wonderfully my strong heart responds!

The sick who were left outside in absence of places called hospitals, have been sent in. Griffith is with us again. The storm over, men have to hunt clothing again for lice. They have become terrible because of forced neglect. G. thinks if they were eatable, we might live on the "fat of the land."

Men just in who attempted escape, report every road and bridge guarded. What will be done with us we are anxious to know; our condition is deplorable. Last evening a man standing by me was shot by a sentry, the ball passing through his wrist and lodging in his side. With others I took him to his friends. This morning he was taken to a doctor. Why he was fired upon, I cannot conceive; we were six rods from the guard line.

South Carolina people are frank, sociable and generous as any I have seen in the South, so far as I have been able to study them. We have seen enough to confirm an undisputed fact that the mass of people are good natured, kind hearted like all Americans. It is only when warped by falsely educated prejudice that they become set on a false track, obstinately, impulsively, recklessly, wrongly determined. Abnormal social and economic conditions fostered by slavery, made free intercourse with the North impossible, if slavery were to be maintained, which had become the paramount policy. Separation socially, made separation politically and geographically imperative if the exclusion of slavery from new territory were to be enforced by national authority. The pet policy of nationalizing slavery according to the Dred Scott edict, could not be longer expected in the Union, and its gradual extinction was but a matter of time—its decadence natural. Secession was the last resort to save and prosper it. This was the Southern hope; for this the war. But to save themselves from military defeat there are those who favor negro emancipation on conditions that slaves bear arms in support of the Confederacy, as an expedient. This is not favored by planters but by ambitious generals and statesmen who shrink from the humiliation of total defeat. To save the personal pride of a few, alone spurs them on. But we shall know each other better through courses opened by this dreadful school of war, and by suffering incident to it which generates a spirit of merciless vengeance that must vanish slowly as war clouds fade from the national firmament. This will be whether we gain our freedom from this "durance vile" by cartel or by death.

A man evidently high in society, not a military man professionally, but assuming an officer's rank, conversed with us today. He is apparently sixty. We expressed our views freely, but in few words, of the Southern cause, when he said: "You say what no citizen dare, or would be allowed to say." We said the force of events will overwhelm the South, when he replied:

"You may be stronger than we but you never can whip us; we never will give up."

"But," says one, "if you cannot feed us now, you will starve. If you free the slaves to enlarge your army, who'll raise the 'grub' to feed the army? You give up the real thing you went to war for—to maintain slavery—and kick out the foundation of your edifice. While this looks like a collapse, still, you will in your fall, build better than you know. You will be at the mercy of the Union government and will have freed the negroes yourselves."

To this hot shot he simply said, with emotion:

"If the Confederacy is not recognized we may; but we are willing to starve, we are willing to starve!"

To nail this argument, Comrade Brock said it reminded him of a story. A man declared if his neighbors did not accede to his insolent demand, he would drown himself. Not complying, he waded into water until it ran into his mouth, nose and ears, when he backed up a little, shook his head, and said, "I can't stand that." Seeing his neighbors laughing at his folly, he went in again; but it was no better and his feet sank in the mud, and he stuck. He couldn't "stand that," and yelled, "Pull me out on conditions so-and-so." His neighbors replied, "We will pull you out on conditions that you stay out and behave, and we will behave, too." So we argue that when Sherman gets through Georgia and the Carolinas, and Richmond falls, and the Confederate government has taken to the dismal swamp, Secessionists will hold up hands and ask Uncle Sam to save them from themselves.

## MISERY.

I've looked on Misery undismayed,
His foul breath on my cheek;
I've felt him crawling where I layed
When wind blew chill and bleak,
And drenching rain fell on my head
And on my body beat,
And starved men, frozen, stark and dead
Lay ghastly at my feet.
I've seen him creeping, mean, ensconce,

To steal my scanty food,
But never suffered him, not once,
To scare me where I stood.
I've fought him upright like a man
That only fears disgrace,
And hit him hard, as best I can,
And scorned him at his face.
I've struggled hard for victory,
In pride, although in pain,
With soul serene and spirit free,
And so I must again.

## TWO REMARKABLE SPEECHES.

That man mentioned in the preceding, is of a passive type; obedient to leadership, trusts unquestioningly; in conscience and thought is superficial; loyal to other men's conclusions; reasoning to none of his own.

Another type came among us; not so mild, but harsh; a fiery, ranting fanatic, half preacher, half gorilla. A fanatical advocate for a good reform is often distasteful, but a fanatical declaimer for a reactionary cause, is inspired by the wildness of savagism; coupled with his religious zeal, reigns the energy of ferocity; his piety is profuse with sacrilege; his honest belief in a bad end to be attained, justifies bad means to attain it. So he gloried in the misery we suffer; prays that we suffer more; said our plight was no comparison to the hell set apart for Yankees in the world to come; God's everlasting wrath is bottled up from past eternity for the wicked; all Yankees are made for a place millions and millions of times hotter than all the powder burned in this war could make it, and that without end, for Yankees are the sum of all sin. While probably more than half of mankind will be damned eternally to the same place, the hottest corner is reserved for Yankees. When the devil shall see Abe Lincoln walk in at the head of his army of hirelings, he will sneak from the throne and take his place in the ranks, for that's the next place Lincoln will be elcted to fill. There had not been such an army of devils on any planet, since the war in heaven, as the infernal Yankee army, that plunder, murder, insult the South, steal niggers decreed by God to be slaves, desecrate religion and disgrace America. He profusely praised the courage, endurance, skill and patriotism of Southern soldiers whose bravery excelled that of any in history, and denounced furiously the baseness and cowardice of Northerners.

This is the substance of his effort which was unique because of its bitterness and vile temper; besides being spasmodic in style of delivery, in language, intellect, passion and bodily contortion that always distinguishes such characters when we let loose, it was a good sample of the stuff that often "fired the Southern heart." His display of chronic wrath and pistols impressed us that a sensible answer would be like laying pearls before swine, and to "answer a fool according to his folly" would be dangerous. But he had drawn a crowd of our men. Several Southern officers, citizens and soldiers of the relief guard crowded as close as possible. Officers and a few citizens were coming through the guard line. It was felt that an opportunity to say something sensible was at hand. Just then a fine looking soldier, just in from our lines, began speaking from an upturned root of a tree who, afterward was called a "prophet from Egypt" who, he told me later, was from that part of Illinois known as Egypt. He said, substantially:

Southern men have proved themselves brave and efficient soldiers. We never doubted that they would. Like ourselves, they are Americans. They rated themselves high; that we did not deny. If they erred in estimates it was in underrating Northern men. They may have suffered for their deficiency, miseducated prejudice, and blind sincerity in judgment. They may have suffered from false and fiery oratory; been misled by irrational zealots who rant and rave, but never fight. Such a one may be smart and be a fool; may be good in heart and wrong in head; may be pious but sacrelegious; may profess patriotism and be a brawl, a panderer. On hundreds of battlefields the courage and prowess of Southern soldiers command the admiration of our forces and the world. But while we admire them for this, we condemn the motive that actuated recreant statesmen and cyclonic idiots who infused into them the spirit of rebellion for a cause that abridges the rights of men to liberty and honest pursuits of happiness. As to the merits of your cause, we differ, hence the war. Upon this hinges real patriotism, honor, heroism. Slavery we esteem unwise. Without it you would not have gone astray. It was the bone of all contention. If you gain, you save that; if you lose the partition that divided will go, and we stand forever united for peace, prosperity, a republic of glory, liberty, strength, a beacon light to the world. None can overthrow us, none can prevail against us, when justice needs our service. Shall Americans, children of Washington, Jefferson and Henry, to whom God has entrusted the aegis of liberty, because

" They find fellows guilty of a skin
Not colored like their own, and having power
To enforce the wrong, belie a sacred cause;
Doom and devote them to be their lawful prey?"

Cowper put part of this in my mouth; if incendiary, see him.

We love you people; we always did. If we had not, we should not have let you had your own way so long. We shall love you better hereafter; you will find reasons which you think you have not, to love us. If we had not loved you we should not have gone after you with guns, scoured the woods, searched regions of the mighty South, raked the sea to bring you back, to save you from the evil that must result from a victory you unjustly seek. We mean you good. It was a case of going to have peace if we had to fight for it. While we admire you as fighters, we love you for that which is better in you, the nobler qualities of freemen where freedom is not denied the humblest. Because we condemn errors of judgment and oppose the execution of it, first at the polls, then in the strenuous arts of war, does not mean that we hate you as fellow men. You are a magnificent people; but we detest a cause you have been misled to espouse. God grant history shall not so wrong humanity as to deceitfully, cowardly, or otherwise seek to veneer an unwise course that has wrought great ruin and compelled such sacrifice as we witness, through false pride and dangerous influences because of the marked ability of your generals, the heroism of your rank and file, and devotion of your citizens, because that would tend to extenuate the evil which this war should exterminate. Had your people truly understood the spirit of the age and the purpose and forbearance of the North, the promoters of your cause would not have risen above a weak but noisy faction. Perhaps if they had had a true sense of the purpose and courage of your Northern brothers, as we had of Southren brothers, they would have been slower to anger, more considerate, less hasty in endorsing a cause with their hearts blood, the merits of which their course of life had never led them to more intelligently examine. If they had, it would have been a truer test of courage than to have gone in ignorant of the vital truths involved, believing that one Southerner was equal in war to five Northern men, as some fanatics wrote and talked. After all, the spring of noblest courage is faith in God; in hope of higher development of men, for wider liberty on a basis of enlightened virtue and social progress open to all of Gods children. He who shuts light and knowledge from any human eye of any race, denies God, sins against men. A belief, a hope, that God cannot, or will not, avoid forever damning the bulk, or a part of mankind; that he doomed any race forever to debasing slavery, is gross, unspiritual, blasphemous.

A courage inspired by Godless sentiment, is blind ferocity, not manly courage. I hope your military prisons are not conducted under the influence of a sentiment expressed today, under guidance of the spirit just manifested; if so, the sequence would be worse than it is. Away with such belief from the brains and hearts of man! Then slavery, war, inequality, brutality will vanish from the earth. Men will be brothers; freedom universal. When God commanded that man should labor He did not mean he should be sold like a steer, or that he would thereby be degraded. Per contra he should be enobled; he should lift from its crudeness the material world, beautify, clarify, make it useful to man, an honor to God, thus demonstrating to the billions who were to dwell thereon. His divinity, His love, His glory, His power, His infinity. Thus was established the divinity of man, the dignity of labor! God worked, created. Is He debased? It is a peculiar view that if white men do labor slaves do, they are degraded and the social scale is tipped against them; especially so because of slavery and because the slave is black, or one or more of his parents were. Is that the meaning of the revolution? Did Washington and his heroes fight for the right of one man to annihilate the rights of others? Look at our vast country. What but labor could have rescued it from wildness, advanced it to an era of civilization? What but labor, intelligent labor,, can continue that work, advance it to the demand of present and coming epochs. Debase the laborer and his God-given mission, and the world retrogrades to darkness, to danger, to medieval times. Always did, always must. It is the spirit of despotism which shuts the way to liberty and enlightenment. Free labor under the reign of freedom on a higher scale, has made the country what it is, though often hampered. Only that can bring us to higher development in industrial and social arts, making more homes, more education, more enjoyment. It takes intelligence, intellectual acquirements. The need of this grows with advancement. You cannot grow figs on thistles; nor can you progress in civilizing arts by means of slavery. Intelligence in all men should be fostered, not denied. That is civilization. To oppress one in a degree, measured by social law, oppresses all. To enslave one race is to brutalize, debase and restrain the better instincts of all races, measured by social law. It is the self-executed judgment of God contained in that law which mankind cannot escape. That is the higher law. Congresses canot repeal nor courts suspend. Slavery cannot last where the social trend is toward universal education. If such is not the tendency and aim in a republic, that republic is on the down grade of retrogression. So slavery is morally, economically, socially, politically wrong—unjust to all mankind. If you seek to exclude from your gardens the dews of heaven and the sun of day, you put yourselves to trouble and show that you love darkness rather than light, deprive yourselves of the resusitating powers of nature; deny yourselves the beneficence of heaven. Those who would shield themselves from the glory, ethical and material growth of liberty and progress, invite disaster, generate conditions whereby it must come. Slavery does that.

Its principles of existence requires the ignorance of the slave. Slavery evoluted into being in the reign of intellectual darkness and moral depravity, stronger individual intellectualities taking advantage of conditions. That is despotism. It cannot continue in the effulgence of moral, social and industrial progress. The slave must not rise, he must remain in subjugation. Yet he must be paramount in the field of labor, ordinarily, which slavery degrades and usurps, a status set up through common misconception. The work of advancing civilization must be done by free, enlightened men. To educate men is to free them industrially and socially. Is not the education of the slave denied him on this principle? So it is a plain fact that a perpetual enslavement of the black race, naturally bars the non-slaveholding white in a slaveholding country from industrial progress, where his labor is his only capital. Is he not also oppressed? He reaps the results of oppression as a logical sequence. Deprived of opportunities his right to life and his pursuit of happiness are hampered; his way to it is debased. Can even the aristocratic master escape breathing the air that pollutes the slave? You say the slave is not oppressed, is property; his owner is interested in preserving the efficiency of his slave. Still he is a slave, a chattel. He is fed, clothed and sheltered for his master, not for himself. The master is not in the same way interested in preserving opportunities and efficiencies for the white who earns his bread by the sweat of his brow, unless he is reduced to a pauper state. There may be no design on the part of the ruling class in this result.; but in all cases it is conditions in which men live that oppress them, or give them liberty and prosperity, provided they are active and ordinarily intelligent.

So do masters for slaves because they are property not men; because they love what slaves are compelled to do for them, not because they are human. All this men do for beasts of burden, if wise. They need not do this even in the spirit of mercy. Men cannot be loved in such a mood. If you love not man whom you see, how can you love God whom you do not see? In such a spirit you cannot know God nor men as they should be known. How then can you love Jesus who manifested the love of God to men by loving men? Liberty means equal chances for men. Civilization means ability in all men to profit by those chances, to enjoy them and enhance their manhood by reason of them.

Men born in a state of society where industrial systems make any sort of labor, if performed by free men, menial and unrespectable generation after generation, become more or less afflicted with physical and intellectual lassitude. This is a socialogic and physiologic fact. Their desire to rise higher in the scale of competence and attainments remain latent, beclouded. The first thing the lower class of people in any country learn to do is to respect the opinion of those more fortunate who constitute elements in society which respect them more in a life of indolent degeneracy than of industriousness, if they come down to the labor level of slavery, for slavery rules public opinion politically, socially, and in a fiscal sense where it exists. An element of strength in slave progagandism is to keep fast in minds of men and women that respectability belongs to the class that owns labor; and those who perform labor rank with the laborers who are slaves and property of those who control the sources of production with facilities for productive labor other than slaves. We hear of infidelity and of Christianity. Yet it is by sanction of some sorts of Christianity that slavery exists, is fostered, enforced, and made the pillar of the church and of an unnatural autocracy. We hear of attempts to make it the backbone of the state, the chief corner stone of an ambitious Confederacy. The arbitrary power that owned the industrial forces of the South aimed to constitute itself above all systems of free labor. The Jews claimed characteristics above other people of earth; assumed to be the chosen of God. By force of that belief they grew oppressive, dogmatic, brutal, dictatorial, warlike, corrupt, aggressively insolent toward people they deemed not of their kind; crossed the shining way of progress, sought to bar it, and fell from their dignified station as an independent people. Early in His day Jesus saw their error; taught that all people are equally the children of God; that the God of the Jews was the God of all people; assailed their religious hypocricy, unjust social and economic systems; and they put Him to death for His truthful candor. He taught the uplifting of the lowly; that a few should not forever rob the mass not born with rich inheritances, to make richer the rich, expand and perpetuate poverty by wicked power, oppressive and degrading; sought to save them from the ruin their course invited by urging them to turn from those sins. He predicted their complete overthrow as a nation, unless their policy be changed. They spurned his philosophy, murdered Him publicly by sanction of Roman authority, but without proving Him guilty of crime. There are many followers of Jesus, but often at long distance, in devious ways never trod by Him. They worship Jesus as the Christ, but heed not His teaching regarding the injustice in the conduct of wordly affairs, as a Christly man, which teachings are as practical and essential today as then and ever will be essential to peace and progress on earth, and to the peace of angels in heaven. Brothers whose policy should be preferred, that of the bigoted, man-hating egoist, or that of the humane, loving altruist? The——

At this juncture a Confederate officer with two guards approached and commanded him to stop and the crowd to disperse. During his talk there had been discussions among the Confederate officers whether he should be silenced. They differed, but as he was civil, and entertaining, though too radical for their mental digestion, he was not, until then, molested, as it was indeed a novelty to listen to an anti-slavery speech so long excluded from the South that they had never heard one. It was a profound, polished statement of that side—a rare speech indeed in South Carolina. The effect was good and much impressed some citizens and two or three officers.

## WHY REBELS WANT AN ARMISTICE.

Wednesday, September 27th.—Every day I practice exercise. It is with a strain of will, nerve and muscle. It is a debatable question, every morning whether I go over the area of the prison daily, or sit or lie; for it seems easier to burrough up and die than to circulate and live. I never dreamed that will power was so marvelous. It braces up against pain, languor, famine and death which has seemed near. So I go today up in front of the commissary shed. I met a nice young man with a nice, clean book in hand. "Hello, what book have you?" I said. "Bunyan's Riches," he replied. He had been trying to sell it to Rebels but could not; had offered it for $1; wanted something to eat; it had fed the "inner man"; he wanted sweet potatoes for the fellow outside, as rations did ont satisfy. "Take it, read it," he said, telling me where he stopped, and his name, Charles L. Johnson, of the 16th Connecticut. After an agreeable talk I hobbled back under the oak to read. Another "love at first sight," I thought. Fatherly Dan Tuttle, I knew in New York, used to say he loved some men well enough to marry and some women too well. Perhaps Johnson is one of Dan's men. I like him; if a man is to be known by company he keeps why should I not? I'm reading the book—selection from John Bunyan's writings. He has been called a prose-Shakespeare. I have not known people here to buy a book, except some blank, or half-written diary, or a "pack of Jacks" some Yankee didn't heave away in going to battle. It is a superstition of soldiers that it would not be well with them to go to battle with cards on them. If killed, it would be evidence of sin unrepented; so they fling them pell-mell when trouble is ahead. But when again settled in camp they beg passes and tramp miles to find a sutler where they can be bought at four ordinary prices, and play all day and after tattoo for stakes, often pledging their next pay. That is a way they have of keeping a clean record to go before the Great Judge.

Evidently two of Bunyan's pilgrims struck a place that in unpleasantness resembled characteristics of Rebel prisons, when they fell into the hands of Giant Despair who held them for trespass, and "put them in his castle, into a very dark dungeon, nasty and stinking to the spirits of these two men," where "they lay from Wednesday morning until Saturday night, without one bit of bread or drop of drink" and were "in evil case * * * far from friends and acquaintance." So are we guilty of trespass, have had a long sniff of a "nasty, stinking" place, have fasted longer than did Christian and Hope who were the wards of Giant Despair whose savage propensities were no more brutal than those of our keepers, and we, too, are far from home and "in evil case."

The man who has immediate charge of prisoners has been disgustingly in evidence for three days. He seems a cross between an idiot and a lunatic. His name is Barrett. Before his name was learned prisoners dubbed him "Red Head," his hair being the color of red sand and coarse as horse tail. He is a lieutenant in the 5th Georgia that served as guard at Andersonville until in the summer. 'Twas there Gen. J. H. Winder learned his bad qualities. Now that about half of the prisoners that were at that place are here, he has detailed him for jailor. The first thing he did was to show his disorderly temper. He is said to be as mean as Wirz. If he knows more, his talent will be used to exasperate his meanness. These traits are commendable in the concepts of Winder. No decent fellow need apply as long as men like Wirz and Barrett can be detailed. Both are cowards at the front; in camp, a Rebel soldier told me, Barrett is hated. He is one of those composits that "to be hated needs but to be seen," for when seen devilishness is manifest. He had not been in charge a day before he ordered up several detachments, one after another, and damned them vehemently with a flourish of his revolver for no conceivable reason. His savage antics are outrageous. He has no gentlemanly qualities like the first officer in charge. Winder is in general charge of Federal prisoners east of the Mississippi; is a base man and means our ruin.

It is not what men outwardly have or want that constitutes their peace or misery, spiritually considered. There are some here who understand it that way. Exposure, nakedness, hunger, abuse and distress of every sort, death itself can be endured when the thought is right and the heart is strong for truth. It is the feeling that injustice is purposely being done us; that perhaps our own government may be ignorant, negligent, thoughtless, or indifferent to the terrible situation into which thousands of good and brave men have been thrown, and leaves them to wicked persecution designed to gratify a low and brutal vengeance because the usages, traditions and opinions of the masters of the South are disregarded by the national administration, the people and the army behind it. Really it is for this we suffer; this is the cause of this dreadful conflict. The prisoners of war are suffering most directly, forcefully, bitterly, revengefully, the savageness of the motive that incited this war. Who can repay?

There are noble men here nerved to the higher standard of human existence, who try to conform living to ideal life; to connect present existence under adverse conditions, to that ideal existence congenial to conditions of equity, justice, love, peace, noble enjoyment, higher unfoldment of spiritual natures, typified by the aims and acts of Jesus as I think they were intended and should be understood. There is not in Nature, or in the plans, or laws of Divinity, a higher ordinance for the soul's salvation from its innate weakness, sinful tendencies and defects, and from unholy environments. Noble virtues! Indeed it is these sublime qualities in the characters of Christly men and women, and he who is worshipped as the Christ, that distinguish them from the sordid, blind, suspicious, superstitious bigots and their blind followers.

I have an Augusta paper, of a Charleston man, which has an article headed, "Armistice." The writer asks the people, and government of the South, why they should not be in favor of an armistice. He adverts to the Chicago resolves in favor of a "cessation of hostilities, that peace may be restored." He says that is what the South wants, and has wanted; but "Lincoln's low cunning" has avoided it. He says now is the grand turning point of the fortunes of the South; nothing can contribute so much to success as an armistice; therefore, the elections North are of momentous interest. If McClellan is elected an armistice can be secured; but if Lincoln is elected, he will push every advantage, and the disasters that will follow cannot be foreseen. An armistice will give them a respite; will be worth 200,000 men and millions of money; will give them credit and influence abroad, and consequent recognition. It would gain the respect of that undecided class of people North, and sever the power of the administration. He defines the nature of an armistice; refers to Wheaton's "International Law," showing it amounts to a temporary peace, but leaves the controversy undecided; that they might do what they could do in time of peace, and is virtually a recognition during the time of the armistice. They may re-enforce their armies, collect provisions, munitions of war, repair vessels and forts, and their ports would be open to the world. Therefore the election of McClellan would be hailed with joy by every Southern man and every friend of the South. But again it should be recollected that McClellan has in his "Letter of Acceptance" declared in favor of the Union, even at the expense of war, should negotiations fail to restore it. But after a few months of peace, the country settled into quietude, the people of the North could not again be aroused to prosecute a war hitherto so disastrous, and now rendered fruitless by their own consent. Or, if they could, they would fight against advantages never before experienced, and without hope, "Lincoln knows that," says he, "but let it be constantly borne in mind that whatever project is favored, whichever party of the North triumphs, the sole project of the South is independence. The war originated for that, and as long as there is a drop of blood to be shed, or a dollar to be spent, it shall be waged for independence."

O, that the people of the North might read these lines and understand the cunningness of the scheme. This may seem right unto men, but the end thereof is death. Talk about peace and union by buying out traitors; chaffering with disloyalty! Demolish every foundation on which their hell-born cause is erected! The people of the North have been long enough deceived. Would to God they might not deceive themselves! The wily spirit of despotism that has pestered and blackened every age now seeks to wind his coils about us. Some are cowed, some are indifferent. But the common sense of the people can defeat these wily schemers. Put your heels upon this copperhead, O, men of the North, and the sunset of this new intrigue is at hand, and the dawn of an invaluable peace is at your door.

Tuesday, September 28th.—A few nights since Boodger, Fred. Clifton and four others, with myself, had planned an escape, having maps marked for East Tennessee, nearer points, such as Washington and Newbern, N. C., having been tried and found unattainable, most every man having been found and picked up. Our plan was to run the guard, risking their firing, and to meet about two miles north, near the Cheraw Railroad. While watching at different points after dark, of a sudden fires were lighted, encircling the entire camp, and a second line of guard was put out beyond, the fire lighting intervening space. The guard has become more vigilant and rigorous, and it is almost certain death to attempt, for the fires are still kept up, and guards have learned to shoot. Serious times indeed. Starvation and numberless other ills stare us in the face. It is too charitable to say they do all for us they can. They do not care if we do suffer. I remarked to a captain today that if we did not have more food men would all die. He said "there are plenty of rations." Not one mouthful have we had today. Tonight there is talk of breaking out. They swear they will die by the bullet before they will starve. Notwithstanding two guard lines, soon after dark they began running; guards began firing; several are wounded, one dead. For fear the guard would be overpowered, the quartermaster notified us that the camp should have good rations as soon as light in the morning.

Wednesday, September 29th.—Meal issued early; mush for breakfast, little past noon we get a piece of sweet potato, rice and molasses. Inducements are offered to take the oath of allegiance. It is said that hundreds have given their names today. Many are desponding, are being starved to take the oath or enlist. God only knows what our fate will be. We are being murdered by inches.

Thursday, September 30th.—Long, wearisome nights; fruitless thoughts fill my mind; I cannot sleep. Heavy dews wet us. Nothing to eat till afternoon. We get a gill each of meal, beans and rice, and a bit of beef; we are so hungry that we eat the beef raw. One scant meal today; we wait its like tomorrow. Rebels think it charitable to give us what they do. O, if there was ever despotism on earth—and destpotism is the meanest, cruelest spirit that ever tortured and crushed mankind, then this military system of the South is despotism in a rage.

Would it ever have occurred to me that fellow-men could look upon such suffering with so little compassion? They look upon these scenes of daily death, and horrible exhibitions of woe, and awful degredation, as a legitimate means justified by the end sought.

We are forced to look on these things ourselves as we had learned to consider common occurrences of life. If men die, it is nothing, nothing to see men dying and laying about our miserable camp eight hours after dead. I have felt a relief when I have seen some disgusting objects borne away, lifeless human wrecks who have suffered long. Others express the same thing. Old tent-mates die; comrades who have toiled for their welfare seem half satisfied when it is over, too conformed to circumstances to give up to broken affection, setting themselves in order as if a new era in prison existence were to begin. Yet there is a faintness of spirit, a sinking of the heart attending this peculiar sternness of our nature. It is a strong, brave spirit, if the heart is not dead to pity, that can keep off "Giant Despair." Hunger, cold and disease welcome ever the vulture death to our bodies. What a grateful providence it is that enables the mind to look upon death with philosophic complacency; to care so little about that we cannot remedy, which otherwise would intensify our woes.

> I know my body is both sick and frail,
> And yet I hope, am often sweetly sure,
> These weakening ills, that do it ail,

It will withstand and happily endure.

I feel my soul has power over ills
That are depressing to my feeble breath,
If I conceive the spiritual law that fills
And lifts my being o'er the law of death.

For I am young, I have not reached an age
When mortal vigor has the line attained
Where the human spirit quits the mortal stage
And has the lesson of its earth life gained.

And yet I know, if mortal threads do break,
My soul, myself, will soar in light away,
As at early morn we from painful sleep awake
To see the glory of another day.

And all true joy which to my nature clings,
Shall clothe my spirit on the better shore;
And all life's sorrows shall be vanished things
That I shall feel, that I shall know no more.

For all the glooms that o'er my spirit float
And fade like clouds, that darken oft the sky,
When sun grows bright and sends his rays remote,
And I know 'twill warm me as it goes more high.

### UNCLE ABE'S ENEMY AT HOME.

Sufficient greenbacks would buy potatoes which seem to be plentiful, but none are given us though other rations are scant and poor. They allow $5 "Confed" for $1 of our money. Men who have most money have preference among traders. If he buys a bushel or two he retails them at great profit to those who have less money. So it is here, as in other conditions in life; "big fish eat little ones," monopolize until everything comes to a standstill.

Jeff Davis is reported as saying recently that his army is badly reduced; that to get his soldiers held as prisoners it may become necessary to recognize "Beast Butler" as an agent, and his claims for the negro. Men are trading clothing for something to eat. I have offered my boots, today; also gloves Griffith has. It is against orders to trade with guards; we have to work sly, changing in the night. They cannot be depended on, so we have slipped up in several agreements, and go hungry.

Saturday, October 1st.—Late in the afternoon we draw rations, and see what the outcry of yesterday about "government rations" amounts to. A few barrels of hard-tack arrived, one hard-tack which we can devour in one minute, with three spoonfuls of meal and five of molasses, are given each man to stop present hunger and stay us for twenty-four hours at least. Leaving with C. L. Johnson his book, I learned his home is in Hartford, Conn. I had a fine time with him. He was taken at Plymouth, N. C. Reported tonight that the sick are to be sent to Charleston for exchange. It comes from Rebels. It is near dark; is raining; signs of a bad night. It is wonderful how patiently men stand or walk with folded hands during a drenching rain.

Sunday, October 2nd.—Foggy and chilly this morning; an uncomfortable night though the rain ceased before morning. About 1,500 men from Charleston arrive. About 9 a. m., orders came to break camp. A cavalry guard appeared. We knew we were to go into the stockade negroes had been building. Binding up a little wood we had, and taking our cooking utensils, we moved by detachments, a mile over an old field grown to weeds and grass, and in sight of a cultivated plantation and houses belonging, I understand, to a Dr. Garrett, a noted planter. On the way men seized rails and sticks, hoping to be allowed to carry them into that hopeless den for shelter. But ere we reached the gate the order came to throw down every stick; guards with bayonets enforced the order. The column was now confused and huddled, so I attempted to smuggle a small rail by attaching it to a strong cord I picked up, dragging it through the grass, not noticing the call to "throw that rail down, sar! Leave the rail, you'ns thar!" till Thompson from behind cried: "North, North! drop it, drop it!" Turning I saw a bayonet close to my skirts, drawing nearer rapidly. I was forcibly impressed that "that had played out," and did "leave go" the rail, and changed my place in the ranks, soon reaching the head of the column. It was remarked that it was no more than fair that we have those rails, as Abe can split more. It is a back place; the walls of the prison are rough, built of trees grown on the enclosure, all of which are used except brush and waste pieces, which are scattered mostly in the swamp, those on dry ground having been removed. The swamp is forty to sixty rods wide, black, and covered with prickley vines. A brook, larger than that at Andersonville, runs through it, which is to supply water which cannot be obtained without going half knee deep in mud. The stockade contains twenty acres. Instead of sentry boxes there is an embankment outside nearly as high as the wall which the negroes are now finishing. The sentry is to walk this, looking down upon us within. Griff. and Glover are sick. I have been trying to get brush and stuff together for quarters; but being hungry and weak, I could go but a rod with a small load without sitting down; have eaten nothing since one half meal yesterday. Johnson, of our company, was among the Charleston men; is destitute of blanket, almost of clothing; stops with us. At dark we drew nearly a pint of meal, two spoonfuls of flour, three of salt, each. After debate how our stuff should be cooked to fill up most, we decided on boiling it for supper, leaving one ration of meal and eight spoonfuls of flour for morning.

Monday, October 3rd.—Cold, dreary rain, wetting to our skins. Rations after dark, and less by half than those of last night. Last night I heard preaching several rods east. In making my way I stumbled in the darkness over what I was impressed was a grave, falling directly across another. This morning I go there. I find several graves, mostly new. Three old ones are small. There are no names, the only indices being the mound; and sticks at head and foot. Several beautiful pines are left standing near. Probably it was a negro burial ground, as negroes (slaves) go into back lonely places in the woods to bury their dead. Edmund Kirke mentions an instance where he attended one of their funerals at night in this State, among the slaves of Col. J.

Negroes are busily packing dirt against the wall. Their curious songs are heard at intervals, night and day. There is something too peculiar in these people, uncouth bondmen as they are, not to excite curiosity and serious thought—an idiosyncrasy, a cult, we almost admire, seldom known to our race—a rude, simple, plain, unmistakable, intuitive sense of something which is, but is not seen—a superstition or a presentiment by the spiritual through the rough exterior. The idiom of their songs, simple, rude, so little in form of language, yet sentimental, strangely, darkly romantic, shadowing the rude, fragmentary traditions of a race, whose history is dark and distant, yet mingling the spirit of the far fatherland and of their far ancestry with their existence now, and the vague, spiritual image of Freedom in gestation glimpsed at in their obscure idea, which is to shape the higher destiny of the race. Poor, despised race, against whom strong, benighted prejudice raves,—sensuous, unnatural, hypocritical hatred! Everything wrong with conservative Northerners is laid to "niggers." If Southerners cannot keep them slaves they are devils. What have they done? They are the most innocent people in the country. Patiently they wait the workings of fate, trusting in Providence, fully believing in its rightful dispensation.

On each corner of the stockade is planted a cannon. Col. Harrison, late from Charleston, was standing by one of these guns today, making us fair promises and kindly answering questions about corresponding with friends. One of our men came up, whom we thought green, or who had forgotton where he was and who he was talking to, said:

"Colonel, does a letter need a Reb stamp on, to go through?"

"A what stamp? Reb!. Young man, you call me a Rebel? What do you mean by Reb?"

"A Rebel stamp,—one of your stamps," replied the man.

"You call me a Reb, you puppy! Young man, I do not stand here to be insulted. I'll learn you all not to call the South Rebels! I will fix you."

Our voices all rose to apologize for the indiscreet act. The Colonel turned, and his agitation having somewhat subsided, said in an earnest way:

"We are not Rebels, we will have you to understand. The people of the South are honorable, besides I claim to be a gentleman, myself, and I am not a Rebel; neither will I suffer such epithets to be used in relation to my people. I exact from all of you proper respect. If I ever hear another man use such language I will take him out and teach him what I can do. I will show him a Rebel in a way he never thought of, by Heavens!"

"Well, I suppose I ought to have said your stamps, or Confed stamps," replied the man.

"Our Government is the Confederate Government. No, I reckon you don't need a Confederate stamp," said the Colonel.

The trite maxim that truth should not be spoken at all times may come under this head, but I "reckon" the Colonel don't like the stamp by the way he squirmed, though he may the act that made "honorable" Southerners the most consumate as well as the most contumacious rebels, and for reasons the Colonel himself cannot define any better than that fat engineer.

Tuesday, October 4th, 1864.—Wrote to A. W. Francis, 117th N. Y., hoping it will find him on Morris Island, S. C. Col. G. P. Harrison, commanding Florence military post, promises fair about letters, boxes, etc., and says anything that our government will send under flag of truce shall be delivered to us. So we are encouraged to send. But that men be turned into a place where nearly one-third of the ground is so swampy that cattle would mire in any part of it, without furnishing the least shelter, and many are without blankets or tents, shoes or socks, and but rags of pants and shirts, perhaps no shirts, and perhaps neither, is in perfect accord with a wicked cause. David never besought God more fervently to "destroy mine enemy" than do we! Stupid and inured to misery as we are, we have not forgotten the iniquity of their ways, and though they wheedle, they have not forsaken their besetting sin. May God destroy them from the face of the earth, or may they turn and live! Northern communities would no more suffer such abuse, such barbarity, to exist under our authorities than they would allow thieves, barnburners, murderers, to go at liberty, and tolerate them in society. But I am now a thousand times convinced that true, full manhood, love of liberty and civilization cannot exist on the soil of slavery. Its perpetuation is the chief object of rebellion. It is the summum bonum of the land policy within its sway; therefore law and every interest spring from it and partake of its nature, as liberal laws spring from liberal interests. Oppression in every form existed prior to civilization. Slave codes are the threatening armor of savageism, to shield the devil from the preaching of saints. The franchises of freemen are monopolized by slave masters and slave breeders who deal out barbarism and oppression in stifling doses to the slaveless ruled. Still they complain as the wolf in the fable complained of the lamb he wished to devour. Still they croak of honor—"the honor of the South"! A stench in the age of progress! A rotten carcass in the way of civilization! A snake in the grass! A girdle around the tree of liberty! A counterfeit quality that disgraces the name of honor! Their whole moral nature is corrupted to the core on this question of slavery. The people are selfish in what they call patriotism; proud of their vanity; haughty to the verge of desperation; emotional beyond reason; deceitful and treacherous; chivalrous unto despotism; vain in what they term the "honor of the South"; glory in the display of the chevalier transmitted from feudal times, to which the stable folk of the South aspire rather than to broader liberty and general progress. Deplorable infatuation! To lean on them in deciding this great crisis is to rest in the coils of a serpent, and to die by its sting.

The swamp is said to be filled with snakes. I saw a large rattlesnake, dead, killed by negroes. These in the swamp and stream are called moccasins. Two men were bitten yesterday by these while in the water washing, and have died. I saw these men; they were bitten in the heel. Several of the snakes have been killed. The sick outside are washing in the stream above. A gang of negroes are working in the swamp; mule teams are passing back and forth, keeping the water constantly black with mud. We are forced to drink it. Three men have been shot within two days, near the north part of the stockade, where we get water.

I askd a guard yesterday if it is necessary to stint us on rations. He answered: "I don't know; I reckon 'tis; we'ns don't get a fo'th part we want; we buy of the people. It's mighty tough on yo'ns fellers; so it is on we'ns; we'ns have to do duty."

A man shot this morning for speaking to the sentry. They say such are the orders now. We have to find all these things out at our peril. They make known to us no regulation that is to control the guard in his connection with us.

Rebel recruiting officers haunt us daily. Several squads have gone out, from 200 to 400 men, and have taken the oath of treason. They are to be put in garrison. It creates great excitement. Parties going out are attacked and stripped of their equipage, such as blankets and cook dishes, if any they have. I have known men to call at the Rebel officers at the gate saying, "When can you take us out? I have starved long enough." Such men are weaker in mind that body, frailties common to this erring world. But as great an incongruity as I have seen is Ireland-born Irishmen packing out to do homage to the New Kingdom of Slavedom, pleasing Rebels by cursing negroes. Irishmen who fled from Ireland, their native land, to gain liberty, blarneying for slavery! Slavery for a race brutally stolen from fatherland, sold like beasts for all time! Honest, intelligent Irishmen should have a more consistent idea of liberty! But "naggers" are black. Indeed! Should the African, whose ancestor was kidnapped, be enslaved for his color any more than the Irishman for his brogue?

Spent several hours with Boodger reading Grimshaw's history of the United States. He touched on events in the sixteenth century, showing how they tend to effect the present; of the sentiments of Oglethorpe, one of the first settlers of Georgia, who was so strongly opposed to African slavery, and by his influence it was ruled out until by the act of the mother country the American feeling was overwhelmed. colonial laws disregarded, and the importation of negroes from Africa became general. Slavery became an institution, and laws relating thereto were enacted. At last slavery seeks to control all laws. It is a truthful charge that the crown is guilty of the entailment of this evil, and of scattering the seeds of despotism on our soil.

Heavy night dews and cold fogs rise from the swamps and rivers on all sides.

Wednesday, October 5th.—Camp organized; laid out in squares, streets passing at right angles, as near as may be from the nature of the ground. Men are put in thousands, as 1st, 2d, 3d, etc. We have been on the tilt nearly all day. I am exhausted. It is now dark; we have had two roll calls, no rations; we are extremely weak and faint. O, something to eat, is the all-absorbing thought. Were we only strong we could labor with the hope of a shelter ere long. Heavy rain clouds hang over us. Met friends John and Sergeant Lee of Hartford. We have known Lee since last summer; a better type of man than we meet everywhere; an earnest defender of our cause, and wavers not at his hard lot. Exchange rumors again—about as good as rations.

Thursday, October 6th.—At dark the rain began to pour heavily, continuing all night. Four of us hover under the old blanket—a poor shield, every shread on us is soaked. The ground is flooded. Not a fire can be kept, though some have wood picked up. How many nights like this must we pass? Cloudy, dreary day. Began work on proposed quarters. Dig two feet into the earth, using sticks, and our half canteens for spades. Intend to cover the hole with brush and sticks, and with mud from the swamp. We dig it out with our hands, making it into balls; bring it up on hods made of brush. Hundreds of men are busily at work all along the banks of the stream. It reminds one of beavers working at their dam. It is by greatest effort we do this; we are both sick and hungry. Awful languor is more and more heavily upon us. Dreary, stormy autumn is upon us; chills of approaching winter are before. We are further north than we were through the summer we must work while our little strength lasts, with hope, well nigh forlorn, to preserve our feeble lives. Daily men die around us, whose lives were as dear, whose hopes were as strong as ours. After consultation I write home for provision and articles of clothing; the letter has gone out. For all we are told it will be delivered we think the chance of receiving it against us. We have not received a word from friends; I think my letters were detained.

Friday, October 7th.—Harsh north wind, chills my thin blood. As feared, we have not brush enough. Everything is faulty about our dirt house. Brush and sticks are closely picked up; stumps are being uprooted for wood; we will try to patch it up. Last night we drew nearly a pint of flour each—nothing else. It made us the best supper and breakfast in a long time. We made it into dough, boiled it. The Colonel is permitting wells to be dug; furnishes a few spades and old axes. Time never wore so heavily. As night comes it grows colder; air damp and chilly. Shirtless, shoeless young men, whom many a Northern lass would like for a beau, come shivering around the splinter fires built for cooking, and ask, "Partner, what are we going to do tonight?" "Do you hear anything about exchange?" Some say: "It is take the oath or die." Others say, "Never! Die a thousand times; never support the bastard concern!"

Sunday, October 9th.—Last night extremely cold for time of year. Lodged uncomfortably in our unfinished hut, suffering with cold; today sickness at the stomach. About four hour's sun. More going out to cling to the slave mother, because she yields so litle milk! Inglorious alma mater! How sweet their rest upon her ravished bosom! One thousand five hundred Andersonville prisoners via Charleston, arrive.

Monday, October 10th.—Weather pleasant. Men going out attacked; blankets taken. Rebel soldiers deployed through camp to protect them. Those I have talked with say they hope soon to escape. Generally they are as strong men as there are here, the starved and sickly being rejected, their physical abilities being examined by surgeons.

Thursday, October 13th.—Nights cold; yesterday we got no rations; today we get a pint of meal and three spoons of molasses.

Friday, October 14th.—Nothing to eat from 2 p. m., yesterday, till night today. We get hominy; they term it grits. A man named Armstrong, from Charleston, is commissioned to sell stuff; he is up today. Lieut. Col. Iverson has issued an order, subjoining a schedule of prices, which are to be adhered to by parties trading. Sweet or Irish potatoes $20 per bushel; other things in proportion. Great activity by Rebels in recruiting; perhaps 100 go out daily to whom the soubriquet of "galvanized Rebels" is attached. This is not a pleasing name to those who divest themselves of blue rags and don Rebel butternut. If they appear after the act, "Ho, Reb!", "Galvanized Yank!", or "Reb!" greet them. It appears to me they who go are "rough-scuffs," simple, weak in spirit.

Saturday, October 15th.—Nearly one pint of grits and a half pint of peas, and we are told: "No more rations till Monday."

Sunday, October 16th.—Griffith gets an ax; we hew wood from stump roots. I am unable to use the ax. No rations; very hungry at night.

Monday, October 17th.—No rations; badly reduced by hunger and sickness; diarrhoea is painful.

Tuesday, October 18th.—Get grits this morning for breakfast; eat raw, no wood. Rain, cold, foggy night. Complaint is made of hunger through Sergeant Kemp, 1st Connecticut Cavalry, who is on parole at the commissary; Colonel orders an "extra issue." It must certainly be a matter of surprise to Col. Harrison that we are hungry today, for we had a bite last Saturday. We get beef, three ounces, and some rice at night.

Wednesday, October 19th.—Feeling exists that lobbyists whose principals center at New York, are as unpatriotic as the venomest opponents of the administration in or out of our lines. From the hour war was imminent, they conspired to control finances, embarrass business, corner specie, hamper government and force the legalizing of schemes for their own enrichment, blocking currency plans independent of Wall Street, and secured unjust advantage over the people through government in financing the war. They first stripped the country of coin and bullion and hid it; suspended specie payment for bank notes issued under State laws and refused loans to government and people. The treasury had been bankrupted by Rebels under Buchanan, and the financiers had deprived the country of all money. Having largely viciated the government plans which it was compelled to consider, for a currency based on national credit rather than on the pretenses of money hangers, they forced legislation that enabled them to put a price on coin, creating demands for it in payment of interest on a public debt to be created, and for custom dues of imported merchantise largely enhanced by war, thus forcing importers to buy their hoarded coin at premium rates entirely determined by its holders. It now stands at nearly three times par. This caused depreciation of currency government was obliged to emit for business and for war purposes, to the extent of coin premiums, and equally the price of bonds in coin, dealers in coin creating the exigencies incident to this policy and the expediencies of war, for their issue. The law also gives coin speculators opportunity to buy the bonds with greenbacks at their face, giving them the advantage of enormous prices for coin and bullion and extortionate discount on bonds. For instance: they sell $1,000 in coin for $3,000 of currency, they buy $3,000 worth of government bonds with it, a discount on government credit of two-thirds of the dollar. The country bears the legitimate cost of war, also this threefold burden imposed to buy the loyalty of money and credit sharks in a time of national stress. They are now reaping a harvest of unholy plots. First they were "dogs in the manger" threatening ruin to the country. Since they coerced the adoption of their plots, they are devouring lions. It is plain how their course has prolonged the war by crippling our resources until they could impose "burdens grievous to be borne," stimulating copperheadism and encouraging treason to persevere. Delay meant millions in the pockets of money sharks; millions out of the toil and valor of the people. Generations must pass before the country can be extricated from these meshes of Shylock. Every hour they are extracting blood; every hour carving flesh! O, baseness of unbridled greed! Ere graves of thousands of boys shall be green, these pretending tricksters will bribe newspapers, prostitute orators, debauch courts and elect congresses and presidents to brace up government evidence of debt they forced and have usurped, after treacherously debasing it, during every hour of bloody struggle. The injustice and cruelty of such selfishness has no counterpart. The men hanged at Andersonville for the murder and robbery of fellow prisoners, were innocents compared with these, and they were justly executed. The group described by Milton—"Devils with devils damned firm concord hold"—can take a back seat!

When peace shall have been restored these demons of finance will take a new turn at their infernal levers. There will come a reaction from this swell of forced inflation of commodity prices, an appreciation of public credit they so meanly traduced and so meanly possess, that will shatter private credit and business and flood industrial centers with people forced from honest pursuits and made needy and idle. Mortgaged farms and their products will drop to "hard pan," the owners bankrupted, to bring to premium, at least to par, bonds and currency debased and monopolized to further enrich the few. These two conditions, brought about by financial jugglery, make this result inevitable. They will shut together like a vise and pinch all except workers of the iniquity. They rob the nation during its peril by discrediting its credit. They will rob it again when legitimate business and labor shall lift its credit from the pit into which they mercilessly plunged it, by bankrupting millions in their private vocations.

Thursday, October 20th.—Days pleasant; nights cold. Disagreeable tentmates; lousy partners; P. G. and Corp. Jim J. do not try to kill their acres of lice; they are demoralized, half devoid of sense. They have no excuse for clothing but coat and pants apiece, split from bottom almost to top, and lying on the bare ground, their flesh has become dirtier than hogs. My God! Who ever saw an ape that was once a man? Some men make fine apes. We have been using "disrespectful language" toward the Corporal. He don't take it to heart, and "dig out"—he digs though. Griff. and I half resolve to leave or eject them. But what shall we do? They claim a share in the hole; none of us can dig another. I believe this is lousier than Egypt, when Aaron stretched out his rod and smote the dust, and all the land became lice. This is triublation indeed. We passed a cold, sleepless, painful night. Rations more liberal, but not liberal. Sanitary goods from the dear folks at home have been here several days. Yesterday blankets were issued, about five to one hundred men. Names of the worst cases taken; blanks and prize tickets were placed in a hat, from which we drew. Five chances in a hundred! Fortune gave me and my lousy partners the biggest chance—a blank. I saw the sentry on post this morning with a blanket on in lieu of an overcoat. U. S. hats are often seen on Rebel heads. Lieut. Barrett, 5th Georgia, having immediate charge of prisoners, sports a sanitary hat on his red pate. He had better thank our Yankee ladies. I would like to lead him into their presence by a rope around his neck. The "red-headed Lieutenant"—"miserable cuss," he is called. He is the scum of Georgia. One of the most despicable, insignificant, fire-weed characters; phosphroic, ill-tempered, hell-infused images of man that ever served a worthless, wicked cause! He will stand at the gate for hours with a revolver in hand, occasionally pointing and snapping it, swearing piratically, calling them "dirty sons of b—s," "lousy hell devils," laughing fiendishly. He often snatches clubs and throws them with all vengeance into crowds of prisoners who come to look at the brute fool, attracted by his loud oaths. He will then call them to come back, not to be afraid; and again jump at them like a mad gander, flourishing sword and pistol. The demon coward!

He is meaner than Wirz, but can't carry it out so logically with a tyrant's grace. Don't know as much—low, shameless, drunk with a little brief authority. Wirz did not care so much to look on the ruin he wrought, the misery he caused, but knew his plans. "Red-head" likes to invite the ladies and go up with them and look down from the wall and hoity toity and simper and giggle, ordering us, fustian style, to do some insignificant thing. At some furtive remark, like "Where did you get your hat," he will go into a spasmodic rage—cold water on a griddle! Presenting his revolver, cocked, with assumed dignity will say:

"Who said that? I dare the son of a b—h, the d—d Yankee, to say that again!"

We suspect this is buncombe, for the high-bred, gay ladies he has the honor to address. They sometimes immodestly laugh at his undignified behavior. Some seem to think it cunning, and tee hee, titter to please. I have noticed some who looked astonished at him, half wishing, I believe, he would fall over the wall. Do Wirz and Barrett embody Southern chivalry? Fit subaltern tools of Davis and several of the bigger devils, to attend to the details of their political pandemonium!

## ON BARRETT.

Barrett: He bears a name as if a man!
Strange if such a thing a man could be!
Beast: I know no beast as mean as he!
Reptile: No viler serpents ever ran!
Viper: None fouler befoul yon sea!
Fool: None so big a fool as he!
Barrett, keeper of this prison pen,
Parades these starved, near naked men
Before women invited as his guests;
Curses and fires in their ranks,
Bestows on them insults and pests,
Venomously shows his apish pranks,
All for torment, naught to please;
Adds insults to their miseries.

Real love for woman much protests
That such a brute should on them fawn,
That to such presence they be drawn
To see men cringe to vile behests;
To hear him swear and act the knave
And like a demon laugh and rave
As though it did these guests amuse
To see an imp us Yanks abuse.
Thank God, the soul of womanhood
A worthless cause can never crush!

Her virtue has these wrongs withstood;
Her scorn revealed, by frown and blush.
But Barrett does not sense or heed
They see but vileness in his deed.

## DAVIS AND WINDER—THEIR WORK.

Sergeant Bourn, Massachusetts, genealogizes Winder, who presides over our pernicious keepers with malicious grace. The gist of it is that his ancestry had the virus of despotism in their blood. His character is rooted in Toryism; his aspiration is warmed by animosity to popular government. Like most Southern leaders who are labeled Democrats, and stole the name to serve the opposite, he is an aristocrat with the instincts of a pirate. He is of the vicious stuff left over from ages of despotism. Our era is sadly burdened with much of that rubbish. It is the fuel of this war. The appointment of John H. Winder by Jeff Davis as commissary general of prisoners has in it more villainy than is imagined. Davis knew him; Davis is Winder's confidant; Winder is his. They are chips from one root. Had Davis wanted a proper man, Winder would not have been in it. His unpopularity with the mass of Southrons who know him, condemned him for any place. Davis is his affinity. He loves his low meanness because it reflects his own. Davis' meanness is his chief characteristic. It is so big he wants this fellow to help him carry it. He is doing it to Davis' notion. Richmond had its fill of Winder as provost general. It howled. Davis saw this place and handed it out. Richmond yelled: " Thank God, we are rid of old Winder, but God have pity on Yanks who come under his sway!" Odious even to noses of Rebels, but not to the nose of the chiefest Rebel. Davis was happier than they, for he had Winder's pledge that he would be "old pizen" to Yankees in "durance vile," as his imp Barrett delights in saying to us of himself. Davis enthroned him to rule over these later prison hells he devised which are worse than the first. He resolved last fall that these prisons should become deadly engines of war, to help fight the battles of the South. Devilish as he is, he is the fit tool of that arch conspirator, Davis. He is pledged to a work of murder. Had it been an honest job, his pledge would never be kept. He is keeping his pledge. Davis saw no humane traits in Winder toward Yankee prisoners. Davis was farther seeing in that conclusion than in any other public act that distinguishes him. His Confederacy will fail. Winder has not failed to murder thousands. That was the covert aim of Davis as a means to success. Just, considerate men were ineligible. Wirz was for Andersonville, Barrett for Florence. Winder knew them; they pleased his ferocity. Two meaner pieces of fiendishness in human flesh cannot be found except Davis and Winder. They are like them, but not as big; not so brainy as the chief culprits. They have no higher conceptions of their positions than to be brutal, harsh, savage, murderous toward Federals. "Ve's cot chu voul!" said Wirz to us. "I'm ol' pizen to G—d d—n Yankees," says Barrett. Their records prove it. They are written in blood, punctuated with agony, embellished in gloom, embossed by the deaths of over 15,000 in two prisons to date. Nothing just or sensible is found in their prison management. Both are addicted to outrageous fits of insane rage. The fit is generally on in their contact with prisoners. They invent pretexts to starve, abuse and persecute. They are reputed no good at the front; but are notorious for killing more men at the rear than forty brigadiers. That suits Winder, Davis approves. If not he would suppress them. Like Davis, all Winder wants "is to be let alone." Davis lets him alone. What devoted loyalty to the cause of human bondage! What unenviable conspicuity!

Saturday, October 22d.—Got a small piece of soap yesterday, the first I know of being issued. Resolve on a general wash, keeping an eye open for snakes. The water is cold. Several hundred suits, or pieces of suits, of clothing from our lines are being issued. They go about four pieces to the hundred men, no man getting more than one piece, whether it is what he most needs or not. The articles are shirts, drawers, pants and hats. To my knowledge no jackets have been received by men inside; some paroled, outside, the healthiest, warmest dressed, have appropriated, by Rebel permit, entire suits. Fatted on "extra grub" they are sound. This afternoon they have been in and strutted through the streets in sanitary goods, among ragged victims, who behold, envy, and despise. Could they not at least have given their old clothes to the naked and suffering? Thus is the work of benevolence and benefaction turned to the account of pimping struts who like too well to palaver around Jonnies. The wind is cold and swift this afternoon, cutting us to the quick. We have been seeking at the gate an opportunity to go out for wood, but have returned to our hiding places without success, crouching and shivering. Few go out but policemen. This police was first organized for our protection but it now serves a purpose of Rebels and themselves. Nevertheless it has done work which would not have been done by Rebels, and have got extra rations. But it does not harmonize well with good sense to "talk turkey" to please low minded Rebs. It all tends to strengthen these green fellows, already biased and led away, who, swaggering, say: "You'ns good Rebels as we'ns, for we'ns only fighting to keep niggers down, and if yo'ns hate niggers, what yo'ns fight we'ns for?"

Sunday, October 23, 1864.—Crouching all night, in our low,

dark place, suffering with cold and gnawed by vile vermin which increase with cooler weather. Stiffness and weakness makes walking difficult. We are routed out at daylight for roll call. The penalty for not being in line is no rations for the day, for the hundred, sometimes the thousand in which we are. The weather has moderated. It is remarkable how well we hold out. How men not as well off as we are with our dirt hut, and no more, or less clothing, can live, I can hardly see. The dead line here at Florence, is simply a furrow made with a plow about twenty feet from the wall. Our roll call is close up to the line. This morning one of our men lay in the furrow dead, shot by sentry in the night. He was a sick man, and had come out of his quarters for a necessary purpose, being close up to the line, when he was fired on. His friends found him immediately afterward, but dare not move him. This morning a lieutenant came, to whom the facts were told. He replied by excusing the guard, saying "men must not come up to that mark."

Dead men were being brought from all parts of the camp and from the hospital ground in the northwest part of the field, and laid below the gate, side by side, heads to the wall. Forty were already gathered. He was carried thither. We took occasion to notice these men. Not one had shoes, socks or coats. Their faces were thin and yellow, but there was a placid expression of countenance common to all who are "where the wicked cease from troubling and the weary are at rest." No barbarous hand or tyrant's chain can drag them down in misery more. But what a scene for their dear ones at home to look upon! Could the wives, the sisters, the mothers look upon them thus, or the fathers or brothers, their hearts would be struck with horror that we cannot even feel. Wards are being built on hospital ground from poles and lumber, by men on parole. The work is slow. Medical supplies received from Columbia, S. C., from the medical purveyor, are less than half the requisitions of surgeons, Drs. Junius O'Brien, David Flood and Strather being the principal in turn. The doctors of the hospitals report delineating the state of affairs, making suggestions of changes that should and could be made for the better. Here there is some attempt at police regulation in prison; the west part is laid out in streets, the camp kept passably clean. Rations are less in quantity; sometimes better in quality. No shelter is given; we are turned in destitute and enfeebled, and with no hope of aid. The hospital is better organized, but no beds or floors. A short distance from the prison are stacks of old straw and acres of wild grass, which men would have gladly pulled had they permitted. Here, too, we are surrounded with pine forests whose dense evergreen boughs invite us, but do not shelter feeble, shivering bodies from the storms of autumn, fogs and blasts of

# CHRONICLES OF A WAR PRISONER.

cheerless nights. Rations are irregular, and denied us with taunts; they trifle with thousands of hungry men with promises never fulfilled.

The folly of Rebels hoping the election of Lincoln's opponent will shorten the war, or give a turn in their favor, is apparent. Lincoln is president until March. Till then the war will be pushed vigorously. The Rebels cannot hold out longer than spring. It will be so nearly over that even McClellan could not find excuse to seek a "new base." He will not have the chance. Leaders hoped, if Lincoln were defeated, for further grace for slavery, and the saving of a few necks. In the matter of hanging none can be more mercifully disposed than Lincoln. "Malice toward none; charity for all." Culprits Wirz, Winder and Barrett if brought to court for compound murder of war prisoners, may swing. The whole Richmond administration is accessory to their crimes. No one will object to self-exile if they run quick enough.

The charge of treason there is no doubt of proving. Public sentiment will not call for extensive use of hemp. Hundreds deserve it; few are worth the rope. The army is not fighting for such ends. The restoration of the Union for freedom, South and North, is the aim. That we will have. The Rebel finger in the presidential pie is an impertinence. If wise they would end the strife now. They never will get terms more to their liking. If just, they would parole every prisoner regardless of exchange. It would be gain, not loss to them. Every hour they hold us, under the circumstances, is to persist in most horrible murder. Their assumed dignity is abominable.

## HISTORY STUDIES UNDER DIFFICULTIES.

### PRISON DAYS.

Our strength is gone, our hearts are almost broken
And but the ghosts of hope to us remain;
And ghastly eyes and feeble sighs give token,
From man to man, of an unspoken pain.

O, prison days, dark prison days of sorrow,
Bring to us only gloom, and pain, and grief,
Bring no promise of a bright tomorrow,
Of any sign, but death, for our relief!

Dusky forms of men, squalid, shrunk and wasted,
Lie cold within the shadow of the wall;
In early prime life's sweet, strong hope is blasted,
And they are mustered on the death-roll call.

O, prison days, dark prison days of sorrow!
Will ever hunger cease to gnaw with pain?
O, will warmer light beam on us tomorrow,
Or bring one hope athwart this mournful plain?

Thursday, October 27th.—For three days my complaints have been more painful; render me almost unable to walk. It is with loathing that I look on the boiled meal and peas we get every two or three days. It is the most contemptible hotch-potch I can think of. The meal is musty, the hog-pea bitter, half gutted by bugs; besides, it is impossible to cook it sufficiently with our allowance of wood. Often the substance is only soaked or scalded till our breath is gone and the wood, too, it being green. At this juncture our repast is ready. There are those more fortunate for wood, a few who get out by influence of police, a few who have money to buy of men who chop and at night bring in a load; but the majority are equally destitute.

Frank Brace, of Company D, 76th Regiment, comes to lodge with us. He is terribly afflicted with scurvy in the mouth, blood and matter issues, emitting an offensive smell continually. He groans night and day. It is very disagreeable to us, but he has a blanket, which we have not, and he is benefited by coming under our earthy roof. The sky is hazy, gloomy. Indications of lingering rain already begun, a dewy drizzle dampening everything. Who can wonder at the outbursts of passion, words declaring that men are absolved from obligations as soldiers, from men enfeebled by long hunger and exposure, constantly stung by pangs of foul, malignant scurvy, and darker, colder days before us? One thing among us seems absurd. Some say were it not for the oath taken when they mustered into the U. S. service, they would enlist when promised plenty to eat and wear. Not but these men are good, brave soldiers, not but they are patriots worthy the name; but they do not exactly comprehend the purpose of the oath. It is not whether the oath is binding, but is our cause still good?

Is the enemy's still bad? Nevertheless, they love "the old flag" enthusisatically, and deeply hate Rebels. But the technicality of oaths, instead of the deeper sentiment binding all men to the cause of God and Liberty, next to hunger and manifold sufferings, seems to stand foremost in mental debate. We are not, in the abstract, serving our government. We wish to preserve it that it may be a blessing in the future greater than in the past. Grant that it has erred in certain details; we can never put on the Rebel gray and fight under a Rebel flag, till Rebels are loyalists and loyalists are Rebels. Among us are those who never took a soldier's oath in form. But that is no excuse. As citizens our duty is the same. It were far better to renounce a lie though we had sworn it and adopt the truth; but the man in blue who absolutely detests the Union cause I have not seen. Nothing could more embitter us against the Southern cause than our sojourn here. These remarks are elicited by a conversation heard this afternoon.

Monday, October 31st.—Weather warm through the day. My health is improved, but I cannot eat the rations, mouth so sore, and my stomach and bowels are so weak. The 28th I exchanged eighteen steel pens at $3 per dozen, for sweet potatoes and nearly a quart of rice, with a Rebel soldier. I am scantily subsisting on these. I keep them very choice; feel that in them is my earthly hope.

Occasionally, soldiers with officers come in to trade some sort of coarse provisions for watches, rings, buttons, etc., officers paying money—$30 and $50 for $2.50 to $5 rings, and from $80 to $130 for common watches—an article scarce now. Staff and New York State buttons are worth $10. An officer was in recently to purchase a button like some he wore on his gray coat. Not finding a full set with the one of whom he bought, he stood in the crowd eagerly inquiring for more, when a shrewd fellow stepped slyly behind and cropped the four that adorned his lordly skirts, which happened to be the number lacking, and soon appeared in front and compared them with the others. They were exactly the thing; he soon had his money and was gone. Another recently "got shut" of his watch and chain. A soldier agreed to give me four quarts of rice for steel pens, but by a trick he got my pens, and refused to give it, saying he "must get a ring with that sho'."

We have a watch fixer, a shoe cobbler, a tinner. The first two are patronized by Rebel officers. The tinner makes cook pans and pails out of old tin and copper, ripped from old car bottoms, without solder. There are small eating stands on two streets, which Lieut. Barrett in some of his freaks kicks over, and which are sometimes raided by famishing men. So we have the genius and the indomitable will to rear a Yankee kingdom, had we material. All around are dense woods. A few hours liberty on parole, would enable us to construct comfortable quarters from pine boughs. Though we can see and think, we cannot touch. Special exchange of 10,000 has been rumored. An officer inside says it is not so, and says we had better improve chances to enlist, as old Sherman had cut off supplies from Georgia, and we shall be "right short on't 'fore a week." He also said we are to remove to another "bull-pen."

Looking at Grimshaw's History today, I noticed this passage on Benedict Arnold:

"Oppression, extortion, and misapplication of public money, furnished him with the means to gratify his ruling passion; treachery and ingratitude afforded the only hope of evading, secreting, and replenishing his exhausted coffers." In this is a lesson to those entrusted with the people's affairs. His imprudence and folly drove him to guilt and madness, and to betray his cause. If the heart is pure, the passions well reined, wisdom flows smoothly in public councils; if not, it is turned to a turbid stream, till its foundation seems dried. True wants can never lead to crime. Excess, extravagance, debauchery, licentiousness, incite moral disease that infect the most gifted minds, blacken the brightest fame, and ruin peace. Though rulers are blessed with intelligence, and boast of honor, they must rely on the common mass for support. The world's experience is that the strongest throne will lose its might and decay, or be overthrown, when the people digress from that standard of integrity, patriotic pride and intelligence that gave it stamina. It is sure to fall unless it renews its virtues, extends its guaranties of justice, submits its interests to the many, and shapes its form and quality to the spirit of the age; for ages move ethically. No tyrant's hold can remain in a land where Liberty dwells.

Days pass quickly, nights unpleasantly. The night air is like a wet blanket wrapped about us. It is dreary to go into our tomb-like abode to wait through darkness, harassed by lice, faint with hunger, aching with pain, shaking with chill, languid with disease till another day. Morning comes invested in a fleecy mantle of fog, and we totter out at the Rebel drum beat for roll call. Such our lot, how long? How long?

The month of October is gone, to me the most beautiful of autumn. These musings occur to me:

  October nights with evenings long,
   How oft I've met those cherished ones,
  And joined them in their gayest song;
   Alas, how strange life's river runs!
  And when October's pleasant nights
   Have come again so fine and gay,
  My thoughts recur with sad delights
   To those I love now far away.
  By change on change how marked the road
   Of life down which we move;
  But Heaven one changeless gift bestowed—
   Memory clings to early love.
  The days of youth go flitting past,
   And youthful friends must part;
  But O Love's memory! thou hast
   A tuft of flowers to twine each heart.
  October nights with evenings long,
   Most pleasant time for toil or mirth;
  To read the news or hum the song
   Around the endeared family hearth.

But do they think of me tonight?
  My seat is vacant at the hearth;
There may be sadness as I write,
  And in my heart there is no mirth.
I join them not in speech or song,
  And yet I strive to cheerful be;
The night is drear, somber and long;
  I hope, yet fear, they think of me.
They read the news, but naught of me;
  I am unheard of, far away!
O, can I ever, ever see,
  The loved at home who for me pray?
I trust it all to fleeting days,
  They may be few that I shall live;
As sad as strange these strenuous ways,
  Yet I will not cease to strive.
I trust it all; my country's fate
  May need this painful sacrifice;
I trust it all, Oh, God! and wait
  For that which in the future lies.
And should I cease to linger here,
  To brook this languor, pain and blight,
I'd soar in peace without a fear
  Clothed in robes of spiritual light!
For it must be as has been shown
  By wondrous vision, holy light!
My soul will not be left alone,
  I will not vanish into night!
O, may they see it as I see,
  Be to my mortal fate resigned;
For death can but my spirit free
  From ills where I have long repined.

## VOTE FOR PRESIDENT.—A FROSTY WAVE.

Friday, November 4th.—Cloudy since last date; forty-eight hours cold rain; forty hours without rations. Our dirt roof was breached, causing a leak. Wm. Walker, 22d N. Y. Cavalry, of New Woodstock, died the 2d. Men are dying all about, death being hastened by inclement weather. Yesterday morning when we crawled out one of the men who lay near us on the top of the ground, way dying, wrapped in a ragged blanket laid close to a faded pine bough, the rain beating mercilessly on his ghastly face. His friends who had laid with him had walked all night to keep from freezing. This is one of many scenes, equally if not more appalling. The sun greets us today for a single hour. Tonight it is piercing cold. We have constructed a fire-place in the bank of our tomb, walling and topping it with clay, found in some parts, which we made into bricks and hardened in the sun. Several attempts have been made to build houses with it, but they can hardly perfect the art; the first rain crumbles it. A smoother, finer quality has been found, of which the boys make pipes in imitation of meerschaum pipes; perhaps with the same facilities of art, this material may be quite as capable of being moulded and finished as that material. It is found in beds or strata. No wood for warmth—barely enough to boil meal, and when that is done we hover over dying coals, keeping them aglow with our breath till they are ashes. I never supposed a single coal of fire or a few hot embers could be so precious, could make me so happy. Wood is put in piles at the gate, so much for each thousand. When divided each man's share is but a small green stick.

Saturday, November 5th.—Thick frost this morning. Saw a man lying near the swamp frozen and dead. Another boy who went from place to place apparently without friends, was stiff and dead, one cheek pressing closely the sand; his hands thrust into the top of his tattered pants just as I have seen him rest them as he walked slowly about the street where he lie. Many of the sick whose clothing was wet and frozen, were chilled, some dead in their uncovered excavations. O, it is a horrible, most ungodly thing—the half cannot be told! Hundreds of naked feet not recovered from sun burn and scurvy, are now inflamed by a touch of frost. Two young men I have seen together for weeks, lie dead at their stopping place where I saw them lying at dark last night, the left hand of one clasped with the right hand of the other.

Officers in recruiting for a pioneer corps, promise plenty to eat; need never shoulder a gun. It is to go with the army to build roads, earthworks, etc. I suppose to take the place of darkies they seriously talk of arming. It is a seductive scheme; numbers take and are going on the strong plea of destitution, exposure and fear of starvation. It is hard to see them turn the tables on Uncle Sam, to drink from the cup Treason holds in the left hand, to stay the jagged knife of starvation held in the right.

Monday, November 7th.—Yesterday the names, ages, birthplace, residence, and time of capture of all prisoners were taken; the motive is a mystery. Great feeling about election; groups of forty to a hundred gather and talk. Great development of sentiment in favor of Lincoln, almost unanimous among those who talk, notwithstanding the total absence of political news from the North. Rebels have done much to discourage by taunts and threats, and are apparently quite hopeful, both rank and file; but one captain in today, told a group of us candidly that it was vain to hope for success through the election, for Lincoln could not be defeated. When he saw the feeling so strong in his favor, and men in our condition praying for his re-election, he could judge of the feelings of the people and soldiers North; that the stake of battle had been laid, and the North would decide it folly to bargain now. The South will find it out so; but he would not express his own wishes.

We have watched with intense interest the result of battles, have felt that the great issue is to be decided tomorrow; that the triumph of a party with which Rebels sympathize, will be a dishonor to our glorious cause, let battles go as they may. We have full confidence in the ability of our army to win the greatest victories ever won for freedom. It is not with our armies that the great danger rests; it is with the people at home. I have not seen a man, though he be for "Mac," that believes that the election of Lincoln would be a detriment to our cause.

Tuesday, November 8th.—It is election day. Early it was announced there was to be a sham election. Accordingly two sacks of beans, white and black, were placed in charge of Sergt. Kemp by the Rebel quartermaster, to be used as ballots, the white to represent McClellan, the black Lincoln. The Rebels are pleased with the idea, having manifested a desire to know how we stand, for they hope if McClellan be elected the war will soon be over with results favoring them. By 8 o'clock the top of the stockade was swarmed with soldiers and citizens, and a few ladies. Beans for ballots were placed inside the dead line, two empty sacks hung on the wall to receive the ballots. Men who wished to vote were marchd in by squads. The Democracy leaders (Irish police) were loud in their cry for "Mac", the Rebels looking on with curious interest. When whole hundreds went in for "Abe" they were very sober; but when a party separated and stopped at the white bean bag shouting "Mac! Mac!" they clapped their hands and gave that shrill Rebel yell heard at the front, with a half laugh and a "bully." Their exultation was but momentary, for the cry often went up, "Colonel, give us another bag of your black beans," and chagrin was written on their faces. But about 1,800 votes were cast, Lincoln receiving about two and a half to McClellan's one. The whole number in camp is about 12,000, five-sixths refusing to vote, saying it was gotten up to please Rebels.

Tuesday, November 15th, 1864.—The dreary days bring no change; existence drags—life and vivacity ebb. Officers generally admit Lincoln's re-election, Prisoners in this morning from Columbia. A few recently from Sherman's lines, belonging to the 120th N. Y., captured on Hooker's skirmish line. I inquired if they ever saw men who had escaped from Andersonville. One said he saw one a few days before his capture who walked out of prison in the guise of a Rebel sergeant, book in hand, one morning after roll call, with several Rebels who had been in to attend to that duty, who belonged to the 7th Michigan. I think this was Henry Damon who escaped in that manner early in August.

J. H. Randell, D, 76th, was seen outside by a member of his company, with a gun on his shoulder. On being recognized, he wept like a child, saying he felt compelled to do so. Yager, Copeland and Duncan, of F, 76th, have gone as recruits. To the credit of the two last, they escaped in September and after several days absence were recaptured and returned in full negro suits, for which they had exchanged their old blue, hoping the more easily to avoid detection. Copeland lay sick in the woods, unable to travel for three days, and was fed by a negro and negress who brought him food in the night. Bewildered, disheartened, weak and alone in a strange country, he went to the residence of a planter, was fed and returned to the nearest military post.

I heard a man relate his experience who attempted escape and was gone from here three weeks. I note it because it is different from cases where men are gone a night or two and are fed by negroes, and then picked up by citizens or provost. He, with a companion, had reached North Carolina, and were traveling one day in dark woods, when they discovered, as they supposed, they were pursued by men and dogs. Hoping to evade them they broke trail and lay down in a hollow and covered in the leaves. It was not long before they heard the pattering of the dogs as they leaped and trotted directly toward them, and presently their whining and snuffing close to where they lay. They stopped, and waited for their masters to come up, which was not long. The men, who proved to be hunters on their own hook, knew very well the meaning, and surprised them by saying they were at liberty to go where they pleased or to follow them for safety, as Jeff Davis had no claims on them; that they, too, had fled from his minions. They followed not far behind the hunters, and an hour later found themselves in a strange sort of camp, surrounded by deep everglades and a dense wilderness, that rendered it a most secluded retreat, and in the midst of strange looking men, women and children, who regarded them with wild, questioning looks at first. There were several pioneer cabins, built of logs and slats from pine. They judged they were many miles from any settlement. It had been given the name of "Devil's Swamp," as called by the Rebels—the home of Union men and their families—refugees from their homes and deserters from the Confederate armies, whence they fled at the first reign of terror, vowing never to fight for a power that had no just cause for existence. Prisoners remained three days, were fed and treated kindly by all, and told they were welcome to remain as long as they pleased. But too anxious, as it proved, to get to our lines in the vicinity of Newbern, they started on their journey, and the second night were captured attempting to cross a bridge that spanned a large stream. His name is Brumer, an Illinoisan; his comrade's name is Hoyt. Approaches to these swamps are guarded by men and dogs. The men frequently going to the settlements for necessary food.

Wednesday, November 16th.—Getting another bit of beef and flour and meal, we thought we would have a fine supper, so sold our beef and bought potatoes, and traded meal for flour. We think a quantity of flour has more nutriment than coarse, musty meal. There are two reasons why: First, with our limited amount of wood we can cook it better; meal is often raw, after fuel is gone.

Second, digestion is so deranged by improper diet that the organs allow meal to pass in the form of chyle, or as eaten, thus its nutritive quality is but partially imparted.

The terrible abundance of vermin is a continuous scourge. We can hardly realize it possible. A great part of the day we are employed in exterminating lice. Next morning they appear as prevalent and lusty. Every rag at times is invested. It impresses me with an appalling sense of degradation, impoverishment, physical wretchedness! No language can interpret it. We have fought it in fear and deathly dread. Now the keener air of autumn makes the task a dread such as we never felt, to strip off tattered garments and feel the chill strike our emaciated frames, stiff and heavy with languor, while we search out with weak and watery eyes, and crush with trembling fingers the miserable, pestering, blood-sucking war beasts of a day! Sitting at that work this afternoon, I heard an unusual hilarity; an uproar in the street where a squad fresh from Sherman had just arrived. Looking that way I saw Thompson approaching, and singing, "Ulysses leads the Van," and clapping his hands in glee. He was coming to tell me news.

"North, North.! I have rich news; Lincoln carried every State but three. The Copperheads are beat out of sight, old Seymour of New York, is driven down without sharpening; Fenton is elected governor of New York by from 30,000 to 50,000. Bully, bully, bully! North! I told you we'd beat."

I had had fears that the people might despond; that Copperheads might manufacture stock out of the great sacrifice of the campaigns, though successful, not completed, and by fusion and secret scheming with Rebel renegades, they might deceive the common heart. But I was not faithless. So I replied enthusiastically:

"Glory to God! It is the greatest triumph the world ever saw. The moral sentiment of the North is truly in the ascendant. The victory is won!" Shouts pealed through the murky air, and satisfaction beamed on faces that had not smiled for weeks. Rebels were greeted with, "Get ready for four years more war." "Mac's gone for a new base." "Copperheads are in the last ditch, dead and buried." "Abe is after you another your years with an abolition beetle, right smart git." "Ho, Johnny, come to limerick." "Three cheers and a tiger for the Union." Rebs are mum, gloomy, sour.

Thursday, November 17th.—Fine weather. Sanitary goods have again arrived; are being distributed to paroled men on duty for Rebels, and the police, except that which is retained for the hospitals. The most needy in camp receive nothing, as before. If Yankees are to do Rebel work let them be clothed as well as fed by them! Let not the aim of charity be thwarted. There are hundreds who have not even a blanket, a hole in the ground, or a stick of shelter. Col. Harrison has been induced to let a few from each thousand go to the woods for poles and brush that a shanty may be built on the ground of each thousand for those entirely destitute of shelter.

This morning the prison was noisy over the return to prison of about 300 galvanized Rebs," (those who went out on oath and enlisted). Wherever they go they are hooted and abused. "O, ye banished from your chosen country!" and other epithets are bestowed. They are a sorry looking squad, from Sommerville, S. C.; have full Rebel uniforms, and to us look contemptible; still we pity them. They, too, are without blankets; stripped of everything, they are turned back into prison, from whence they perjured themselves to escape. Knowing the boys were coming, Col. Harrison had the loyal prisoners working for the "Rebel poor," as the boys call them, building shanties on the pretense of sheltering the sick; and now these "galvanized Rebs" come pouring in, enough to four times fill the huts he has let us build, and the shelterless for whom we intended them, get no relief. No one knows why they were turned in. They say it was because they stole a bull and chickens to get a "square meal."

We have an energetic man near us, nicknamed "Slick." His name is Brown, from Georgia. He was confined with us at Andersonville. He left his home to escape Rebel rule, and joined the army of the Cumberland; has been a prisoner ten months; had an interview with a sister at the prison gate last August, when Lieut. Davis was in command, during Wirz's sickness, and received a few articles of apparel and food. His expressions against the Rebel cause are bitter. For a while during the summer he was placed in a dungeon. He goes outside to chop, On return at night choppers are searched, not allowed to bring in anything except wood or a bundle of wild grass, unless they buy it of the sutler. Citizens are anxious to trade, but are forbidden. "Slick" and one other I know, make a sly trade now and then, and splitting a large piece of pine they scoop out one of the halves in the form of a trough, and frequently bring in a peck of beans or potatoes or something that fits the cavity, concealed by replacing the pieces.

Not far away is a group of Tennessee men. Among them is a man apparently fifty-five; a prisoner since Chickamauga; has been in the Union army since the spring of '61. He left his home and family and a well-to-do estate in the mountains; traveled by night to join our army. He is more than ordinarily intelligent, of placid nature, an example of loyalty, an exemplifier of the love of that people for republican government, against the hateful oligarchy under which they had lived. In the sunshine of the day often several gather about him to hear him talk; his melodious bass voice, and fatherly words touch our hearts. We call him "Uncle." Such men are the mettle of every golden age—metal without alloy, though fame may not be stamped on their characters, the true ring will thrill the nation's heart in time to come, vibrate in the diviner realm of our nature and wake our souls to gratitude. They are the true among the false.

I was up to the gate this morning (18th), noticing some of Barrett's spasmodic gymnastics. Quite a crowd was present, observing the choppers going out, others wishing an opportunity to go. One of his maneuvers was to rush wildly up to men in front, shake his revolver in thir faces,then fire it over their heads, saying with an oath, "I'll make you get up and git!" The adjutant of his regiment, a tall, slim, good-natured, laughing fellow,—never cross or mopish,—with a big flop hat, had charge of the wood squad and was going with them. Barrett interposed, remarking to the adjutant that it was foolish to laugh or make fun for them.

## BARRETT'S STARVATION ORDER.

Wednesday, November 23d.—The 19th it began raining; continued till the night of the 21st, and grew cold; froze last night; water at our door iced half an inch. In pools along the swamp I saw ice an inch thick. The morning of the 21st, while eating our last morsel in the form of flour gruel, our shanty came near collapsing. The banks, softened by rain, flaked off at the top letting the rafters down. Incidents often save accidents; fortunately we had obtained a piece of rail of Sibley, a chopper, and laid it from bank to bank to keep it from being stolen, which saved the whole weight of dirt from covering us.

Today, and for two days and nights, there are six of us in our hut five feet square and about three feet high to the arch, having taken in two who were shelterless. No rations have been issued since Sunday morning (20th), when we received one day's only— about three gills of flour. Three days have passed; we have waited, watched and prayed, but no rations yet. Lieut. Barrett announces from the gate that no rations will be issued until a tunnel and spades are found, adding that it is by order of Col. Iverson, and not a G—d d—d thing will be brought in; but if the tunnels were exposed we would get double rations tonight. This is the first we had heard of a tunnel. To satisfy this malignant spirit over 12,000 men are brought to the verge of starvation, for nothing for which they are to blame. Knowledge of a tunnel is confined to a few, perhaps a dozen, and they have a perfect right to escape. So every man's hole has been hunted by the most active of our men, hoping to reveal the secret and get needed rations. It is now late in the afternoon; while writing it has been announced, "Tunnel found!" Rations are being sent in. O, God, it is gladsome news! With feeble shouts of joy it is hailed from dead line to dead line. Monday night, Wright, Boodger and Fred Clifton, worthy of remembrance, gave us a pint of meal, out of about four quarts hoarded for an emergency (two of their mess being on police). It made a light meal for four. Noble fellows, I shall ever be grateful. Since then, forty-eight hours, we have not tasted or seen a crumb. A great part of the camp has not had anything since Sunday.

There is a sad sequel to this story. But few of thousands who rejoiced at the coming of rations after the elapse of seventy-five hours of famishing, realize how dearly they were bought. Barrett's vicious edict that no rations should be sent in until a suspected tunnel should be disclosed and the diggers surrendered, was madly adhered to. Seventy hours had passed since the last issue when men comprehended that thousands had reached the brink of starvation. Every means had been exhausted to gain concessions. Our sergeants who handle rations inside, counseled as to what could be done to locate the supposed tunnel and those connected. No new tunnel was found, of course, no one who knew of one. But relief must be had. A tunnel was started and exposed. Men were called to volunteer to face his insane wrath and to save their comrades. A score reported. None questioned but the punishment would be as cruel as the base wretch could inflict. High courage, physical and moral, was required and was manifested. Four was deemed sufficient to feed the ferocity of Brute Barrett. They were selected by lot. Accompanied by the sergeants they went to the gate and delivered themselves to Barrett who thereupon sent in one day's rations of meal and strutted in brutal pride over his murderous triumph. Many men ate it raw, mixed in cold water, ravenously. They were in the fever of starvation, their brains pulsating with delirium.

The sun shone this afternoon, the first since Friday, the 18th. During these dreary, cold days of famine, the issues of wood have been more liberal, and by economy we have been able to keep up a little fire during the coldest, which we have hovered over till we are besmeared with pitch smoke.

A report that Sherman had taken Macon with 6,000 prisoners, and was pushing for Savannah, is all we have had from without to cheer us. One man in our hundred was found frozen this morning. Three other men were frozen to death last night that I know of. To add to our misery, all the wells in the camp are ordered filled, compelling us to go to the swamp brook for water. Every man was ordered in line and kept standing, many barefooted, all ragged, for over an hour while it was being done. On the stockade near our hundred (the seventh of the third thousand), Lieut. Barrett, with three dressy ladies with jaunty hats, appeared to give directions to the police in doing the work, making some broken remarks to the ladies and a show of authority. He had come out with his sanitary hat on, the brim looped up blusteringly, set back on his red pate, in his usual swearing mood for one of his delectable show-offs, we his subjects; the ladies his audience. At first we were prompted to retire from the presence of ladies, our toilet and attire being imperfect; but his old revolver and threats kept all in line, whether cold or modest, and finally we concluded modesty might be something different among those upper-tens from what rude nature taught us, so we submitted to their scrutiny. But his delicate ear was shocked by voices, now here, now there, uttering groans, "Red head," "Sanitary, where did you get that hat? Perhaps those ladies would like to know," and like exclamations, when he would verily hop from the ground, swearing madly and brandishing his revolver, not knowing how to vent his wrath. He would point it cocked directly toward us and say, "Who said that? G—d d—n you, who said it? I dare the son of a b— to say it again—I dare—what? what?—say it agin—I dare you to say it—G— d—n you—I'll put some of you under the ground!" Between these exclamations he would pause for a sound. Not long after breaking ranks, the lieutenant and the ladies retired. Rations—nearly a pint each of meal and rice and a spoonful of salt, after dark.

Thursday, November 24th, 1864.—A chill on the air, but pleasant. Report that an order is received to cut down rations. The colonel said at the gate if we get one pint of meal a day we will be well off. Indeed, better off than we have been at all times under his fostering care! Today a new avenue of freedom is opened. The Rebs want bookkeepers to go to Charleston and other points. Those wishing to go write their names and hand them to an officer at the gate, probably a broker. Large wages proposed, they are to be considered citizens of the South, leaving it optional with us whether we be exchanged. A pretty vocation! Several of us were urged to go, but declined on the ground that we would not assist the enemy of our country, come what may. "They never fail who die in a great cause; their spirits walk abroad."

Saturday, November 26th.—News comes of a sudden that hospital sick are being paroled. It is said that 350 are to leave on Monday.

Steward Brown, paroled at the hospital, tells the fate of the four martyrs who went out to save the camp. They were put in the guard house the first night and given a supper. In the morning, Lieut. Barrett, half drunk on sorghum whisky, ordered the heroes brought out and strung up. A strong hemp cord was looped around their thumbs, then drawn over ends of poles projecting from the guard house roof, three guards to each of the victims, pulling them clear from the ground. The agony caused was a terrible crucifixion. They had resolved not to please their satanic persecutor by crying out. But the pain was so excruciating it was beyond both nature and will to endure silently. They shrieked in frenzy. The agony was so apparent that a couple of the guard involuntarily protested and were ordered arrested by Barrett. The men begged to be shot. Barrett laughed, sneered, and swore in fiendish delight; answered their agonized supplication with vile ridicule, vulgar boasting, savage denunciation, murderous threats, swaggering about with drawn sword, saying it pleased him best to let them die in their present plight; that he had authority and proposed Yankees find it out. While he would delight to shoot them he preferred to let them die slow in swift misery. His profane and vulgar rant is unfit for and impossible of repetition. Paroled Union men were near enough to witness the outrage, hear their screams. An hour later they learned they had been cut down after fainting and almost dead, when taken to the hospital by a surgeon, where they are in a state of prostration and distraction. These men suffered to save prison comrades; are as innocent of having committed a wrong as any of us. Their act is the very highest exemplification of the principle of love for mankind. It was devoid of motive for self gain or gratification. They knew they were walking directly under the sway of a man who was determined to cause them suffering, perhaps death, their motive being, in the face of this, to alleviate the suffering of others. Indeed this is real martyrdom!

Sunday, November 27th.—The first thousand is marched out, and a number of the worst cases are selected for parole, no doubt, though all sorts of stories are afloat. It seems like a dream. Shall we soon awaken to a real existence? Is deliverance nigh? Notwithstanding about 1,500 from Savannah and some from Sherman arrive, confirming election reports. Lincoln is elected—a great movement from the heart of the people.

Orderly Sergeant Matteson, Burton and Boodger, of my company, pass for parole. The brass band, the first we have to acknowledge since we left Gen. Lee's lines, is playing, "Bonnie Blue Flag," "Dixie," and other pieces.

Tuesday, November 29th.—My thousand called for critical inspection, but is sent back. More prisoners from Blacksheare, Ga., who report exchange "knocked in head."

Thursday, December 1st.—The camp is astir again today, marching all on the west of the run to the east; then all back to the west, counting us to ascertain the exact number, to prevent any drawing double rations, taking nearly all day. The column was moving over the long corduroy road across the marsh, when Lieut. Barrett came running toward the stream with the pomposity of a brigadier. Attempting to cross, he slipped and tumbled in. The boys laughed. He no sooner got on the bank, wet and daubed with the black mud, than he drew his revolver and snapped it. It missed; shouts increased; snapped again; again it missed. Pulled again the cap went, but missed fire. The crowd became tumultous and provoking; he grew excessively mad. Fired with passion, he leaped the stream, ran through the swamp to one of his guard, seized his musket and fired quite at random, though he intended to hit, for his bullet whistled along the line, grazed a man's arm, and entered the dirt roof of a shanty, but seriously injuring none that I know of.

Friday, December 2d.—Go to sick call with Con. Corbett, get a decoction of wild cherry bark. The steward dealt it out to whoever came with a tin cup, or bottle, until it was gone, not a half who applied getting any. He had two kinds in pails and some pills. He asked which I wanted. I told him no difference. One was a decoction of wild cherry, the other white oak bark and sweet fern. It is laughable to see the poor fellows drink it down, thinking perhaps it will do them good. This is the usual way the medicine is given out.

I succeeded once, some time ago, in passing the guard with Sergeant Springer, of Ohio, and getting a view of the interior of the hospital. To go and lay among those skeletons on the ground, without bed or covering is not hospitable; conditions are but little improved except in rations, which are mostly of wheat and rice. To call such miserable sheds "hospitals" is a perversion of language. To go to a hospital here is lying down by one's grave to wait for the ebbing of life. The majority admitted are past hope. No floors, no straw, though it could be easily had. Emaciated, sickly, loathsome frames are stretched on the ground wrapped in old blankets, swarming with vermin, often covered with scurf. The attendants appeared willing, some kind and sympathetic, doctors generally humane in address. Dr. Fludel, in charge, is a neat, gentlemanly appearing man. It is said he can boast of being an original signer of the ordinance of secession of South Carolina. He appears unwilling to disgrace his profession, but it is difficult to see how he can grace it here. There has never been a full supply of medicine, scanty as doses are; besides, it is impossible to cure a single case without removing causes, viz., exposure, starvation, and the powers are against it.

Monday, December 5th.—Those who went from here to Savannah on the 3d returned, military operations preventing procedure in parole. Many were crestfallen over it, but likely if that point is obstructed and the general terms are satisfactory, another place will soon be agreed on. Charleston is talked of. Those same men are ordered out today. The train moves down the Charleston road. A tendency to dropsy increases. When I arose cheeks were much swollen, one eye nearly closed, feet and limbs puffed. I shambled about, feeling as though a heavy weight were on me, wound tightly about my person from head to feet. Clyde and Townsend, belonging to the second thousand of the 100th Regiment New York, whom we took in to save from freezing, are gone, taking their blankets, leaving us entirely destitute. 'Twas well we sheltered them in cold and storm; I would do much more if possible. But they are very thoughtless to leave us without a thing, lugging their lousy, ragged duds to our lines, to be thrown into the sea. There are more unconsciously ungrateful than consciously bad. Hepworth, of the 1st Vt., who has been turned away by S. and N., who chop and do not like to have him share their extras, lays with us tonight. He is destitute of covering, being stripped when captured. What a load of selfishness men carry on their hearts? In the world charity is scarce as gold unless it is counterfeit; generally there is a premium on that. Some hearts fear lest charity enter their doors; with others it is boundless as the world. Here it is narrow as our prison bounds; it is shut out by its walls; it is as coarse and sparse as our begrudged subsistence. Disease and hunger gnaw our frames; selfishness goads our spirits.

Tuesday, December 6th.—My detachment is entered to be ready for inspection in the morning; it is a trial to see who shall go or stay. We are baking our meal into a cake tonight. I shall go with a heart for any fate. Friends tell me I am sure to pass.

## ON TO CHARLESTON HOMEWARD BOUND.

Wednesday, December 7th, 1864.—My thousand was marched inside the dead line early this morning, and examined by hundreds.—Standing at open ranks, the surgeon passed down the front rank, feeling the arms of men, sometimes examining their breasts, sending the most feeble to the gate. He passed down the rear rank the same way till near me, then passed several of us without noticing us at all. Vexed at being so slighted, I determined to plead my case, feeling I had a strong one. So I immediately said, in a feeble, plaintive tone, not assumed: "Doctor, I am sick." "What?" said he, glancing at me sharply. "I am sick." "What is it? What ails you?" "General debility," giving him briefly causes and results, among them dropsy. "You can stand it till the war is over, I reckon, eh? Time out, eh?" "Can't go it long, doctor, sure." The truth was prima facia, for I was bowed, and one side of my face was bloated, one eye closed, and mouth inclined to one side. With a side glance he said sharply, motioning with his hand, "Go out." A look of good-bye to friends and comrades in distress, and I hobbled away. In mute happiness I found myself beyond the gate, with a squad, squalid and miserable like myself, moping toward headquarters to be paroled. Stopping in front of the log buildings, I looked back toward the gate; I saw J. B. Hawks, 7th Michigan, limping toward us. He was the only man in the squad I had learned to love and prize, intimately. We naturally agreed to be companions on the road, or in any future fate, for still we braced ourselves against disappointment, determined that if again cast into prison it should not surprise us or kill us with despair. The same spirit, with calculations of probable possibilities, and a hope that rested on entities which awakened calmness, courage and strength, has borne us through the trying scenes, the unnatural gloom and suffering, and cheered us in a den of death. Friends were often vexed and counted me stubborn, incredulous, faithless, because I ridiculed frivolous reports, rejected partial views one way and the other. I knew that nothing was lost by it; I knew the mutability of affairs at such an epoch, how slight a circumstance might change the course of events, and had they paroled us and then drew us up in line before a detail of armed soldiers and read our sentence to be shot, I'd not have been shocked. I had no fears; I did not feel an impulsive gladness, was not so exquisitely happy as we had talked about months before, when we should have signed the parole. Yet others were childishly so, and as childishly miserable on slight disappointment. Still I felt assured that the glorious day was not far away, that the blissful change was nigh, and my heart warmed in my bosom and beat a few times like a live man's. But it was with great effort that I could put my thoughts clear over on the bright side. I could vaguely imagine it, almost vainly stared to see it; the deadly shadow of late existence had dimmed my sight, ingrained itself into my mind. So physically wretched, so chained in spirit in my present phase of life, that I had but a dim idea of what I was.

During the night a squad of 170 men had arrived from Sherman's army; they were drawn up in single files, submitting to a rigorous search. While awaiting the process of paroling I watched the proceeding, and it is more particularly worthy of note because of the season of the year, and the fact that there might be a possibility of their release. They were forced to undress, stripping off even their drawers. Tents, overcoats, blankets, all extra clothing was thrown in piles, and then they were roughly ordered to dress hurriedly, and were marched into the prison from which we had just escaped, leaving blankets and changes of clothing. It seemed to us that nothing but a merciless, hellish feeling of revenge could have prompted such an inexcusable action on the part of the Rebels.

After the clerk had written our names, company and regiment (we merly touched the pen), underneath the parole, which was in substance a pledge not to take up arms or serve in any branch of military service of the United States, or to do any duty usually performed by soldiers, until duly declared exchanged, we moved to the railroad to await the return of the train from Charleston.

Several soldiers came near us with cooked sweet potatoes and inimitable wheat and corn cakes to exchange for rings and the like. My hunger was past keenness—it was morbid. I tried to trade an old hair brush; could find but one man who would look at it; he didn't want it. He was a man about five-and-forty, and held two small biscuit in his hand. I insisted he should take the brush and examine it; he did, and at the same time I wished to "heft the biscuit" and took them and made off to the best of my ability, leaving Mr. Johnny to find out the superior qualities of the brush, crying, "Har, sar! I wants a ring or buttons for 'em ar!—you'ns!" "Not so bad as I do these," was the thought, and before reaching poor Hawks I had hoggishly devoured both, and felt that I could have eaten a peck, easily.

Near night a guard was placed over us, and scanty rations of sour bread issued. I traded my small pen-knife, having kept it very choice, with a soldier, for pieces of bread and bacon, worth, he said $5, not more than a man's ration for a day. This time Hawks shared.

The exercise of the day had quite exhausted me and caused

my feeble limbs to swell and pain badly. Around small fires that seemed like our own camp fires, without blankets, we waited all night, in chilling fog and drizzle, but got no sleep.

In the course of the night I had occasion to pass a group of guards engaged in jovial talk, and seeing me they said:

"Ho, Yank! you needn't be in a hurry; we want to talk!"

I remarked that I did not know but it was against orders to be with them.

"No, you can go where you please. You won't run away, now, I reckon; you are going home."

They began a series of questions about the North, taking a deep and curious interest in my explantions, which were candid and plain as I could make them, for I found that in important respects they were idealess. I wanted to leave a good impression. Their local conceptions of us were extremely erroneous. Were I a farmer? Did farmers work? Do their wives and daughters and sons work? Thought one man could do but little on a farm; did all of us own farms; what do we raise; how large are our farms? They were mystified at the idea that men who work for wages ever become independent farmers. Did young ladies teach school North? Were interested to hear about our school system. I told them it was open to all classes, and was more indispensible to us than our legislatures. Too feeble to talk more, having lost my voice, I started back, but they urged me to stay and talk. Excusing myself on account of health, they expressed sympathy, I proffered my thanks and returned to the fire.

They were fine looking young men, in neat gray suits, roundabouts, and caps, all South Carolina boys, sons of wealthy merchants and planters, apparently well bred and educated. They had never seen service in the field, and thought their duty here extremely hard. They knew as little of the merits of the issue as innocent children; appeared as free from partisan principles, but actually supposed they were on the right side, because on the South side.

Never shall I forget that boyish, winsome group of handsome, cleanly-dressed young men, leaning on their bayoneted muskets, or swinging them playfully, standing about my figure stooping with disability, shivering in dirty rags, and listening to my broken voice, and speaking to me kindly.

Thursday, December 8th.—About three o'clock in the morning we had a cold rain bath. At five o'clock we went aboard the train and steamed for Charleston. The day was bright, but we had a slow, tedious, all-day passage among the everlasting pine. Indeed, it was painful. I could not raise up without assistance. Disease seemed to have increased with exercise, for the first in my imprisonment I expected to die and gave up for a time. Our cars were those used for transporting stock and grain, without seats, and packed with men, squalid, enfeebled with months of prison misery, clothing soaked with the night wet, and reeking with vermin. Our condition was horrible; I felt it keenly. My gaunt frame was now bloated almost to hardness—the griping pain and oppressive weight and morbid hunger which no amount of food could repress, gnawed my vitals like a cancer.

About 8 o'clock in the evening, having accomplished a hundred miles in fifteen hours, we arrived at Charleston. Weather had turned cold; icy winds blew fiercely off the sea, chilling even Rebel soldiers to the core. One hard tack apiece was given at 10 o'clock p. m. No fires allowed, staid aboard the cars till welcome morning, hoping it would be the last hard night of prison life, for we were told we would go aboard the flag-of-truce boat at 7 o'clock next morning.

Friday, December 9th.—Quite early this morning we go to the wharf, the sickest conveyed in drays and ambulances, and go aboard the Confederate transports, about 1,100 men. The tide was out, the wind incessantly blowing in, meeting the waves, billowing them up and dashing their spray like ten thousand boiling fountains. O, it was a grand sight to look upon—that broad, deep bay, the narrow channel between us and liberty, life and death—and see the mad struggle of wind and tide. But the tide would not ebb till the appointed hour, though the wind bloweth where it listeth. Over the wave, through the mist, beyond this seething channel, over the bar stood our Moses. The red and frowning earthworks of Morris Island, that had vomited fire upon this Sodom town, now smiled on us from the promised land. We could not see our streaming banner, but we felt it, though out of sight. We could not hear a voice saying "Peace, be still!" but we knew salvation walked upon the sea. The storm grew more violent; after fearful delay Capt. Hatch, assistant agent of exchange, ordered the planks down and the prisoners ashore. Reluctant to go, many wept and begged to stay, asking "Why don't she shove out?" It was explained that it would be impossible to reach our fleet, but some had to be actually driven off by the soldiers and officers, the while peevishly begging not to be returned to prison.

The wharf at this point extends perhaps 300 yards into the water. During this delay some of the boys climbed down to the water and picked oysters from the timbers and stones, and when we went back to the city and were under cover of the gas works buildings, where we were allowed to remain a while, a few had a delicious feast.

About 11 o'clock a. m., we were ordered out. Passing up a long deserted street and through shorter ones, decorated by crumbling walls, paneless windows, broken blinds and swinging doors, walls with breaches larger than cart wheels, in some buildings a dozen of them, where our shell had entered. In several places large buildings were dead heaps of ruins—brick and dust. Sidewalks torn up with shell, weeds higher than my head close by where we walk, and in the burnt region there was almost a wilderness of tall, rank, dead weeds, and among them fragments of broken lumber and brands. Every step of streets and walks, every door and window, pillar and veranda, post or sign, was desolation. Stupendous ruins on every hand! Battered, dusky walls, leaning and gray with premature decay, reminding me of a land of ruins, of cities fallen five centuries ago. We were utterly amazed; no one can imagine or conceive the awful wreck. No pen can write, no pencil paint, no tongue tell. Every shade was loneliness, the air dreamy, ancient. Could ruin be more complete? An age of downfall has perched on this proud city. It is not Pompeii nor Thebes; but it is our own architecture, built by our own fathers, even ourselves, in our own age and generation, and in our new world, in ruins as awfully sublime as they.

Hotels were without a guest, without a host; within was a hollow echo, without, cracking, gaping walls, piles of dirty rubbish, and wild weeds had grown and were gray with autumn decay. Commercial houses rang emptily at our stumbling tread. Glancing through broken doors we saw masses of rubbish fallen from roofs and ceilings.

Few people were seen in this vicinity, once the principal business part of the city.

Overdone and weak, hundreds fell behind, and the column was scattered. Assisted by Hawks and B. F. Madison, of Plainfield, Otsego County, New York, we had chosen the sidewalk, allowed to take our time. We were limping up the rusty pavement, gazing thoughtfully at desolate scenes, when a man appeared at the door of a large, broken establishment and accosted us in an insolent way:

"Ha, wall; wah isn't what it's cracked up to be, ha,—after all, is it?"

I suggested: "By the cracks, you have got around here, I guess it is."

He seemed exultant over our wretched condition. After more than an hour's windings we entered Roper Hospital, a large commodious building that had been used to confine Federal officers in, but was dirty as a barn. It was surrounded by a high iron fence. The guard was placed outside the fence and we had access to front and rear. "Sisters of Charity" with something to give and colored women with coarse eatables to sell or exchange for notions or photographs. I traded a photograph of Gen. Grant for a little cooked rice, the first rations received from Grant in a long time,

A sister kindly acting as agent between me and aunty. One fellow traded a likeness of a lady, representing it to be Queen Victoria. Men whose names excited interest in negroes, shared the same fate. These pictures excited loud talk and a brisk stir among them, which would have been laughable had we felt like it. Many ladies of Charleston, who also came to us are hospitable, often went beyond the guards' orders to give or exchange something; but the "Sisters" represented that they were destitute, and the little we could buy or beg was but a drop in the cup of want.

We had barely began to feel that we were getting comfortable, having large stoves in one or two apartments, and were calculating on a night's sleep under a roof, when just before dark all able to walk were ordered out and marched through the penitentiary into a back yard enclosed on all sides by buildings and high walls. Quarter rations were given, the proportion given us while we remained, and two loads of wood. Nothing had been issued since the night before. What they calculated for twenty-four hours was hastily devoured. The air was hazy, cold; the ground dirty, rough and hard. The sheds would not hold a quarter f us—consequently many were exposed to the cold rain. December 10th it rained severely all day. Most of us had not even an old blanket. We were informed that a car load of prisoners had arrived from Florence, and the storm having subsided they had taken our places on the Frankfort and we would be sent to the stockade at Florence. In the forenoon, Dec. 11th, we again went to the streets and took a shorter route to the Custom House wharf. Everything about it looked old from disuse. The large, handsome buildings were closed and silent. I climbed up the steps and looked through the large window, but it was desolate. In about an hour the Confederate transport steamed around and we went aboard. The harbor was empty. There was not a forest of masts nor a continuous puffing of steam tugs. I saw two or three boats, only of minor account. Even from these the Confederate flag waved not. We took a deep interest in everything around, but a deeper interest in heaving ahead. The thick clouds had fallen away, the sun shone brightly, the rippling water glistened, and with a keen, steady breeze we set out for the offing where our vessels were waiting. Standing upon that crowded deck, we watched eagerly for our flag, and finally we descried it just above the water, before the ship that bore it appeared. Meanwhile we glanced at Castle Pinckney and Fort Moultrie, lingered long on the ruins of Sumter, a shapeless mass of broken, fallen walls, a great pile of rubbish that bore but little resemblance to a fort as we viewed it, except points facing Charleston and Moultrie, where portions of the wall was standing. But on the latter side, Dupont had left his marks in April, 1863, and a vast number of logs were piled along the harbor and against the wall. The side opposite Fort Wagoner, whose works were quite plain, was in ruin. The rebels have exhibited remarkable tenacity in clinging to that wreck, where rebellion first embarked.

The city of Charleston is located on a flat, even surface, a peninsula formed by the Ashley and Cooper rivers, west and north, and the bay on the southeast and south, and from the water it was like looking down upon it and finally it seemed to sink leaving only steeples; four or five miles out I lost sight of these. We were on historic waters, a straight between the widening bounds of loyalty, and narrowing cape of treason. True the miserable Rebel rag hung over the ruined structure where Anderson pulled down the broad stripes, and bright stars under the guns of Beauregard; but it was a proud thought that we had survived unheard of sufferings and were looking triumphantly on the renowned city where secession had its inception. About noon the U. S. flag of truce boat with the commissioners on board, met and hailed us and were answered that we were paroled prisoners from Charleston, 670, 500 being left to be returned for. About 1 o'clock p. m. we were in the midst of several large streamers. One the "Star of the South," laden with released Union soldiers newly attired in clean, bright blue, was weighing anchor for Annapolis. The decks of another was thronged with ladies from Hilton Head and other points, and never did women look so beautiful. Shout upon shout rang over the broad water, old caps and new caps were thrown up, the ladies continually waving handkerchiefs and little flags, all seeming to realize the boon of blessed deliverance—as glad to see us as we were to be seen. We obeying the impulses of our poor glad hearts; they manifesting the joy of generous souls and noble natures impassioned by love fraternal. O, how deeply our cause is loved, how deeply dear to the hearts of those who met upon the wave. No suffering, no peril could drive it away. How beautiful that flag; never so bright before! It never so thrilled us with the joy of freedom of which it is emblematical. The old flag! O, it is a new flag forevermore! Its stars are stamped on every heart; its folds entwine our lives; in its character is our sacred honor; all our noblest deeds are there embalmed. And that sweet white flag that floated softly above it, that had hushed the booming cannon gently for a time, spoke peace to troubled spirits. Ceremonies over, a band sent forth sweetest anthems from the ladies' ship. I thought then we had surely got to God's country. Spellbound in ecstacy we watched that splendid steamer as it took its departure southward with its blessed burden. We were now alongside the "New York," the "receiving ship," and helped aboard. Crazy with delight, the boys indulged in wild exclamations about, "Reb bull pens," "corn meal," "meal beer," "How are your hardtack and cofee, pork and beans, we'll not want anything better!" "Meal rations tonight, boys," "That's played"; a continued uproar of soldier phrases. But more soberminded ones were looking calmly on, or talking with the ship's hands about affairs, finding their confidence in the government fully justified. We drew more than double the amount of rations for supper that we had ever drawn in Rebel lines for a whole day, that which was entirely wholesome, and nearly a quart of hot coffee and an onion. Owing to the swell of the sea that the remainder of the day and all night rocked the boats, nothing further was done. We remained on the "New York" till the middle of the forenoon of the 12th, when we drew clothing and passed to the "United States," where we divested ourselves of prison rags, which were immediately thrown overboard, and surprised our backs with a new rig throughout, then embarked on the "Crescent," and about 2 p. m., she bore away for Annapolis, Maryland. All this joy had not been felt without pain. A new suit and plenty to eat did not altogether remedy our wretched physical state. Excitement over, old stupor and pains returned, and with many prison malaria redoubled its ravages—apparently working with increased food. Hunger could not be stopped; ravenous appetites seized whatever came in reach. Even old grease from barrels and tubs, where boiled pork had been packed, was swallowed by some, by handsful; men quarrel over it like starved dogs over a carcass. From morn till noon, from noon till night were the cooks watched, teased, begged, and cursed to give them something. Chronic diarrhoea, so terribly prevalent, thus received new impetus. It was by great vigilance that boat hands and soldiers able to perform duty kept the decks any way passable. Is it asked, were you not reasonable beings? Should you not have been prudent and controlled yourselves? Reasonable! Scarcely rational! Men deprived of manliness as much as degredation, physical and moral abuse can force them from it! Disease, hunger and temptations such as men never knew before possessed us; wretchedness it would seem impossible to endure, and but for that long, bright, suffering hope of the future, how sweet would have been annihilation months before!

Some were violently seized with fever. Doctor ordered rations reduced the second day, for all that was eaten beyond a moderate quantity, incrased our morbid hunger. It was deemed advisable to make them less than usual allowance. Most of us, perhaps, felt how easy it would be to end life by over-eating; but the hunger and temptation was there just the same; the thoughtless impulse to eat, and eat, and still be unsatisfied; to eat continually, if "grub" could be had, with a stingy fear that we should not get enough; feeling that we were being cheated; eating beyond comfort, still madly, morbidly hungry, feverishly longing with the starved man's powerlessness!

On the evening of the 13th there was the unceremonious but solemn spectacle of burial of dead men at sea. In the forenoon of the 14th several more were brought up wrapped in blankets, and lowered into the water and parted from us forever. Men on the boat, may it be recollected, were from prison not from hospital, according to Rebel regime, considered inadmissible; men who were considered healthy, strong enough to subsist on coarsest fare, a mere bite, as we may say, for it is an actual fact, from day to day, at no time a sufficiency had been given. On hospital boats, I was told by persons who came on them, the burial of from 12 to 30 was common during the voyage from Savannah and Charleston.

Fortunately, perhaps for myself, I early sickened of rations, or they became tasteless; for most part I subsisted on crackers furnished by the Christian Commission; the doctor gave the worst a drink of hot whisky punch three times a day, or a dose of Jamaica ginger tea supplied by the Soldiers' Aid Society. But nothing checked my complaints, and owing to dropsical tendency, that made me sluggish and clumsy, my complaint was all that saved my life in the end; for while the operations of the urinary system were entirely checked, laxity of the intestinal organs nature seemed to demand. The boat was uncomfortably crowded, and selfishness, the human hog, deprivation and pain had served to develop and stimulate to monopolize better parts, covering as much space as possible, for some persisted in spreading their blankets at all times, and stretching at full length and breadth without regard to others' rights or wants, and were ready to fight it out on that line—a class of men who rejoiced as loudly when free as any, though perhaps less grateful for respect and kindness shown by friendly strangers, who took every little tenderness, every expression of affection, every service and sympathy, and devoured and forgot, or trampled them under foot. Few among this class, however strong—and they were among the strongest—gave their places to weaker ones. They were the stoutest and they would stay. Shall we say this is but the world over again? Sea sickness among some, added no beauty to the scene. "Crowded in the rank and narrow ship," nothing of the fair and exquisite did we behold in our strange voyage. But through the stormlike mist and threatening wintry wave the "Crescent" plowed its way, bearing us to the loved North, our homes, our friends, we half unconscious of happy destiny. We kept far out from land; the crew talked much about the stormy waters of Cape Hatteras; we felt a dread, not really fearing, but not liking a rough time.

Late the second night, lying on the upper deck, I heard the watch announce "Cape Hatteras Light House." The feeblest on deck raised their heads; men came from below, and we saw far shoreward, through fog and darkness, a red light glimmering, then standing steady, larger, brighter than Venus. It was from North Carolina's most seaward coast.

I shall always remember the feeling of wonder and gratitude as I kneeled upon the deck, wet with the spray of the sea, and beheld that friend of the seamen on the shore, and felt assured that we had nearly rounded the cape. It was said we were sixty miles at sea, deeming it less dangerous at such distance. All was deemed safe, still waves rolled high, the wind-swept sea roared, the vessel rocked and rose and fell with them, but worked steadily on. We did not see the incomparable spectacle of a clear sunrise at sea for it was cloudy and foggy all the way.

Late in the afternoon of the 14th, before reaching Fortress Monroe, we met Porter's great fleet, whose destination proved to be Wilmington. I merely raised my head (lying on the deck) and gave a sidelong glance, and heard the glorious shouts of heroic men as we swept by. There is no grander sight than a vast fleet, the decks thronged with men, and the thought that they were friends whom we had left, going from battlefield to prison, that we were going for rest and quiet and resuscitation, they for labor and battle-strife. Remembrance of the past and hopes of the future combined to produce a romantic feeling of pride, of joy and fear, of a character seldom men's lot to realize.

That evening we saw the light of Cape Henry, and those in the vicinity of Fortress Monroe, and on the renowned waters of Chesapeake Bay we rocked gently between the Virginia shores. Fifteen months before I passed over these waters to Alexandria, to engage in scenes that cost many noble lives, much suffering and my own capture and imprisonment, and having been dragged through the self-styled Confederacy, return emaciated and impoverished, but still alive.

The afternoon of December 15th we came in view of the city of Annapolis and moored our vessel at its wharf. The Marine Band was playing a welcome and the passage-way for quite a distance from the wharf, was lined with men and women. On leaving the vessel, agents of the Christian Commission distributed tobacco, towels and handkerchiefs, giving to every man who would receive. As we passed, the ladies waved handkerchiefs and said: "Welcome home, boys"; "We are glad to see you, boys"; "God bless you, boys; may you soon get home to your friends," and other kindly greetings, so pleasant that I never can tell, and never can forget how it blessed and comforted; the sweetest words, the kindest looks, that women ever gave. But I cannot tell my wretched state, none wish to hear, I do not wish to pollute the page. I only wondered then, as now, that I had any feelings of a man, I wonder that I lived; felt my degredation deeply, my loathsomeness and corruption, unfitness, self disgust! Then the oppressed soul within lifted its head from wearied nature's breast and sighed a living breath.

By the assistance of Hawks and Madison, I succeeded in reaching College Green Barracks. Here each State's troops went together. Hawks bade me good-bye, and with Madison and Montgomery I went to barracks occupied by New York men.

An entire new suit and change of clothing, with blankets, were given every man.

Those taken from prison hospitals come on separate boats and are in the Naval School and St. John's College Hospital. New arrivals are being sent to Parole Camp Hospital, two miles from the city.

I acknowledge a debt of gratitude to James B. Hawks, Wakeshma, Kalamazoo County, Michigan, whose brotherly care, and faithful services, and patient forbearance toward me, while suffering pain himself, did much to relieve and comfort, and quite probably may have saved me from a watery grave. Also Benjamin Frank Madison, whose kindness was like a father's.

>
> Out of darkness, out of din,
>   Unto realms of peace I rise;
> From a den of woe and sin
>   Where squalid misery filled my eyes.
>
> A have risen from the night,
>   From the worst of mortal hells;
> From its fumes and from its blights,
>   'Gainst which every thought rebels.
>
> In that clutch of circumstance
>   Strong men winced and cried aloud
> 'Gainst bludgeoning of hate and chance;
>   Yet my soul is strong, unbowed.
>
> There is no spot of wrath or tears,
>   Or horrors worse than that foul place;
> The suffering for the sin of years
>   That brought the Nation deep disgrace.
>
> There is no crime that men commit
>   That brings to peoples more distress;
> Nor mightier war fires e'er were lit
>   The wrath of Treason to suppress.

Born of war shall come new fate;
Great wrong is blotted from the roll;
The future yet shall compensate
For sin that stained the country's scroll.

## CONCLUDING SKETCHES FROM DIARY.

From College Green Barracks, I was taken, with others to Parole Camp Hospital, Ward 3, December 17. Several acres are occupied for prisoners and hospital wards are being added, the need far exceeding expectations, for more than half of those from the prisons need medical attention that cannot be given in camp barracks. Here I remained until February 9, 1865, being confined to my cot for over six weeks. The place seemed a heaven; my notions of Union hospitals became exalted, though filled with starved and sickly men from the prisons of the South. The change was so marked that my existence verily seemed ecstatic. As natural functions began to resume their activities, they met the resistance of disordered systems and brought great pain, fevers, spasms, bloat, and eruptions, conditions very rare in medical practice. Friends of patients from the North frequently arrived to take them home. Generally patients were adjudged unfit to be removed. Christmas and New Year days are remembered for death scenes near my cot. In the ward were five men unrecovered from wounds received in battles of May and June, 1864—broken bones not knitted, flesh unhealed in cases where they were taken prisoners and were not properly treated, all doomed to end fatally. The endurance of these men under the circumstances, is a marvel to our doctors, owing to the poison diffused through their bodies which no known treatment can remove. The last of January I began to recover. But when the crisis had passed ravenous cravings of morbid prison hunger prostrated me, increasing with my strength. Nothing satisfied however plenty and good. This was true with all. Months elapsed, even after leaving the hospital, before I dare eat a common meal. The act of "filling up" did not stop the gnawing. It seemed to increase the abnormal hunger while it enervated and inflamed the system.

Books were furnished by Mrs. Carey and Miss Phillips, who resided near to deal out goods furnished by Sanitary and Christian Commissions. These ladies were from Massachusetts. Truly did they perform their labors of love. Ladies from other parts, some established at Washington, came on the same mission—ladies of culture, high character and intelligence, whose conduct made us feel they were comforters and teachers. It is but an expression of gratitude to say that theirs was the noblest part. Manly bravery and hardihood faced the dangers of battle, but womanly love and kindness, through many sacrifices, dealt with horrors left thickly behind.

The evening of February 8th the chief clerk brought my thirty days' furlough. I had not been out of my ward, but the next morning I ate my ration of bread, steak, milk and egg, and dressed for a start. Calling on Miss Phillips I found her unpacking clothing, bandages and the like. She had invited all to call who had been furloughed, to bid her good-bye. She was efficient as a mother in ascertaining the wants of "my boys," as she called us. She gave me underclothing, a scarf, gloves, and insisted in putting up crackers and candy—"Innocent little things to gnaw on the way. They will be good for you," she said, and she came around and crowded them into my pockets.

While this leaves the impression that the lady is kind and philanthropic to unfortunate soldiers, I am constrained to note, also, that she is a pretty young woman—a beautiful blonde. Mrs. Carey is an older woman, perhaps forty-five, a lady of culture, gentility and ripening womanly graces that compel respect and admiration.

I was off at 9 a. m., but did not leave Baltimore till evening. The train was crowded with invalid soldiers, accompanied by friends. At Harrisburg depot at midnight I found a lady and gentleman sitting besides a soldier son, whom they had been to Washington after. He had been wounded and a prisoner, having a broken leg which had not healed. They were Ohio people. While waiting for the train, he expired.

It was five days and nights before reaching my home in New York, having to stop at Binghampton to recruit. The proprietor and ladies of the hotel were extremely kind to me. Fifty days, twenty more than my original furlough, I was under the care of two doctors, getting to the door for the first to listen to booming cannon, April 10, celebrating the surrender of Lee to Grant. April 11th I started for Annapolis, Md., via New York City. April 14 I left that city in the afternoon. Reaching Baltimore about 3 a. m., April 15, the train was stopped in the suburbs, and boarded by officers and all doors locked, no reason being given, until daylight when news of Lincoln's assassination was announced and the doors were opened and all cars emptied. There were probably 100 furloughed soldiers. A crowd of rough men, of the degraded class, confronted us and began to jeer and shout "Good news this morning," and rejoice at the murder of the president. We immediately formed as if by impulse, and with canes and revolvers charged them. They ran for their lives, scattering into alleys and behind buildings until all had disappeared. The movement was earnest; every soldier meant business; and citizens cheered as they saw us rush up the banks and chase the ignorant traitors.

It was announced that no trains would leave Baltimore that day. It was apprehended that the assassins were in the city. Trains were coming in, but all were retained. The city was filled with people from other sections. Many Union soldiers. It was estimated that 40,000 Ex-Confederates were there, all in uniform, to be paroled. We mingled freely with them, they rejoicing with us that the war was over and most of them freely condemned the shooting of Lincoln. Citizens universally mourned; buildings were draped, flags hung low. Great change of sentiment among the more intelligent since the April of four years ago was apparent.

Many pathetic scenes occurred. Ladies filled the yards of residences, anxious to converse with Union soldiers and learn the latest bulletin from Washington, expressing sympathy and regret. It was a warm day with frequent quiet showers. As we were talking with a group, one lady with hands clasped before her said: "See, the heavens are weeping for Abraham Lincoln!" The excitement continued the next day. On the morning of April 17 trains again moved South, and at noon I arrived at the hospital, my extended furlough two days over due, and reported. As none from hospitals were allowed to report to their regiments, I was placed in charge of a ward; later detailed as clerk to the office of W. D. Stewart, Surgeon General of U. S. V., in charge, where I remained until June 24, 1865, assisting in the discharge of soldiers.

It was a sad sight after four months in hospital to look through sickly wards still filled with yellow, rigid victims. It is fearful to think that the grim visage of disease and death was stamped upon so many by a wanton, studied system of revenge. Out of 3,000 Union prisoners, arriving the 10th of March, 1865, over 1,500 were sent to hospitals. On the 11th, another installment of 802 arrived, 540 of whom were sent to hospital. These were men taken from prison, not from hospitals. The burial of twenty and thirty a day was frequent; fifty-four were buried one day. I state these as coming within my knowledge, not as a whole. The horrors of prison life were not all left in Georgia and South Carolina. One mile from the city of Annapolis, in the national cemetery, are graves of many victims of "Camp Sumter" and other prisons. Among them is Waldo Pinchen, a personal friend, and of my company.

Richmond, Danville, Salisbury, Florence, Millen, Savannah, and Charleston, as well as Andersonville, attest the barbarity of the treatment of prisoners, and will stand on historic pages as dark and loathsome spots. Not till the sea shall give up its dead and the hidden entombments of those who died in transit, shot by the way, or mangled by dogs in attempting escape, of which there is no account, will it all be revealed.

I have alluded to some acts of kindness of some people of the South, for which I was and am grateful. There were acts of brotherly kindness shown by Southerners on the field towards captives, but prison life was a scourge, a horror, a merciless slaughter pen. At Lynchburg, Va., Greenboro, Salisbury, and Charlotte, N. C., Augusta, Ga., Charleston, S. C., and other points there were unmistakable tokens of friendliness. When I speak of the barbarity of the South I mean that ruling spirit that first concocted the nefarious scheme to subvert the government to an instrument of oppression, finally to overthrow it.

The funeral obsequies for President Lincoln whom most soldiers esteemed as a loving father is esteemed, as well as the most lovable of public men, were in progress at Washington, and the wailing thunder of cannon was heard from the Potomac to the Chesapeake, on the forenoon of April 19th, 1865. Walking among the trees near my ward, deeply feeling the great solemnity of the occasion, these lines were composed:

### LINCOLN.
#### To Conquor is to Live, Enough.

Arise, ye sons, of brave Columbia, rise
And pay a tribute to a martyred son!
Let tear drops fall, like soft rain from the skies,
Bedewing the earth where our own Lincoln lies,
As great and good as our own Washington.
Ye daughters rise and let your voices sound,
In solemn anthems chant a people's grief;
But sound the glorious tidings far around,
Again the lost Atlantis has been found,
Though deeply now we mourn our noble chief.
Long he strove to check thes welling tide
That flowed to undermine the Nation's hope,
Leviathan struggling at its bleeding side
To swallow up all Freemen's hope and pride;
He drew the sword heroic'ly to cope.
He fought, Oh, bravely fought and well;
The maddened waves were dyed with running gore!
The monster raved, but wounded often fell,
So firm did Lincoln stand its power to quell;
He saw the monster fall to rise no more.
The land rejoiced and sounded o'er the sea
Good tidings gladdening every foreign shore.
He saw the light of peace glance o'er the Southern lea,
Heard trumpets swell, "America is free;

Slavery's power is broken, evermore."
He would sought his rest, but still the helm of State
He truly guided with a master hand;
But a foul assassin, mad at Treason's fate,
Cut short his reign while smiling at the gate
To welcome back the erring of the land.
    Most surely he condemned foul Treason's crime,
    But not in hate, or cruel lust, but love;
    He prayed for country, for liberty sublime,
    For unison and peace, o'er all our glorious clime;
    His virtuous heart his patriot labors prove.
Most nobly he from humble station rose;
Step by step he forced the brambly way,
His homely honor winning all his foes
Till the Nation's life in his firm hands repose,—
He saved the Nation in its dying day!
    He denied the traitors' mean and unjust claim,
    He fearless stood as if a host alone;
    He looked to God and millions praised his name,
    And, stepping from the niche of truest fame,
    He sits in peace beside the highest throne.
How oft it's been that purest men have died
To prove the truth of some great, holy cause,
To seal the life that all exemplified
Their lofty teachings unjust powers denied;
So Lincoln lived and died for Freedom's laws.
    What nobler deeds have heroes ever wrought,
    Who conquered worlds and trampled strong rebuff?
    He grandly rose to victory Treason sought;
    To win and conquer all was Lincoln's lot;
    To live and conquer is to live enough.
Then sleep, thou hero, thou wast truly free
Because thou willest none should be enslaved!
Sleep, honored ashes that no more shall be
Urn of the spirit now so heavenly!
Rest, for thy flag in triumph still is waved.
    Millions unborn will read the lofty tale,
    Will bless thy spirit in eternal skies,
    Exult in thee as sadly now we pale,
    Point to thy name whose luster ne'er shall fail,
    Name patriots love and traitors did despise.
So, fare thee well, chief of the patriot band;
A mighty land is weeping for thee now!
Missed is the guidance of thy steady hand!
Twice thou wast crowned to rule with Freedom's wand,
A wreath of glory crowns thy spirit brow.

## VISITED CLARA BARTON.

While in hospital at Annapolis, I answered inquiries made on printed slips caused to be posted by Clara Barton, regarding missing soldiers, and received letters from her in acknowledgement, one of which asked information about Andersonville prison and cemetery, stating that she had authority to go there to arrange and beautify the cemetery, and desired an ex-prisoner to accompany her, and invited me to visit her in reference to her mission after my discharge. On June 25, 1865, I called on Miss Barton in Washington and was pleasantly received, she extending her hand and thanking me as gratefully for my letters as though I had done her a personal service instead of giving slight aid to her efforts to serve hundreds of people she had never known. She had been made the head of a special bureau with the title "General Correspondent for the Friends of Paroled Prisoners," having been appointed by President Lincoln, March 11, 1865. I related to her all I thought might assist her. She asked if I could go. I doubted my ability owing to prison ailments. She asked me to go with her to a physician for examination which I did. He strenuously advised against my return to Andersonville.

It was a pleasure to meet Clara Barton. She is noted for humane and heroic service to suffering soldiers and their friends. I judge the lady thirty-five years of age, medium height, dark eyes and hair, slim, graceful form. She is not what society people esteem a fascinating beauty. Her face is plain but bearing about it that which is better than physical beauty—a sweet convincing expression of kindliness, self reliance and trustfulness, and when her interest is aroused it is lighted, her eyes become calmly brilliant and impart a charm that commands admiration due a soul whose love knows not narrow bounds. It is a face of firm intelligence which with other graces inspire associates in the work to which she has been highly devoted. Her purity of purpose and fidelity to her mission, has led her to know no danger, to dread no experience she must have met in the years she witnessed what no woman or man had seen in this generation. I felt impressed that her lofty unselfishness and the spirituality of her mind are saintly; that we need not seek in the mazy past, about which we little know and little feel, to find heroines and heavenly spirits.

Yet she is only one of many noble women engaged in alleviating the pains and sorrows of war. Both sides of the struggle have witnessed this saintly effort in a dreadful work to which men never dreamed gentle women would so heroically, yet so tenderly become devoted. In a lofty sense they knew no foe if foe came within their ministrations. Theirs has been a mission as high as the causes for which belligerents warred. While I have not been situated to know much about it personally until after leaving Charleston, S. C., yet I am thrilled with admiration and gratitude beyond expression. Miss Barton seems to be distinguished as an organizer and manager of the work so as to have influence in the government, and has been assigned to finish it according to plans she devised. Indeed she is recognized as the main organizer of the work to which so many grand women have given beneficent services in the war.

### FOUND HER BROTHER'S GRAVE.

In 1878 a considerable part of my diary was published in The Parish (N. Y.) Mirror, of which I was editor and proprietor, to which the writer of the following letter, whose husband was a major in a New York regiment during the war and later a resident of Georgia, was a subscriber:

Editor Parish Mirror:

Dear Sir: I presume none of your patrons have read your "Diary of a War Prisoner," with more interest than myself, as a brother of mine lost his life in the Andersonville prison and his remains rest in the cemetery at that place. * * *

In my home I often hear from the cemetery, and the year after my removal to Georgia, in company with a lady friend from Skaneateles, New York, we made a trip to Andersonville and gave the place a thorough inspection.

A night's ride from home brought us to Macon, where we parted company with my husband and proceeded alone the rest of the way. We had been told there was a little "inn" there where travelers could be entertained, and, so great was my desire to see the noted place, that I dared to undertake it. At that time the old bitterness between the North and South had not faded away, as it has now, and we sat quietly by ourselves in the car, feeling that we were indeed "strangers in a strange land"

I had with me a huge bunch of flowers that I had collected in my own grounds before leaving home, thinking that, for once, my brother's grave should be decorated. All unwittingly, I had pitched upon the day set apart for Confederate decoration. I was frequently asked if I was going to decorate, to which I replied in the affirmative, but when the conductor came for our tickets he glanced at the flowers which were swinging from the bracket over our seat, then at the tickets, then at us, when the following dialogue took place:

"Are you going to Andersonville?"

"Yes ,sir?"

"Have you friends in that cemetery?"

"Yes, sir; a brother."

"Are you a Northern woman?"
"Yes, sir. Are you a Southern man?"
"Yes."

After giving me a searching look he said: "Well, you have come a great way to find your graves, and I will help you all I can"; which he did not forget to do when we arrived at the station, for he waited his train until he found the man who had charge of the cemetery, and also the records, which he left me searching. The grounds are in charge of a superanuated regular army sergeant, who was exceedingly polite and accommodating. He informed us it was his duty to entertain any persons who came to visit the place, but I found there was a contraband school kept by two ladies from the North, in a building that used to be a Confederate hospital in prison days, and I went there and threw myself on their mercy, and passed a pleasant time with them; they being, evidently, as glad to see some person from the North as we were to get quarters. In a short time the old sergeant and his wife arrived at the school with a pair of mules and a cart, with the familiar brand U. S. on both vehicle and animals, and filled some hay in the box. We all got in (five ladies) and took seats on the bottom, and were driven away through the pen, and up the rise of ground to the cemetery. I feel that you will readily see how we looked and where we went, for all will be familiar to you. Arriving at the gate we were astonished at the beauty of everything around; the lodge just outside (the sergeant's home); the architecture of the gate, over which was a large board on which was printed an order from Washington, framed in language so plain and pointed that no one would be left in doubt as to the penalty that would be inflicted on any one who dared by any means to desecrate those grounds.

The carriage drive was wide and beautifully kept, rising in the center and sloping away on either side to a handsome piece of brick masonry which is to serve as a drain; for you must remember how the land will gulch and gully here after the hard rains. A white picket fence encloses the whole, inside of which is an osage orange hedge. Just in the center of all, in the main carriage drive, is a tall flag staff, and I believe Clara Barton had the honor of hoisting the first flag. A large handsome one was slowly flapping in the breeze that day and seemed to be guarding the spot where so many slept.

The records had told me the number of my brother's grave was 11854 and the sergeant commenced the search among the acres of the dead, as if it was a trade of his. We would look at the first head board of every row and said we must go to the eleven thousand rows. Finally, upon reaching those, he would seem to make a calculation as to how many was in the row, when he would say,

"No; it will run out at the end"; until reaching one he said, "It will about come in this," when, to be sure, following along until four graves of the end, we found it. I can never describe to you my feelings upon looking at his name, date of death, his company and regiment, all plainly printed on that head board, so many miles from his home on the sandy plains of Georgia, and I had at last been permitted to meander to the spot. I could only think if it were possible for him to know that one member of the family had sought all there was to find, it would in part atone for his having to close his eyes alone—bereft of every friend. I placed my floral offering on his grave, gathered some wild flowers that were growing on it, and turned away to look at other parts of the ground. Fine young trees were growing in every part, magnolias, water oaks, sweet gum, and other varieties peculiar to these latitudes, and I thought that at last the shade would come that they so much desired when it would have benefited them. At intervals roses were planted, and other Southern shrubs, some of them in perfect bloom. Government has made every reparation in its power, since they have been able to reach the spot.

In one place I found six graves, in a row by themselves, and on the headboards were inscribed "Hung! Hung! Hung!" In horror I asked, "Who hung these men?"

"They were hung by their own comrades," was the prompt reply, and he then proceeded to tell me the same tale I found in your record, and I must confess I have always remembered it with grains of allowance, until testified to by yourself. A handsome weeping willow was drooping its branches over them, which the sergeant informed me he placed there with his own hands, for said he: "Madam, had they not souls as well as the rest?" On glancing at the names on the boards and listening to his own peculiar brogue, I could perceive his particular friendship for them.

After obtaining the number of graves in the cemetery—13,716 Federals, and 118 Confederates—we visited the old stockade, or "pen. We found it slowly rotting away. The stockade was falling down, but the old sentry boxes still stood. The hospital buildings had tumbled over, and there was debris of brick and mortar, which they told me was where they had ovens. The stream was running through the pen, and looked cool and clear, and I felt that, if they had chosen to have it so, you might have been quite well fixed for a prison. The country is far more healthful than where we reside. I should judge but little malaria there. I stopped at the large wells dug by the prisoners, and peeped to the bottom. There was no water in them, and wild vines, clambering up and down the sides, presented a pretty appearance. The little spring you wrote of was bubbling up and has become quite large. I was told the same tale about its bursting forth, and had a cool draught from it in a gourd dipper. They now call it "Providential Spring." We looked about the grounds for some relics the poor fellows had left behind, but could see nothing but old shoes twisted and blackened by the suns and rains, until my friend picked up a button that had been lost from some coast. We were told that trinkets of all sorts, forks, spoons, buttons, etc., were plenty at one time; but too many had been there before us.

One thing I noticed in particular, was the color of the soil or sand, which resembles iron ore,, and from the soiled condition of our clothing after walking about the stockade, (now covered with grass), we calculated what your chances might have been for cleanliness, after the soil had been ground fine, as it naturally would be, trodden by so many feet. I gathered some in a paper and brought it away, and enclose you part, which will no doubt awaken reminiscences of your brick-colored "linen." * * *

After spending a day and night in Andersonville we left for Macon, with feelings of satisfaction I never expected to experience in relation to my brother's grave. We had always hoped we should be permitted to finally lay him to rest in the family lot in our native village, but every appointment about the "National Cemetery" was so appropriate and beautiful that I felt content to let him lie with those who suffered and died with him. I could see but one improvement that I could make: That would be to place a marble stone at his head, which would be more enduring than the wooden headboards; but government has even done that for us, and the friends of those who lie there may know that there is at least a bright side now that is in contrast with the uncertainties and agony of mind they endured when their friends were there, and in no earthly way could they reach, comfort, or aid them.

MRS. H. C. DEVENDORF.

Doctorstown, Ga., December 10, 1878.

## PRISON PSALMS.
### No. 1.

Arise for our help, and redeem us for Thy mercy's sake.—Psa'ms 44:26.

> Heavenly Father, we adore Thee,
> In affliction fall before Thee,
> Humbly bow and supplicate,
> Trusting Thou wilt guide our fate.
>
> To Thee, O, Lord, our sins confess,
> All our guile and wickedness,
> And come to Thee, now weak and poor,
> Asking alms, Lord, at Thy door!

# CHRONICLES OF A WAR PRISONER.

And from this bondage seek release
And go where love and joy increase!

And then I've thought it could not be
  This world is a redeemless place;
  That man is out of reach of grace;
And then I checked the thought in me,
And sighed, and thought, and felt more free;

Thought of all so dear to me,
  Of many a happy, peaceful day,
  Of loving friends, far, far away
And knew their hearts did yearn for me;
Then hoped that soon I might be free.

Then I thought to die would not be sweet,
  Imprisoned, exiled, and oppressed;
  To die unheard of and unblessed
And all my fondest hopes defeat;
My life would seem too incomplete.

And I've resolved to struggle still,
  Strive not to faint and not to tire,
  O'er towering peaks still looking higher,
Trusting in God's most holy will
To make me strong to brook each ill.

Is there no happiness below?
  Should I deplore my birthright here?
  Who knows the joy for every tear?
O! Who should fear to live and do
The work to God and men we owe?

Swift rush the currents to the sea,
  And clouds come lowering o'er the way,
  The dust of worlds in carnal fray;
And now I trust, but scarce can see,
A higher growing destiny.

I trust, I hope, I almost know
  It is the coming of the Lord,
  His chariots through the centuries heard,
Leavening the sodden world below;
To prepare the way His armies go.

Pestilence and death are here,
Day and night are lurking near,
And thousands wither in the blast,
Unsheltered into prison cast.

Men steeped in sin of deepest dye,
Sin with a savage hand and high;
With theft and murder in their hearts,
All love of God and man departs.

Scenes too horrid for the gaze,
Of nightly plunder, daily frays;
Too horrid for the human eye,
Or hearts not void of sympathy.

Heavenly Father, Thou knowest the sin,
All without and all within;
Thou knowest our wants and Thou canst give;
We thank Thee, Father, that we live!

Thank, yet from our fearful hearts
Some yearning deep to Thee departs;
For midst affliction, night and day,
What can we better do than pray?

Pray and lift our thoughts above
In hope, and faith, and trust, and love.
Save us from the wiles of sin;
Purify the man within!

And from disease our bodies save
Lest soon they languish to the grave!
Shield us, Heaven, from all we fear;
O, may we brook these ills severe!

Deliver, from affliction's ban,
To Thy glory and the good of man;
Lift up the right, confuse the wrong,
Teach men the ways of peace ere long!

But if foul disease and sapping pain,
Should rend these selves of ours in twain,
Then take us home unto Thy breast,
Great Father! and eternal rest.

Andersonville Military Prison, (Ga.) June 19, 1864.

## No. 2.

For he shall give His angels charge to keep thee in all thy ways.—Psalms 91:11.

Lord, Thou hast been our dwelling place
  Since Time's first note was beat,
Since Nature by Thy power and grace,
  Rolled grandly at Thy feet.
And when all elemental things,
  The Creative mandate heard,
From sphere to sphere the music rings
  Of that All Potent word...

On earth Thy power is all supreme,
  All Heaven owns Thy sway;
And all Thy goodness's like the beam
  Of Thy perpetual day.
The Heavenly hosts around Thy throne
  Sing anthems in their bliss,
And angels from their happier zone
  Note all the ills of this.

From their bright elysian bowers
  They watch our earthly race,
And scatter in our course sweet flowers
  To help us on to grace.
O! who shall say they do not oft
  Descend to us in love,
Glimpsing to us, in visions soft,
  The world that is above!

How oft they'd satisfy our wants
  And soothe us in distress,
As heaven's shining pursuivants
  Bring messages to bless,
If our poor aching souls could know
  Their heavenly presence near,
(As oft in psychic realm they do),
  And their cheering voices hear,

If 'twere not that these mortal coils
  And baser passions bind,
And keep us from the higher toils
  That sweet communions find.
Yet round our paths they linger still,
  When midst the darkest din
We stumble oft, on life's steep hill,
  To save us from our sin.

They keep us in our better way,
  Though wayward oft we be,
Though prodigal may go astray
  And blinded cannot see.
They seek to call us back in love
  And heal our leprous sight;—
There's rejoicing in the world above,
  When sinners turn to light.

But there are those whose sin and wo
  Their presence may not reach—
Such poor benighted souls below—
  Sweet heavenly lore to teach;
And so we grovel, knowing not
  Their constant mindfulness.
They'd guide us to our better lot,
  And fit us for its bliss.

O, raise the veil from this dim sphere,
  And let me look beyond,
And to my prayers, O! let me hear
  Their voices sweet respond!
O, let their everlasting hymns
  My pining spirit raise
To join the songs of seraphims,
  God's gracious love to praise!

Military Prison, Adersonville, Ga., July 18, 1864.

## No. 3.

I've almost wished that I was dead
  And far beyond the woe and din
  Of this dark world and all its sin,
Nor cared where lay my weary head,
Nor whose rough hands prepare my bed.

I've sometimes thought it would be swe
  When sore affliction did oppress,
  And all around me was distress,
For my strong heart to cease to beat;
In the deathly realm to seek retreat.

O, let my spirit soar in peace,
  And know no more of war and strife
  That mar all happiness of life,

Pestilence and death are here,
Day and night are lurking near,
And thousands wither in the blast,
Unsheltered into prison cast.

Men steeped in sin of deepest dye,
Sin with a savage hand and high;
With theft and murder in their hearts,
All love of God and man departs.

Scenes too horrid for the gaze,
Of nightly plunder, daily frays;
Too horrid for the human eye,
Or hearts not void of sympathy.

Heavenly Father, Thou knowest the sin,
All without and all within;
Thou knowest our wants and Thou canst give;
We thank Thee, Father, that we live!

Thank, yet from our fearful hearts
Some yearning deep to Thee departs;
For midst affliction, night and day,
What can we better do than pray?

Pray and lift our thoughts above
In hope, and faith, and trust, and love.
Save us from the wiles of sin;
Purify the man within!

And from disease our bodies save
Lest soon they languish to the grave!
Shield us, Heaven, from all we fear;
O, may we brook these ills severe!

Deliver, from affliction's ban,
To Thy glory and the good of man;
Lift up the right, confuse the wrong,
Teach men the ways of peace ere long!

But if foul disease and sapping pain,
Should rend these selves of ours in twain,
Then take us home unto Thy breast,
Great Father! and eternal rest.

Andersonville Military Prison, (Ga.) June 19, 1864.

### No. 2.

*For he shall give His angels charge to keep thee in all thy ways.*—Psalms 91:11.

Lord, Thou hast been our dwelling place
　Since Time's first note was beat,
Since Nature by Thy power and grace,
　Rolled grandly at Thy feet.
And when all elemental things,
　The Creative mandate heard,
From sphere to sphere the music rings
　Of that All Potent word. ..

On earth Thy power is all supreme,
　All Heaven owns Thy sway;
And all Thy goodness's like the beam
　Of Thy perpetual day.
The Heavenly hosts around Thy throne
　Sing anthems in their bliss,
And angels from their happier zone
　Note all the ills of this.

From their bright elysian bowers
　They watch our earthly race,
And scatter in our course sweet flowers
　To help us on to grace.
O! who shall say they do not oft
　Descend to us in love,
Glimpsing to us, in visions soft,
　The world that is above!

How oft they'd satisfy our wants
　And soothe us in distress,
As heaven's shining pursuivants
　Bring messages to bless,
If our poor aching souls could know
　Their heavenly presence near,
(As oft in psychic realm they do),
　And their cheering voices hear,

If 'twere not that these mortal coils
　And baser passions bind,
And keep us from the higher toils
　That sweet communions find.
Yet round our paths they linger still,
　When midst the darkest din
We stumble oft, on life's steep hill,
　To save us from our sin.

They keep us in our better way,
  Though wayward oft we be,
Though prodigal may go astray
  And blinded cannot see.
They seek to call us back in love
  And heal our leprous sight;—
There's rejoicing in the world above,
  When sinners turn to light.

But there are those whose sin and woe
  Their presence may not reach—
Such poor benighted souls below—
  Sweet heavenly lore to teach;
And so we grovel, knowing not
  Their constant mindfulness.
They'd guide us to our better lot,
  And fit us for its bliss.

O, raise the veil from this dim sphere,
  And let me look beyond,
And to my prayers, O! let me hear
  Their voices sweet respond!
O, let their everlasting hymns
  My pining spirit raise
To join the songs of seraphims,
  God's gracious love to praise!

Military Prison, Adersonville, Ga., July 18, 1864.

### No. 3.

I've almost wished that I was dead
  And far beyond the woe and din
  Of this dark world and all its sin,
Nor cared where lay my weary head,
Nor whose rough hands prepare my bed.

I've sometimes thought it would be sweet,
  When sore affliction did oppress,
  And all around me was distress,
For my strong heart to cease to beat;
In the deathly realm to seek retreat.

O, let my spirit soar in peace,
  And know no more of war and strife
  That mar all happiness of life,

And from this bondage seek release
And go where love and joy increase!

And then I've thought it could not be
  This world is a redeemless place;
  That man is out of reach of grace;
And then I checked the thought in me,
And sighed, and thought, and felt more free;

Thought of all so dear to me,
  Of many a happy, peaceful day,
  Of loving friends, far, far away
And knew their hearts did yearn for me;
Then hoped that soon I might be free.

Then I thought to die would not be sweet,
  Imprisoned, exiled, and oppressed;
  To die unheard of and unblessed
And all my fondest hopes defeat;
My life would seem too incomplete.

And I've resolved to struggle still,
  Strive not to faint and not to tire,
  O'er towering peaks still looking higher,
Trusting in God's most holy will
To make me strong to brook each ill.

Is there no happiness below?
  Should I deplore my birthright here?
  Who knows the joy for every tear?
O! Who should fear to live and do
The work to God and men we owe?

Swift rush the currents to the sea,
  And clouds come lowering o'er the way,
  The dust of worlds in carnal fray;
And now I trust, but scarce can see,
A higher growing destiny.

I trust, I hope, I almost know
  It is the coming of the Lord,
  His chariots through the centuries heard,
Leavening the sodden world below;
To prepare the way His armies go.

O, I would live to see that day,
  Of which prophets spake and sages wrote,
  In great historic days remote;
O, I'd go farther on the way,
  Till Freedom's laws all men obey.
Andersonville, (Ga.) Military Prison, August 6, 1864.

### No. 4.

O, Thou who was all else before,
  Above all else extant,
Whom angels reverence, saints adore,
  Who knoweth every want,
We turn to Thee in darkest day
Knowing not the way!

In prison cast, afflicted sore,
  Where help of man could scarce be found,
With death and misery at the door,
  We felt Thy goodness still abound.
In Thee we hoped for our release,
Only in Thee had peace.

Long days of suffering passed away,
  Many sank to nameless graves,
But the closing of an autumn day
  We heard a cry my heart still craves.
At dawn the gates were open thrown.
A light momentarily shone.

Out poured the famished, sick and lame,
  O'erjoyed to breathe a purer air,
Till to this prison den we came
  To feel anew our hearts despair.
Hope sank low, still murmuring run
Like rills ,hid from the sun.

It was relief our hearts to bless,
  To come forth from that deadly pen;
To gain some respite from distress
  That whelmed that host at Anderson;—
To hasten many miles from there
To fight this new despair.

They bore by scores the dead men forth
  Each day—and hundreds worse than dead;—

Once stalwart men, and men of worth,
　　From youth and prime the life-glow fled.
Midst filth and vermin, spite of pride,
　　As they had lived they died.

Ah! We had hoped to see no more
　　Of such dark woe, and yet we feared;
But it is here, e'en at the door
　　To blast the thought forlorn hopes cheered.
Still we are prisoners and the foe
Will not, will not let us go.

Yes, these hard trials come anew,
　　And famine stares us in the face;
Horrors thicken 'round the place
　　Making sad and dark our view.
Yet, dear Lord, we look to Thee
For our salvation free.

Deliver us, good God, we pray,
　　From the hands of bitter foes
Who seem delighted by our woes;—
　　O, haste deliverance day!
'Tis hard to linger thus distressed,
Though trusting, yet unblessed.

Unblessed except in faith in Thee,
　　Knowing Thou rulest o'er all, Most High!
E'en though we faint, and rot and die.
　　A bird so worthy of Thy note?
　　The fall of sparrows Thou dost see?
From Thee am I remote?

Thanks and praise unto Thy name,
　　O, Great and Holy One!
We bow contritely at Thy throne
　　Whence all life and being came.
Keep us from famine and from cold;
Be with us as with those of old.

Purge our hearts from sin, good God!
　　And seal them with Thy seal;
There's grace and wisdom in Thy rod
　　'Tis justice oft to feel—
Oft turned us on the better road,
Oft light and peace bestowed.

Military Prison, Florence, S. C., September, 1864.

## No. 5.

"Lead me, Father, holding by Thy hand,
I ask not whither; for it must be on."
MacDonald.

Trials dark, afflictions sore,
Have burst upon my soul anew
But Thou canst safely bring me o'er
As Israel's tribe the Red Sea through.
By fiery pillar piloted,
The sea rolled back its watery bed,
While through the deep and dread abyss
The chosen children strode
Safely to the shore of peace,
Beyond the raging flood
That wrapped their swift Egyptian foes,
Confused, and broken as they close.
From Gilead Mount did Gideon
To Jezreel vale, with faithful band,
Descend to the hosts of Midian
Whom the Lord delivered to his hand.
'Neath an oak in Ophrah came the word;;
There sat an angel of the Lord.
How oft was Israel, when oppressed,
Though found upon an evil way,
Delivered from her foes, and blessed,
By faith in Thee from day to day.
And such deliverance I pray that we,
God of heaven! soon may see.

O, give us faith, be it our guide,
As Abraham had faith in Thee,
To offer up his son, when tried,
A living sacrifice and free;
Yet meek as Isaac, only child,
Submissive, patient, undefiled.
Thou'lt send an angel to embrace;
Thou wilt withhold the fatal rod!
What e'er Thou wilt, oh, give us grace
And lift us to some blest abode!
Like Enoch translated to the skies,
So let our aspirations rise.

Confederate Military Prison, Florence, S. C., October, 1864.

## No. 6.

God of our fathers! O, God of all!
  In Thee we live forevermore.
In all our hearts sweet peace install,
  And make us welcome at Thy door.

Forgive each soul that wrongly stept,
  That it shall seek the rightful way.
If in the wrong our spirits slept,
  Awake them by Thy heavenly ray.

Thy mercies send our lot to bless;—
  We feel that e'en this woeful place
Thou fillest with Thy righteousness
  And lightest with Thy holy grace.

For in our hearts doth still abide
  Thy word of truth, and light, and cheer,
And whatsoe'er may us betide
  We'll trust Thy goodness still, nor fear.

Here weak with pain and gaunt our frames,
  Slow fading in this earthly blight;
Famished we chill, then feverish flames
  Unnerve by day, disturb by night.

Yet every heart in Thee may trust
  To free our souls from every taint;
We know Thou lovest, Thou art just,
  That Thou dost hold us when we faint.

Florence, (S. C.) Confederate Military Prison, November 8, 1864.

[These poems, written as indicated by dates, are inserted in deference to the opinions of a few friends.]

### OF FAR AWAY.

The dreary winds come murmuring on
And in the old woods roar,
And the faint November sun
Cold in the west doth lower,
And shadows thicken round the door
Where I have sat at noon's bright ray,
And I think of those now all the more;
Who made me happy then and gay,
For I am sad and far away.

The Gothic house, its windows low,
Its rattling rods for lightning drest,
The chamber where I used to go
To read, to write and rest;—
Old fondled schemes my thoughts infest!—
The old grey barn, the chosen site
Where martin's build each huddled nest
And gambol with a strange delight,
All haunt my thoughts this lone twilight.

The red schoolhouse, the watering place,
The penstock in the yard;
The stubbled hills, that southward face,
In summer time so dry and hard;
The wood tops looking brown and bared;
The Gilead by the picket fence;
The mountain ash the cattle marred,
Near the wall where lingers fragrance
And maids have twined bouquets, perchance.

The cold west wind sweeps 'cross the field
And o'er the old causeway;
The frost-bit leaves in silence yield
Unto the Autumn's sway;
The orchard's bare that bloomed in May.
White curtains o'er the windows fall,
The red rays on the carpet lay
And break against the farther wall;
These scenes my longing thoughts recall.

Light steps upon the kitchen floor!
The cistern spout I seem to hear
Where softly silver waters pour!
My mother's form is at the door,
And other forms appear.
My father, ripe with many a year,
Moves up the dooryard from the gate;
A loving voice his heart doth cheer;
My sister doth upon him wait,
The pride and stay of the estate.

Now, sitting by her bedroom door
One grown venerable and fair,
As she was wont in days before,—
Sits in her high-back rocking chair;
And her brow seems worn with care.

She speaks of those dear to her heart,
Of one far away she knows not where;
Of both with whom 'twas hard to part,
And from her eyes tears often start.

Now when the evening draweth nigh,
Twilight's grey stream is poured,
Shadows come o'er earth and sky
Like curtains softly lowered,
They gather round the family board—
My father's board was always free;
Who would might share the riches stored
By dint of virtuous industry;
How gladly would they share with me!

But the sun will rise and set again,
I know not how many times it will;
November's fog and cheerless rain
Will float and fall upon the hill;
The vale below may flow and fill,
And winter snows as they have been,
And I may be here still,
Within this cold and dreary den;
A living tomb, a hell of men.

Florence, S. C., Military Prison, November, 1864.

## PILGRIMAGE.

Childhood has its golden charms,
  Meandering through the maze,
And thought of it I know disarms
  The cares of later days.

The softest dews of verdant morn,
  The tenderest April showers,
Wake from its mold the germ forlorn
  And lift the happiest flowers.

The warm sun comes, the warm bright sun,
  And all the day it shines
Till waning in the west sky run
  The sunset russet lines.

Day light gone, the twilight come
  Then cooler, darker shades;

Then bright white stars set in the dome
   As mild as modest maids.

Then deeper glow, then glitter clear,
   An azurer hue the ray,
And later, still, more bright appear,
   Too gentle for the day.

The herbage springing all the night,
   The roots more lucious grow,
And at the soft, clear orient light
   There is a fresher glow.

Pastures green are grown more green,
   Meadows begin to wave;
The grain, and corn, in sweet serene
   The dews anoint and lave.

Then dark, thick clouds bedim the west,
   And darken Southern sky.
And breezes mild, that lulled to rest,
   Have fierce winds grown and high.

Then thunders roll and jar the air,
   And rain in torrents fall;
Thick hail cut down the blossoms fair
   And beat against the wall.

Then lulls the storm, the dreary storm,
   The clouds break off in sheets;
The atmosphere does quick reform
   And dries the pebbly streets.

The sunshine comes again, again
   The storm-beat, drooping heads
Of flower, and grass, and corn, and grain
   Raise from their watery beds.

Bright days are warm and warmer grow,
   The earth is mantled o'er,
And fruitful fields all living flow
   Rich harvests at your door.

The fruit trees, that the gale had bent,
   Have bought their good supplies;

The air is rich with sweetest scent
  Borne to the evening skies.

And everywhere there is a beam
  Of happiness and love;
The storms that once did adverse seem,
  Have helped to lift above.

The spring of life, the summer come,
  The harvests' glorious show;
I would my life were such a tome
  For all the winds might blow.

I would it were?—oh, may it be!
  Would I be spared the lore
That makes the spirit truly free
  When its pilgrimage is o'er?

No; I must toil from door to door,
  Nor lay aside my staff,
Nor think my day's toil is all o'er
  While yet unfinished half.

The angel, that I seek afar,
  Throws open wide her door,
And becks me on from star to star,
  And smiling will no more.

Oft clouds grow dark and rough the way,
  Betimes I cannot see,
And I have sighed, ah, many a day,
  Hard is the lot for me.

Then lulled the storms that rolled above;
  There glows a beam more fair;
I stronger grow in my sweet love
  E'en fainting with despair.

O, shall that Paradisal hour
  E'er greet my panting soul,
When like a full matured flower
  I shall have gained the goal?

But the angel sought is far away,
  Sits smiling at her gates.
And says to me: "This is the way;"
  And watches, chides and waits.

Andersonville, Ga., Military Prison, June 22, 1864.

## APPENDIX.

## CONFEDERATE TESTIMONY.

### Statement of Dr. Jones, Professor in the Medical College of Georgia

Beginning on page 588, serial number 121, of the War Records, is a report as to the condition of Andersonville in the summer and autumn of 1864, prepared by Dr. Joseph Jones, Professor of Medical Chemistry in the Medical College of Georgia, at Augusta, Georgia, by authority of Surgeon-General Moore of the Confederacy, and was to have been presented to him at Richmond, but the ending of hostilities prevented. It fell into Federal hands and was sent to the United States War Department and used by Judge-Advocate W. P. Chipman as evidence, Dr. Jones also being a witness to show the competence of this report as evidence and its accuracy, against Henry Wirz in his trial before the military commission, accused of murder of Union prisoners while in charge at Andersonville. Wirz was convicted and hanged November 10, 1865. Coroborative of my diary, I use the substance of that report which is remarkable for frankness in stating the truth, and in the absence of any defense of our keepers for the terrible condition that prevailed, unqualifiedly putting the responsibility upon his own government. It being loosely written its value is preserved in condensed form in which the language used is that of the Confederate doctor, eliminating superfluous sentences, and omitting complicated tabulations which simply confirm plain statements. The significance of the document lies in the candor with which it tells some of the facts relative to the management and consequent conditions at Andersonville, which had its weight in the conviction of Wirz. Dr. Jones states that it was in Richmond that he heard of the horrors at Andersonville; so it is indisputable that the Confederate authorities were cognizant of the situation. Dr. Jones began:

"Hearing of the unusual mortality of Federal prisoners confined at Andersonville, Ga., in August, 1864, during a visit to Richmond, Va., I expressed to the surgeon general, S. P. Moore, Confederate States of America, a desire to visit Camp Sumter, with the design of instituting a series of inquiries upon the nature and causes of the prevailing diseases. * * * It was believed that a large body of men from Northern United States, suddenly transported to a Southern climate, and confined upon a small portion of land, would furnish an excellent field for the investigation of the relations of typhus, typhoid, and malarial fevers. The surgeon general of the Confederate States of America furnished me with the letter of introduction to the surgeon in charge (Isaiah H. White) of the Confederate States Military Prison at Andersonville, Georgia,"

After describing the constructive features of the prison which are previously stated, he says:

"Within the circumscribed area of the stockade Federal prisoners were compelled to perform all the offices of life. * * * Prisoners were crowded into the confined space, until in the month of June the average number of square feet of ground to each prisoner was only 33.2 or less than four square yards. These figures represent the condition of the stockade in a better light light than it was; for a considerable breadth of land along the stream, flowing from west to east between the hills, was low and boggy, and was covered with excrement, and rendered uninhabitable, and useless for every purpose except that of defecation. * * * No shade trees were left in the stockade. With their characteristic industry and ingenuity, the Federals constructed for themselves small huts and caves, and attempted to shield themselves from the rain and sun and night damps. * * * In the location of these huts no order appears to have been followed; regular streets appear out of the question in so crowded an area; especially as large bodies of prisoners were from time to time added suddenly without previous preparations. * * *

"The large number of men confined soon covered the surface of the low grounds with excrements. The sinks over the lower portions of the stream were imperfect in plan. The volume of water was not sufficient to wash away the feces, and as they accumulated in such quantities in the lower portion of the stream as to form a mass of liquid excrement. Heavy rains caused the stream to rise, and as the arrangements for the passage of the increased amounts of water out of the stockade were insufficient, the liquid feces overflowed the low grounds and covered them several inches, after the subsidence of the waters. The action of the sun upon this putrefying mass of excrement excited rapid fermentation and developed a horrible stench. * * * As the forces of prisoners were reduced by confinement, want of exercise, improper diet, scurvy, diarrhoea, and dysentery, they were unable to evacuate their bowels within the stream or along its banks, and the excrements were deposited at the very doors of their tents. * * * The accommodations for the sick were imperfect and insufficient. From the organization of the prison, February 24, 1864, to May 22, the sick were treated within the stockade. In the crowded condition of the stockade it was impossible to secure proper ventilation or to maintain necessary police. The hospital was, on the 22d of May, removed to its present site without the stockade, and five acres of ground covered with oaks and pines appropriated to the use of the sick. The supply of medical officers has been insufficient from the foundation of the prison. * * *

"From the want of proper police and hygienic regulations it

CHRONICLES OF A WAR PRISONER.    21

is not wonderful that from February 24 to September 21, 1864, nine thousand four hundred and seventy-nine deaths, nearly one-third the entire number of prisoners, should have been recorded. I found the stockade and hospital in the following conditions during my pathological investigations, instituted in the month of September, 1864:

"At the time of my visit to Andersonville a large number of Federal prisoners had been removed to Millen, Savannah, Charleston, Florence and other parts of the Confederacy, in anticipation of an advance of General Sherman's forces; however, about 15,000 remained confined in the stockade and hospital. * * *

"Each day the dead from the stockade were carried out by fellow-prisoners and deposited upon the ground under a bush arbor, just outside of the southwestern gate. From thence they were carried in carts to the burying ground, one-quarter of a mile northwest of the prison. The dead were buried without coffins, side by side, in trenches four feet deep.

"The low grounds bordering the stream were covered with human excrements and filth of all kinds, which was alive with maggots. An indescribable sickening stench arose from these fermenting masses of filth.

"There were near five thousand seriously ill Federals in the stockade and hospital. Deaths exceeded one hundred per day. Large numbers of prisoners who were walking about, and who had not been entered upon the sick reports, were suffering from severe and incurable diarrhoea, dysentery, and scurvy. The sick were attended almost entirely by fellow-prisoners, appointed as nurses, and as they received but little attention, they were compelled to exert themselves at all times to attend calls of nature; hence they retained the power of moving about to within a comparatively short period of the close of life. Owing to the slow progress of diseases most prevalent, diarrhoea and chronic dysentery, the corpses as a rule are emaciated.

"I visited two thousand sick within the stockade, lying under long sheds erected late in August, which had been built at the northern portion for themselves. At this time only one medical officer was in attendance, whereas at least twenty medical officers should have been employed.

"Scurvy, diarrhoea, dysentery, and gangrene were prevailing diseases. I was surprised to find but few cases of malarial fever, and no well marked cases of typhus or typhoid fever. The absence of the different forms of malarial fever may be accounted for in the supposition that the artificial atmosphere of the stockade, crowded densely with human beings and loaded with animal exhalations, was unfavorable to malarial poison. * * *

"Effects of scurvy were manifest on every hand, in all its

various stages, from the muddy, pale complexion, pale gums, feeble, languid muscular motions, lowness of spirits, and fetid breath, to the dusky, dirty, leaden complexion, swollen features, spongy, purple, livid, fungoid, bleeding gums, loose teeth, oedematous limbs, covered with livid vibices, and petechiae spasmodically flexed, painful and hardened extremities, spontaneous hemorrhages from mucous canals, and large, ill-conditioned, spreading ulcers covered with a dark purplish fungus growth. I observed that in some cases of scurvy the parotid glands were swollen, to such an extent as to preclude entirely the power to articulate. Dropsy also appeared. * * * Severe pains and livid patches were associated with swellings in various parts, especially in the lower extremities, accompanied with stiffness and contractions of the knee joints and ankles, often preventing the motion of the skin over the swollen parts. * * * I observed numerous cases of gangrene, and spreading scorbutic ulcers, which had supervened upon slight injuries. The scorbutic ulcers presented a dark, purple fungoid, elevated surface, with livid swollen edges, and exuded a thin, fetid, sanious fluid, instead of pus. Many ulcers which originated from the scorbutic condition of the system become gangrenous. * * * From the crowded, filthy condition, bad diet, and dejected, depressed condition of prisoners, their systems had become so disordered that the smallest abrasion of the skin, from the rubbing of a shoe, effects of the sun, the prick of a splinter, from scratching, or a mosquito bite, in some cases, took on rapid and frightful ulceration and gangrene. The long total deprivation of vegetables and fruit are the chief causes of scurvy. I carefully examined the bakery and the bread furnished the prisoners, and found that they were supplied almost entirely with corn-bread from which the husk had not been separated. This husk acted as an irritant to the alimentary canal, without adding nutriment. * * * I strongly urged the preparation of large quantities of soup made from the cow's and calves' heads with the brains and tongues, to which a liberal supply of sweet potatoes and vegetables might been advantageously added. The material existed in abundance for the preparation of such soup in large quantities with but little additional expense. Such aliment would have been not only highly nutritious, but it would have acted as an efficient remedial agent for the removal of the scorbutic condition. The sick within the stockade lay under several long sheds. These sheds covered two floors which were open on all sides. The sick lay upon the bare boards, or upon such ragged blankets as they possessed, without any bedding or even straw.. (Building of these sheds is mentioned in my Chronicle in August).

"The haggard, distressed countenances of these miserable, complaining, dejected, living skeletons, crying for medical aid and food, and cursing their government for its refusal to exchange prisoners, and the ghastly corpses, with their glazed eye balls staring up into vacant space, with the flies swarming down their open and grinning mouths, and over their ragged clothes, infested with lice, as they lay amongst the sick and dying, formed a picture of helpless, hopeless misery which it would be impossible to portray by words or by brush. A feeling of disappointment and even resentment on account of the United States government upon the subject of the exchange of prisoners, appeared to be widespread, and the apparent hopeless nature of the negotiations for some general exchange of prisoners appeared to be a cause of deep and injurious despondency. * * * A hundred or more prisoners had been released from confinement in the stockade on parole, and filled various offices as clerks, druggists, carpenters, etc. * * *

"Patients and attendants, near two thousand, are crowded into this confined space but poorly supplied with ragged tents. Large numbers without bunks lay upon the ground, oftimes without even a blanket. No beds or straw appeared. The tents extend to within a few yards of the small stream, the eastern portion of which, used as a privy and is loaded with excrements. I observed a large pile of corn-bread, bones, and filth of all kinds, thirty feet in diameter and several feet high, swarming with myriads of flies, near the pots used for cooking. Millions of flies swarmed over everything, covered the faces of sleeping patients, crawled down their open mouths, and deposited their maggots in the gangrenous wounds of the living, and in the mouths of the dead. Mosquitoes infested the tents; many patients were so stung by these insects, that they resembled those suffering from measles.

"The police and hygiene of the hospital were defective in the extreme; attendants * * * seemed to have in many cases but little interest in the welfare of their fellow-captives. They certainly appeared to neglect the comfort and cleanliness of the sick shamfully, even after making due allowances for the difficulties of the situation. Many of the sick were literally encrusted with dirt and filth and covered with vermin. When a gangrenous wound needed washing, the limb was thrust out and water poured over it, and all the putrescent matter allowed to soak into the ground floor of the tent. The supply of rags for dressing wounds was very scant. I saw the most filthy rags which had been applied several times, and imperfectly washed, used in dressing wounds. Where gangrene was prevailing, it was impossible to escape contagion. The results of the treatment of wounds in the hospital were of the most unsatisfactory character, from this neglect as well as from various other causes. I saw gangrenous wounds filled with maggots. * * *This want of cleanliness appeared to be the result of carelessness and inattention, rather than of malignant design, and the whole trouble can be traced to the want of proper police and sanitary regulations, and total absence of system. In extenuation of these abuses it was alleged by medical officers that Confederate troops were barely sufficient to guard prisoners; that it was impossible to obtain experienced nurses from Confederate forces.

"The manner of disposing of the dead was calculated to depress the desponding spirits of these men, many of whom have been confined for months, even for nearly two years in Richmond and other places, and whose strength had been wasted by bad air, bad food, and uncleanliness. The dead-house is merely a frame covered with old tent cloth and bushes, situated in the southwestern corner of the hospital grounds. When a patient dies, he is laid in the narrow street in front of his tent, until he is removed by Federal negroes detailed to carry off the dead; if a patient dies during the night, he lies there until the morning, and during the day the dead frequently remained for hours in these walks. In the dead-house the corpses lie upon the bare ground, and were covered with filth and vermin.

"The cooking arrangements are of the most defective character. Five large iron pots similar to those used for boiling sugar cane, were the only cooking utensils furnished for the cooking of two thousand men; and patients were dependent in great measure upon their own miserable utensils.

"The air of the tents was foul in the extreme. The entire grounds emitted a nauseous, disgusting smell. I entered nearly all tents and carefully examined cases of interest, especially cases of gangrene, during the prosecution of my pathological inquiries at Andersonville, and enjoyed every opportunity to judge correctly of the hygiene and police of the hospital.

"There appeared to be almost absolute indifference and neglect of personal cleanliness; the persons and clothing of patients, in most instances, especially of those suffering with gangrene and scorbutic ulcers, were filthy in the extreme and covered with vermin. Patients were received from the stockade in most deplorable conditions. I saw men brought from the stockade in a dying condition, begrimed from head to foot with their own excrements, and so black from smoke and filth that they resembled negroes rather than white men. * * *

"During six months, the 1st of March to the 31st of August, 42,686 cases of diseases and wounds were reported. No classified record of the sick in the stockade was kept after the establishment of the hospital without the prison. This fact, in conjunction with those already presented relating to the insufficiency of medical officers nad the extreme illness and death of many prisoners in the stockade, without any medical attention or record beyond the bare number of the dead, demonstrate that these figures, large as they appear, are far below the truth. * * *

"We observe a progressive increase of the rate of mortality, from 3.11 per cent. in March to 9.09 per cent. of mean strength, sick and well, in August. The ratio of mortality continued to increase during September, for notwithstanding the removal of one-half of the entire number of prisoners during the early portion of the month, one thousand seven hundred and sixty seven (1,767) deaths are registered from September 1 to 21, and the largest number of deaths upon any one day occurred during this month, on the 16th, viz.: one hundred and nineteen.

"The entire number of Federal prisoners confined at Andersonville was about 40,611; and during the period of near seven months, from February 24 to September 21, 9,479 deaths were recorded; that is, during this period near one-fourth, or more, exactly one in 4.2, or 23.3 per cent., terminated fatally. This increase of mortality was due in great measure to the accumulation of the sources of disease, as the increase of excrements and filth of all kinds, and the concentration of noxious effluvia.

### His Conclusions.

"The great mortality among Federal prisoners confined in the military prison at Andersonville was not referable to climatic causes, or to the nature of the soil and waters.

"The chief causes of death, were scurvy and its results and bowel affections—chronic and acute diarrhoea and dysentery. The bowel affections appear to have been due to the diet, the depressed, dejected state of the nervous system and moral and intellectual powers, and to the effluvia arising from decomposing filth. The unvarying diet of corn-meal, with but few vegetables, and imperfect supplies of vinegar and syrup, were manifested in the great prevalence of scurvy. This disease, without doubt, was also influenced to an important extent in its origin and course by foul emanations.

"From the sameness of the food and the action of poisonous gases in the densely crowded and filthy stockade and hospital, the blood was altered in its constitution, even before the manifestation of actual disease. In both the well and the sick the red corpuscles were diminished; in all diseases uncomplicated with inflammation, the fibrous element was deficient. In cases of ulceration of the mucous membrane of the intestinal canal, the fibrous element of the blood was increased; while in simple diarrhoea, uncomplicated with ulceration, it was diminished or remained stationary. Heart clots were common, if not universally present, in cases of ulceration of the intestinal mucous membrane, while in the complicated cases of diarrhoea and scurvy, the blood was fluid and did not coagulate readily, and the heart clots and fibrous concretions were almost universally absent. From the watery condition of the blood, there resulted various serous effusions into the pericardium, ventricles of the brain, and into the abdomen. In almost all the cases which I examined after death, even the most emaciated, there was more or less serous effusion into th abdominal cavity. In cases of gangrene of the extremities, and of the intestines, heart clots and fibruos coagula were universally present. * * *

"The fact that gangrene appeared in the stockade first, and originated spontaneously without previous contagion, and occurred sporadically all over the stockade and prison hospital, was proof positive that this disease will arise whenever the conditions of crowding, filth, foul air, and bad diet are present. The exhalations from the hospital and stockade appeared to exert their effects to a considerable distance outside of these localities. The origin of gangrene among these prisoners appeared clearly to depend upon the state of the general system induced by diet, and external noxious influences. The rapidity of the appearance and action of gangrene depended upon the powers and state of the constitution, as well as upon the intensity of poison in the atmosphere, or upon the direct application of poisonous matter to the wounded surface. This was further illustrated by the fact that gangrene, or a disease resembling it in all essential respects, attacked the intestinal canal of patients laboring under ulceration of the bowels, although there were no local manifestations of gangrene upon the surface of the body. This mode of termination in cases of dysentery was quite common in the foul atmosphere of the Confederate States Military Hospital, in the depressed, depraved condition of the system of Federal prisoners.

"A scorbutic condition of the system appeared to favor the origin of foul ulcers, which frequently took on gangrene. Scurvy and gangrene frequently existed in the same individual. In such cases, vegetable diet, with vegetable acids, would remove the scorbutic condition without curing the gangrene. * * * As in the present case of Andersonville, so also in past times when medical hygiene was almost entirely neglected, those two diseases were almost universally associated in crowded ships. In many cases it was very difficult to decide whether the ulcer was a simple result of scurvy or of the action of prison gangrene, for there was great similarity in the appearance of ulcers in the two diseases."
* * *

After saying that in this foul atmosphere amuptation, though freely practiced for gangrene, did no good; that the disease returned and patients died from it, and from prevailing bowel troubles; that ordinary medicines did no good owing to bad conditions, he continues:

"I endeavored to impress upon the medical officers the view that in this disease treatment was almost useless, without an abundant supply of pure, fresh air, nutritious food, and tonics and stimulants. Such changes, however, as would allow of the isolation of the cases of gangrene appeared to be out of the power of the medical officers.

"Finally, this gigantic mass of human misery calls loudly for relief, not only for the sake of suffering humanity, but also on account of our own brave soldiers now captives in the hands of the Federal government. Strict justice to the gallant men of the Confedrate armies, who have been or may be so unfortunate as to be compelled to surrender in battle, demands that the Confederate government should adopt that course which will best secure their health and comfort in captivity or at least leave their enemies without a shadow of an excuse for any violation of the rules of civilized warfare in the treatment of prisoners."

### EDITOR'S COMMENTS.

The last paragraph of Dr. Jones provokes a smile, wherein he urged the Richmond government to remedy the great evils he describes, so that the Federals would find no excuse to violate the laws of war in the treatment of prisoners. He may have been unaware that his honest, humane plea virtually accused his government of being guilty of such violation. His report proved it guilty beyond question.

The variation from month to month of the proportion of deaths to the number living is interesting. Facts taken from the offical report, show:

In April one in every sixteen died.
In May one in every twenty-six died.
In June one in every twenty-two died.
In July one in every eighteen died.
In August one in every eleven died.
In September one in every three died.
In October one in every two died.
In November one in every three died.

Think of the magnitude of this horror. Did any one ever hear of an epidemic so fatal that one-third of those attacked by it in one month died; one-half of the remnant the next month, and one-third of the remainder the next month?

Dr. Jones' report from prison records, puts the total number of Federals imprisoned at Andersonville at 40,611. The cemetery records show 13,716 deaths nearly one-third of the number entered. Only 26,895 came out alive. Of these doubtless 10,000 died in prisons to which they were transferred, and in transit, and after reaching our lines because of disorders contracted in this and the prisons to which they were mercilessly transferred when the better policy for the South, from every point of view, would have been to paroled them.

General Winder felt the force of his remark when he said, with a fiendish chuckle:: "I'm doing more to kill off Yankees than twenty regiments at the front." The number "killed off" at Andersonville was 13,716 men in about nine months, though one-half of those living were sent to other prisons early in September. No twenty Rebel regiments of long service ever killed 13,000 men, or one-fourth that number. More than 25,000 Union prisoners under Winder's jurisdiction were starved, shot and pestered to death after his assignment to the position of commissary general of prisoners by Jefferson Davis who knew his character and because of that fact he chose him. His cold blooded cruelty was a desirable qualification, though it often disgusted many Rebel officers. Colonel D. T. Chandler of the Rebel War Department, sent on a tour of inspection to Andersonville, reported from there August 5, 1864, as follows:

### Colonel Chandler's Testimony.

"My duty requires me respectfully to recommend a change in the officer in command of the post, Brigadier General John H. Winder, and the substitution in his place of some one who unites both energy and good judgment with some feelings of humanity and consideration for the welfare and comfort, as far as is consistent with their safe keeping, of the vast number of unfortunates placed under his control; some one who, at least, will not advocate deliberately, and in cold blood, the propriety of leaving them in their present condition until their number is sufficiently reduced by death to make the present arrangements suffice for their accommodation, and who will not consider it a matter of self-laudation and boasting that he has never been inside of the stockade—a place the horrors of which it is difficult to describe, and which is a disgrace to civilization—the condition of which he might, by the exercise of a little energy and judgment, even with the limited means at his command, have considerably imrpoved."

In his examination as witness, touching this report, Colonel Chandler says::

"I noticed that General Winder seemed very indifferent to the welfare of the prisoners, indisposed to do anything, or to do as much as I thought he ought to do, to alleviate their sufferings. I remonstrated with him as well as I could, and he used that language which I reported to the Department with reference to it—the language stated in the report. When I spoke of the great mortality existing among the prisoners, and pointed out to him that the sickly season was coming on, and that it must necessarily increase unless something was done for their relief—the swamp, for instance, drained, proper food furnished, and in better quantity, and in other suggestions which I made to him—he replied to me that he thought it was better to see half of them die than to take care of the men."

### Editor's Comments.

It was Winder who issued the order July 27 to open the Florida battery on helpless prisons, elsewhere printed, (See page 104), when it was supposed that General Stoneman was approaching Andersonville.

Th s order to butcher Union prisoners, the reports of physicians and military officers, and Col. Chandler's report was on file in Davis' War Department; yet men undertake to believe that the policy of murder in Southern prisons was not known at Richmond, and that Wirz was the only guilty man, or that ex-prisoners lie about the situation!

It has been noticed that Dr. Jones does not attribute prison diseases to climate or other natural causes, but wholly to artificial conditions resulting from vicious prison management. Colonel Chandler was of the same opinion.

## AS SEEN BY SENATOR BLAINE.

When the general amnesty bill to Southern leaders was pending in the Senate, James G. Blaine, in debate on the bill, said:

"I except Jefferson Davis on the ground that he was the author, knowingly, deliberately, guiltily and wilfully, of the g'gant'c murders and crimes at Andersonville. I have taken occasion to read some of the historic cruelties of the world. I have read over the details of the atrocious murders of the Duke of Alva in the Low Countries, which are always mentioned with a thrill of horror throughout Christendom. I have read the details of the massacres of Saint Bartholomew that stands out in history as one of the atrocities beyond imagination. I have read anew the horrors untold and unimaginable of the Spanish Inquisition; and I here, before God, meaning my words, knowing their full extent and import, declare that neither the deeds of the Duke of Alva in the Low Countries, nor the massacre of Saint Bartholomew, nor the thumb-screws and engines of torture of the Spanish Inquisition, begin to compare in atrocity with the hideous crimes of Andersonville!"

## EDITOR'S LAST SAY.

What better can be said of Florence and several other Confederate military prisons.

The sudden death of Winder as he was entering a banqueting tent for officers at Andersonville the evening of January 1, 1865, doubtless saved him from the fate that later overtook Wirz. And if Davis had been tried as an accessory to the fact, what would have been his end? In fact were not Wirz, Winder and others accessories, and was not the principal at Richmond as Mr. Blaine saw it?

## ADDENDA.

The quotation on page 126 escaped proof reading and was not credited. It should read:

> Seeing too much sadness has congealed your blood
> And meloncholy is the nurse of frenzy.
> \*     \*     \*     \*     \*     \*
> Frame your mind to mirth and merriment,
> Which bars a thousand harms and lengthens life.
>                                     Shakespeare.

The 'word "Gorrilla," for the use intended, should have been spelled "Guerrilla." A few other slight errors escaped attention in proof correction.

## INDEX.

| | |
|---|---|
| Dedication | 2 |
| Prelude | 3 |
| Preface | 4 |
| Causes Leading to Civil War | 5 |
| Events Following Election of 1860 | 13 |
| Opening Campaign in 1864 in Virginia | 22 |
| Opening Great Wilderness Battles | 25 |
| Surprised and Made Prisoners | 28 |
| Behind Enemy's Guns—Lee and Longstreet | 30 |
| Leave Battle Lines for Prison—Interview | 32 |
| Incidents at Gordonsville | 37 |
| Virginia Girls of Sweet Sixteen | 41 |
| Lynchburg to Danville—Drew Enemy's Fire | 44 |
| Danville to Columbia—Wayside Notes | 49 |
| In Slavedom (Poem) | 52 |
| South Carolina Capitol and Onward | 53 |
| Arrive at Andersonville | 55 |
| Prison Scenes, Incidents, Etc | 60 |
| Stories of Four Days | 64 |
| Is This Paradise Lost? | 69 |
| Facts and Rumors Journalized | 73 |
| Prison Cleaned of Raiders | 79 |
| Prison Annex—How We Celebrate | 82 |
| Scenes Among Sick—Raiders Convicted | 85 |
| Hanging the Chief Raiders | 88 |
| Niggers in the Exchange Fence | 90 |
| Berilla Shows Pluck—Georgia Patriotism | 97 |
| Poems,—Prisoner's Song; Stack Arms | 99-101 |
| Rain Knocks the Stockade | 102 |
| Winder's Murder Order | 104 |
| Ode to Wirz—A Few Days Doings | 105 |
| Men of Tennessee (Poem) | 109 |
| Hospitals, Their History | 110 |
| Women Prisoners—Providence Spring—Deyo | 113 |

Interesting Records and Comments..................118
Night of Jubilee......................................123
Girls With True Southern Hearts...................126
Homeseekers' Excursion in Dixie....................128
ExNorthern Man, Etc..............................131
Arrive at Florence..................................135
Prisoners Overrun Guards.........................136
Nine Days' Storm, Etc.............................138
Two Remarkable Speeches.........................141
Why Rebels Want Armistice.......................147
Uncle Abe's Enemy at Home.......................153
Davis and Winder..................................163
History Studies, Etc................................166
Vote for President—A Frosty Wave...............170
Barrett's Starvation Order.........................176
On to Charleston—Homeward Bound..............182
Concluding Sketches from Diary....................193
Poem, Lincoln .....................................196
Visited Clara Barton...............................198
Found Her Brother's Grave........................199
Prison Psalms ................,....................202
Of Far Away.......................................210
Pilgrimage ........................................212
Confederate Testimony ...........................215
Editor's Comments ...............................223
As Seen by Senator Blaine.........................225
Editor's Last Say..................................226

----, J Jim 161 John 157 P G 161
ABE, 153 172 175
ABOLISH, 24
ABRAHAM, 48
ANDERSON, 188 Maj 16
ARMSTRONG, 159
ARNOLD, Benedict 168
ATHERTON, David 93
AXTAL, Stephen 58

BALDWIN, 82
BARRETT, 162-164 166 176 Lt 161 177-180 Red Head 148
BARTON, Clara 198 200 Miss 199
BEAUREGARD, 188 Gen 20
BEVERLY, Ira 78
BLACK, Attorney Gen 19
BLAINE, James G 225 Mr 226
BOGLE, Albert 63
BOODGER, 123 136 150 157 177 180 W 58
BOURN, Sgt 163
BOURNE, Sgt 115
BRACE, Frank 167
BRECKENRIDGE, 76
BREKENRIDGE, John C 14
BROADER, Henry 118
BROCK, Conrade 140
BROWN, John 10 97 133 Slick 175 Steward 68 98 103-104 179
BRUBER, Jacob 8
BRUMER, 174
BUCHANAN, 17-18 21 47-48 72 159 Lt 51 President 13 20
BUELL, 109
BUERILA, 98
BUNYAN, 148 John 147
BURNSIDE, 23 72
BURTON, 180 O W 58 136 Sgt 107
BUTLER, 31 Beast 152

CAHILL, Lt 28
CALHOUN, 33 40 Jack 133
CALL, Homar 51 Lt 28
CAREY, Mrs 193-194
CARLTON, 124
CARPENTER, Adjutant 74
CARY, 76
CHANDLER, Col 6 224-225 D T 224
CHEESEMAN, Lt 51
CHEESMAN, Lt 27-28
CHIPMAN, W P 215
CLAY, Henry 49
CLIFTON, Fred 15O 177
CLYDE, 181 Capt 28-29 51
COBB, 19 21 66 Howell 15 72
COLBY, 118
COLLINS, 89-90 William 87
COOK, Lt Col 74
COOPER, 14 Samuel 13
COPELAND, 173
CORBETT, Boston 93 Con 180
CORD, Thomas A 93
COWPER, 142
CUMMINGS, L H 93
CURRILL, Maj 108
CURTIS, 88 90 Charles 87

DAMON, Henry 173
DANTE, 86
DAVIS, 14 72 77 96-97 162 164 226 Jeff 39 85 132 152 163 173 Jefferson 13 15 224-225 Lt 82 88 116 175
DECKER, Billy 85
DELANEY, Patrick 87
DEVENDORF, Mrs H C 202
DEYO, 113
DOUGLAS, 98
DUKE, Of Alva 225
DUNCAN, 173
DUPONT, 187

EARLY, 115
EGGLESTON, Willie F 125
ELLIS, Reuben 119
ENGLISH, James 92
EWELL, 26 91

FENTON, 174
FLOOD, David 165
FLOYD, 13 21 J B 13 John B 16
FLUDEL, Dr 181
FORREST, 76-77
FRANCIS, A W 155
FREDERICK, 93
FREEMONT, 95
FREMONT, 74

G, 139
GARRETT, Dr 153
GARRISON, W L 10
GLOVER, 136 153
GODDARD, J L 74
GRANT, 29 32 47 52 65 72 74
    85 103 108 115 123-124 167
    194 Gen 24 186 U S 77
GRENNELS, William 119
GRIFF, 122 153 161
GRIFFITH, 37 70 94 135-136
    138-139 152 159 H B 58
GRIMSHAW, 157 168
GROVER, Col 74

HAMDY, Doris 13
HAMILTON, 14
HANCOCK, 23 125
HANSON, 107
HARRIMAN, 70 78 91 Anna E
    93 W H 62 93
HARRIS, Isham 109 Isham G 13
HARRISON, Col 154 159 175 G
    P 155
HATCH, Capt 185

HAWKS, 183 186 J B 71 182
    James B 50 125 192
HENRY, 35 142
HEPWORTH, 181
HICKS, Thomas H 15
HILL, 29
HIRST, 100
HOOD, 92-94 123-124
HOOKER, 53 172
HOYT, 174
HUCKLEBY, Charles 78
HUGO, Victor 123
HUNTER, 76

IVERSON, Col 177 Lt Col 159

J, Col 154
JACKSON, Claiborne F 15
    President 11 Stonewall 134
JEFF, 56
JEFFERSON, 8 14 35 40 142
    Thomas 41
JOHN, Ellis W 16
JOHNSON, 154 C L 153 Charles
    L 147
JOHNSTON, 14 53-54 59 65 85
    92 94 100 Joe 73 98 Joe E 77
    Joseph E 13
JONES, Dr 223 225 Joeseph 215
    Joseph 6

KELLOGG, Robert H 93
KEMP, Sgt 159 172
KERR, John W 93
KEY, Leroy L 81 Sgt 82 87
KILPATRICK, 72 92 120
KIRKE, Edmund 154
KLINE, William 104

LEE, 22 26-27 34 37 45 47 52 72
    77 85 91 108 123-124 194
    Bobby 29 120 Gen 30-33 137
    180 Robert E 14 Sgt 157

LESLIE, 124
LETCHER, Gov 20
LINCOLN, 14-15 17-18 20-21 36
   48 50 53 74-75 95-96 98 102
   116 149-150 166 171-172 174
   180 194 Abe 35 141 Abraham
   5 12-13 49 195 Mr 127
   President 49 124 196 198
LONGFELLOW, 84
LONGSTREET, 31 51-52 Gen
   30 40
LYON, Nathaniel 15

MAC, 172 175
MACDONALD, 209
MADISON, 14 35 107 B F 186
   Benjamin Frank 192
MAGOFFIN, Gov 15
MARION, 13O
MATTESON, Sgt 180
MATTISON, 79-80 G W 28 58
   136
MCCLELLAN, 29 35-36 120
   123 149-150 166 172 1O2
MEADE, 87 Gen 24 37
MERRITT, H D 97 107 Harvey
   Deyo 113
MILLER, M H 93
MONTGOMERY, 192
MOONEY, 76 80
MOORE, S P 215 Surgeon Gen 6
MORSE, Hiram 69
MOSEBY, 87
MUIR, 90 A 87
MULFORD, Maj 123

NORTH, 153
NORTHROP, Henry 91 J W 6
   John H 91
NORWOOD, Wesley 94

O'BRIEN, Junius 165
OBERLY, Maj 63

OGLETHORPE, 157
OULD, Judge 123 Robert 21

PARSONS, Col 72
PELOT, Dr 113
PENDELTON, 123
PHILLIPS, 91 Miss 193-194
PICKETT, 52
PINCH, 85
PINCHEN, 65 70 119 Waldo 58
   195
PLUMER, William 10
POLK, President 9 133
POLLARD, Edward A 16
POLLOCK, 70
POMEROY, G W 93
PORTER, 191
PRESTON, Senator 10

RANDELL, J H 173
RANDOLF, Edmund 53
REEVES, Dr 113
RICE, 27 Gen 25 43 51 Gen J C
   25
ROBINSON, Gen 43
ROSECRAN, 59
ROSECRANS, 109
RYAN, Tony 90

SAILOR, Jack The 87
SARSFIELD, John 87
SCOTT, Dred 139 Gen 20
SEDGWICK, 23
SELDEN, 77-78
SEWARD, 12 17
SEYMOUR, 174 Brigadier Gen
   51 Gen 54 Horatio 36
SHAFFER, Peter 71
SHALER, Brigadier Gen 51 Gen
   52 54
SHEPARD, Rev T J 93
SHERIDAN, 115

SHERMAN, 59 73 80 85 92 94
   100-101 103 123-124 127 140
   168 172 174 178 180 183 Gen
   121 217
SHULTZ, Frederick 119
SIBLEY, Sgt 123
SIEGEL, 62
SIGEL, 76
SLICK, 176
SPENCER, 115
SPRINGER, Sgt 180
STANTON, Secretary 74
STEPHENS, 133 Alexander H 15
   33 54 Mr 127
STEWART, W D 195
STONEMAN, 104 Gen 225 Maj
   Gen 97
STONEWALL, 25
STRATHER, Dr 165
STUART, Gen 47
STURGIS, Gen 76
SULLIVAN, 76 79-82 89-90
   Cary 87 Terrence 87
SWAN, Capt 23 27-29 51

TANEY, Roger B 8
THOMAS, 53
THOMBURG, Dr 113
THOMPSON, 32 50 59 61 64-65
   72 79 84 93 100 153 174
   Lloyd G 58
TOOMBS, 66 100
TOWNSEND, 181 W M 107

TURNER, J O 93
TUTTLE, Dan 147
TWIGGS, Gen 16

ULYSSES, 174

VICTORIA, Queen Of England
   187

WADDLE, B N 93
WADSWORTH, Gen 24 41 43
WALKER, W M 170
WARREN, 23 Elon J 123 Gen 24
WASHINGTON, 14 35 40 142
   144
WHEATON, 149
WHEELER, 121
WHITE, Isaiah H 215
WILLIAMS, 8 106 Alex 106
WINDER, 122 164 166 225-226
   Gen 73 104 J H 148 John H
   72 104 163 224
WIRZ, 64 69 72 82 100-101 148
   162-164 166 175 225-226
   Capt 57 73 76 79-80 85 88 91
   116 Henry 61 215
WISE, Henry A 10
WITHERSPOON, Rev T S 10
WRIGHT, 136 177
YAGER, 173
YANCEY, 40 66
YOUNG, John W 51

www.ingramcontent.com/pod-product-compliance
Lightning Source LLC
Chambersburg PA
CBHW060602230426
43670CB00011B/1934